HOLT SCIENCE & TECHNOLOGY

Short Courses

   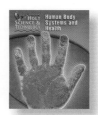

Teacher Edition WALK-THROUGH

Student Edition CONTENTS IN BRIEF

HOLT, RINEHART AND WINSTON

A Harcourt Education Company

Orlando • **Austin** • New York • San Diego • Toronto • London

Designed to meet the needs of all students

15 Short Courses

Holt Science & Technology: Short Course Series allows you to match your curriculum by choosing from 15 books covering life, earth, and physical sciences. The program reflects current curriculum developments and includes the strongest skills-development strand of any middle school science series. Students of all abilities will develop skills that they can use both in science as well as in other courses.

STUDENTS OF ALL ABILITIES RECEIVE THE READING HELP AND TAILORED INSTRUCTION THEY NEED.

- The *Student Edition* is accessible with a clean, easy-to-follow design and highlighted vocabulary words.
- Inclusion strategies and different learning styles help support all learners.
- Comprehensive **Section** and **Chapter Reviews** and **Standardized Test Preparation** allow students to practice their test-taking skills.
- **Reading Comprehension Guide** and **Guided Reading Audio CDs** help students better understand the content.

CROSS-DISCIPLINARY CONNECTIONS LET STUDENTS SEE HOW SCIENCE RELATES TO OTHER DISCIPLINES.

- **Mathematics, reading,** and **writing skills** are integrated throughout the program.
- Cross-discipline **Connection To** features show students how science relates to language arts, social studies, and other sciences.

A FLEXIBLE LABORATORY PROGRAM HELPS STUDENTS BUILD IMPORTANT INQUIRY AND CRITICAL-THINKING SKILLS.

- The laboratory program includes labs in each chapter, labs in the **LabBook** at the end of the text, six different lab books, and **Video Labs.**
- All labs are teacher-tested and rated by difficulty in the *Teacher Edition,* so you can be sure the labs will be appropriate for your students.
- A variety of labs, from **Inquiry Labs** to **Skills Practice Labs,** helps you meet the needs of your curriculum and work within the time constraints of your teaching schedule.

INTEGRATED TECHNOLOGY AND ONLINE RESOURCES EXPAND LEARNING BEYOND CLASSROOM WALLS.

- An **Enhanced Online Edition** or **CD-ROM Version** of the student text lightens your students' load.

- **SciLinks,** a Web service developed and maintained by the National Science Teachers Association (NSTA), contains current prescreened links directly related to the textbook.

- **Brain Food Video Quizzes** on videotape and DVD are game-show style quizzes that assess students' progress and motivate them to study.

- The **One-stop Planner® CD-ROM** with **Exam View® Test Generator** contains all of the resources you need including an *Interactive Teacher Edition,* worksheets, customizable lesson plans, **Holt Calendar Planner,** a powerful test generator, **Lab Materials QuickList Software,** and more.

- Spanish Resources include **Guided Reading Audio CD** in Spanish.

CHAPTER RESOURCE FILES FOR

Inside the Restless Earth

Skills Worksheets
- Directed Reading A
- Directed Reading B
- Vocabulary & Notes
- Section Reviews
- Chapter Review
- Reinforcement
- Critical Thinking

Assessments
- Section Quizzes
- Chapter Test A
- Chapter Test B
- Chapter Test C
- Performance-Based Assessment
- Standardized Test Preparation

Labs and Activities
- Datasheets for In-Text Labs
- Datasheets for Quick Labs
- Datasheets for LabBook
- Vocabulary Activity
- SciLinks® Activity

Teacher Resources
- Teacher Notes for Performance-Based Assessment
- Lab Notes and Answers
- Answer Keys
- Lesson Plans
- Test Item Listing for ExamView® Test Generator
- Teaching Transparencies
- Chapter Starter Transparencies
- Bellringer Transparencies
- Concept Mapping Transparencies

Life Science

 A MICROORGANISMS, FUNGI, AND PLANTS

 B ANIMALS

PROGRAM SCOPE AND SEQUENCE

Selecting the right books for your course is easy. Just review the topics presented in each book to determine the best match to your district curriculum.

C CELLS, HEREDITY, & CLASSIFICATION	D HUMAN BODY SYSTEMS & HEALTH	E ENVIRONMENTAL SCIENCE
Cells: The Basic Units of Life • Cells, tissues, and organs • Populations, communities, and ecosystems • Cell theory • Surface-to-volume ratio • Prokaryotic versus eukaryotic cells • Cell organelles	**Body Organization and Structure** • Homeostasis • Types of tissue • Organ systems • Structure and function of the skeletal system, muscular system, and integumentary system	**Interactions of Living Things** • Biotic versus abiotic parts of the environment • Producers, consumers, and decomposers • Food chains and food webs • Factors limiting population growth • Predator-prey relationships • Symbiosis and coevolution
The Cell in Action • Diffusion and osmosis • Passive versus active transport • Endocytosis versus exocytosis • Photosynthesis • Cellular respiration and fermentation • Cell cycle	**Circulation and Respiration** • Structure and function of the cardiovascular system, lymphatic system, and respiratory system • Respiratory disorders	**Cycles in Nature** • Water cycle • Carbon cycle • Nitrogen cycle • Ecological succession
Heredity • Dominant versus recessive traits • Genes and alleles • Genotype, phenotype, the Punnett square and probability • Meiosis • Determination of sex	**The Digestive and Urinary Systems** • Structure and function of the digestive system • Structure and function of the urinary system	**The Earth's Ecosystems** • Kinds of land and water biomes • Marine ecosystems • Freshwater ecosystems
Genes and Gene Technology • Structure of DNA • Protein synthesis • Mutations • Heredity disorders and genetic counseling	**Communication and Control** • Structure and function of the nervous system and endocrine system • The senses • Structure and function of the eye and ear	**Environmental Problems and Solutions** • Types of pollutants • Types of resources • Conservation practices • Species protection
The Evolution of Living Things • Adaptations and species • Evidence for evolution • Darwin's work and natural selection • Formation of new species	**Reproduction and Development** • Asexual versus sexual reproduction • Internal versus external fertilization • Structure and function of the human male and female reproductive systems • Fertilization, placental development, and embryo growth • Stages of human life	**Energy Resources** • Types of resources • Energy resources and pollution • Alternative energy resources
The History of Life on Earth • Geologic time scale and extinctions • Plate tectonics • Human evolution	**Body Defenses and Disease** • Types of diseases • Vaccines and immunity • Structure and function of the immune system • Autoimmune diseases, cancer, and AIDS	
Classification • Levels of classification • Cladistic diagrams • Dichotomous keys • Characteristics of the six kingdoms	**Staying Healthy** • Nutrition and reading food labels • Alcohol and drug effects on the body • Hygiene, exercise, and first aid	

Earth Science

F INSIDE THE RESTLESS EARTH	**G** EARTH'S CHANGING SURFACE
CHAPTER 1		

CHAPTER 1

Minerals of the Earth's Crust
- Mineral composition and structure
- Types of minerals
- Mineral identification
- Mineral formation and mining

Maps as Models of the Earth
- Structure of a map
- Cardinal directions
- Latitude, longitude, and the equator
- Magnetic declination and true north
- Types of projections
- Aerial photographs
- Remote sensing
- Topographic maps

CHAPTER 2

Rocks: Mineral Mixtures
- Rock cycle and types of rocks
- Rock classification
- Characteristics of igneous, sedimentary, and metamorphic rocks

Weathering and Soil Formation
- Types of weathering
- Factors affecting the rate of weathering
- Composition of soil
- Soil conservation and erosion prevention

CHAPTER 3

The Rock and Fossil Record
- Uniformitarianism versus catastrophism
- Superposition
- The geologic column and unconformities
- Absolute dating and radiometric dating
- Characteristics and types of fossils
- Geologic time scale

Agents of Erosion and Deposition
- Shoreline erosion and deposition
- Wind erosion and deposition
- Erosion and deposition by ice
- Gravity's effect on erosion and deposition

CHAPTER 4

Plate Tectonics
- Structure of the Earth
- Continental drifts and sea floor spreading
- Plate tectonics theory
- Types of boundaries
- Types of crust deformities

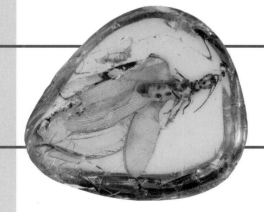

CHAPTER 5

Earthquakes
- Seismology
- Features of earthquakes
- P and S waves
- Gap hypothesis
- Earthquake safety

CHAPTER 6

Volcanoes
- Types of volcanoes and eruptions
- Types of lava and pyroclastic material
- Craters versus calderas
- Sites and conditions for volcano formation
- Predicting eruptions

H WATER ON EARTH

The Flow of Fresh Water
- Water cycle
- River systems
- Stream erosion
- Life cycle of rivers
- Deposition
- Aquifers, springs, and wells
- Ground water
- Water treatment and pollution

Exploring the Oceans
- Properties and characteristics of the oceans
- Features of the ocean floor
- Ocean ecology
- Ocean resources and pollution

The Movement of Ocean Water
- Types of currents
- Characteristics of waves
- Types of ocean waves
- Tides

I WEATHER AND CLIMATE

The Atmosphere
- Structure of the atmosphere
- Air pressure
- Radiation, convection, and conduction
- Greenhouse effect and global warming
- Characteristics of winds
- Types of winds
- Air pollution

Understanding Weather
- Water cycle
- Humidity
- Types of clouds
- Types of precipitation
- Air masses and fronts
- Storms, tornadoes, and hurricanes
- Weather forecasting
- Weather maps

Climate
- Weather versus climate
- Seasons and latitude
- Prevailing winds
- Earth's biomes
- Earth's climate zones
- Ice ages
- Global warming
- Greenhouse effect

J ASTRONOMY

Studying Space
- Astronomy
- Keeping time
- Types of telescope
- Radioastronomy
- Mapping the stars
- Scales of the universe

Stars, Galaxies, and the Universe
- Composition of stars
- Classification of stars
- Star brightness, distance, and motions
- H-R diagram
- Life cycle of stars
- Types of galaxies
- Theories on the formation of the universe

Formation of the Solar System
- Birth of the solar system
- Structure of the sun
- Fusion
- Earth's structure and atmosphere
- Planetary motion
- Newton's Law of Universal Gravitation

A Family of Planets
- Properties and characteristics of the planets
- Properties and characteristics of moons
- Comets, asteroids, and meteoroids

Exploring Space
- Rocketry and artificial satellites
- Types of Earth orbit
- Space probes and space exploration

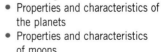

Physical Science

INTRODUCTION TO MATTER	INTERACTIONS OF MATTER
CHAPTER 1	
The Properties of Matter	**Chemical Bonding**
• Definition of matter	• Types of chemical bonds
• Mass and weight	• Valence electrons
• Physical and chemical properties	• Ions versus molecules
• Physical and chemical change	• Crystal lattice
• Density	
CHAPTER 2	
States of Matter	**Chemical Reactions**
• States of matter and their properties	• Writing chemical formulas and equations
• Boyle's and Charles's laws	• Law of conservation of mass
• Changes of state	• Types of reactions
	• Endothermic versus exothermic reactions
	• Law of conservation of energy
	• Activation energy
	• Catalysts and inhibitors
CHAPTER 3	
Elements, Compounds, and Mixtures	**Chemical Compounds**
• Elements and compounds	• Ionic versus covalent compounds
• Metals, nonmetals, and metalloids (semiconductors)	• Acids, bases, and salts
• Properties of mixtures	• pH
• Properties of solutions, suspensions, and colloids	• Organic compounds
	• Biomolecules
CHAPTER 4	
Introduction to Atoms	**Atomic Energy**
• Atomic theory	• Properties of radioactive substances
• Atomic model and structure	• Types of decay
• Isotopes	• Half-life
• Atomic mass and mass number	• Fission, fusion, and chain reactions
CHAPTER 5	
The Periodic Table	
• Structure of the periodic table	
• Periodic law	
• Properties of alkali metals, alkaline-earth metals, halogens, and noble gases	
CHAPTER 6	

FORCES, MOTION, AND ENERGY

 ELECTRICITY AND MAGNETISM

 SOUND AND LIGHT

Matter in Motion
- Speed, velocity, and acceleration
- Measuring force
- Friction
- Mass versus weight

Introduction to Electricity
- Law of electric charges
- Conduction versus induction
- Static electricity
- Potential difference
- Cells, batteries, and photocells
- Thermocouples
- Voltage, current, and resistance
- Electric power
- Types of circuits

The Energy of Waves
- Properties of waves
- Types of waves
- Reflection and refraction
- Diffraction and interference
- Standing waves and resonance

Forces in Motion
- Terminal velocity and free fall
- Projectile motion
- Inertia
- Momentum

Electromagnetism
- Properties of magnets
- Magnetic force
- Electromagnetism
- Solenoids and electric motors
- Electromagnetic induction
- Generators and transformers

The Nature of Sound
- Properties of sound waves
- Structure of the human ear
- Pitch and the Doppler effect
- Infrasonic versus ultrasonic sound
- Sound reflection and echolocation
- Sound barrier
- Interference, resonance, diffraction, and standing waves
- Sound quality of instruments

Forces in Fluids
- Properties in fluids
- Atmospheric pressure
- Density
- Pascal's principle
- Buoyant force
- Archimedes' principle
- Bernoulli's principle

Electronic Technology
- Properties of semiconductors
- Integrated circuits
- Diodes and transistors
- Analog versus digital signals
- Microprocessors
- Features of computers

The Nature of Light
- Electromagnetic waves
- Electromagnetic spectrum
- Law of reflection
- Absorption and scattering
- Reflection and refraction
- Diffraction and interference

Work and Machines
- Measuring work
- Measuring power
- Types of machines
- Mechanical advantage
- Mechanical efficiency

Light and Our World
- Luminosity
- Types of lighting
- Types of mirrors and lenses
- Focal point
- Structure of the human eye
- Lasers and holograms

Energy and Energy Resources
- Forms of energy
- Energy conversions
- Law of conservation of energy
- Energy resources

Heat and Heat Technology
- Heat versus temperature
- Thermal expansion
- Absolute zero
- Conduction, convection, radiation
- Conductors versus insulators
- Specific heat capacity
- Changes of state
- Heat engines
- Thermal pollution

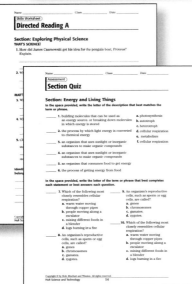

Program resources make teaching and learning easier.

CHAPTER RESOURCES

A *Chapter Resources book* accompanies each of the 15 *Short Courses*. Here you'll find everything you need to make sure your students are getting the most out of learning science—all in one book.

Skills Worksheets
- Directed Reading A: Basic
- Directed Reading B: Special Needs
- Vocabulary and Chapter Summary
- Section Reviews
- Chapter Reviews
- Reinforcement
- Critical Thinking

Labs & Activities
- Datasheets for Chapter Labs
- Datasheets for Quick Labs
- Datasheets for LabBook
- Vocabulary Activity
- SciLinks® Activity

Assessments
- Section Quizzes
- Chapter Tests A: General
- Chapter Tests B: Advanced
- Chapter Tests C: Special Needs
- Performance-Based Assessments
- Standardized Test Preparation

Teacher Resources
- Lab Notes and Answers
- Teacher Notes for Performance-Based Assessment
- Answer Keys
- Lesson Plans
- Test Item Listing for ExamView® Test Generator
- Full-color Teaching Transparencies, plus section Bellringers, Concept Mapping, and Chapter Starter Transparencies.

SPANISH RESOURCES

Spanish materials are available for each *Short Course*:

- *Student Edition*
- *Spanish Resources* booklet contains worksheets and assessments translated into Spanish with an English Answer Key.
- Guided Reading Audio CD Program

ONLINE RESOURCES

- *Enhanced Online Editions* engage students and assist teachers with a host of interactive features that are available anytime and anywhere you can connect to the Internet.
- CNNStudentNews.com provides award-winning news and information for both teachers and students.
- SciLinks—a Web service developed and maintained by the National Science Teachers Association—links you and your students to up-to-date online resources directly related to chapter topics.
- go.hrw.com links you and your students to online chapter activities and resources.
- Current Science articles relate to students' lives.

ADDITIONAL LAB AND SKILLS RESOURCES

- *Calculator-Based Labs* incorporates scientific instruments, offering students insight into modern scientific investigation.
- *EcoLabs & Field Activities* develops awareness of the natural world.
- *Holt Science Skills Workshop: Reading in the Content Area* contains exercises that target reading skills key.
- *Inquiry Labs* taps students' natural curiosity and creativity with a focus on the process of discovery.
- *Labs You Can Eat* safely incorporates edible items into the classroom.
- *Long-Term Projects & Research Ideas* extends and enriches lessons.
- *Math Skills for Science* provides additional explanations, examples, and math problems so students can develop their skills.
- *Science Skills Worksheets* helps your students hone important learning skills.
- *Whiz-Bang Demonstrations* gets your students' attention at the beginning of a lesson.

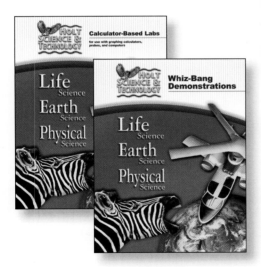

ADDITIONAL RESOURCES

- *Assessment Checklists & Rubrics* gives you guidelines for evaluating students' progress.
- *Holt Anthology of Science Fiction* sparks your students' imaginations with thought-provoking stories.
- *Holt Science Posters* visually reinforces scientific concepts and themes with seven colorful posters including **The Periodic Table of the Elements.**

- *Professional Reference for Teachers* contains professional articles that discuss a variety of topics, such as classroom management.
- *Program Introduction Resource File* explains the program and its features and provides several additional references, including lab safety, scoring rubrics, and more.
- *Science Fair Guide* gives teachers, students, and parents tips for planning and assisting in a science fair.
- *Science Puzzlers, Twisters & Teasers* activities challenge students to think about science concepts in different ways.

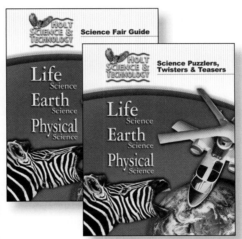

TECHNOLOGY RESOURCES

- *CNN Presents Science in the News: Video Library* helps students see the impact of science on their everyday lives with actual news video clips.
  - Multicultural Connections
  - Science, Technology & Society
  - Scientists in Action
  - Eye on the Environment
- *Guided Reading Audio CD Program*, available in English and Spanish, provides students with a direct read of each section.
- *HRW Earth Science Videotape* takes your students on a geology "field trip" with full-motion video.
- *Interactive Explorations CD-ROM Program* develops students' inquiry and decision-making skills as they investigate science phenomena in a virtual lab setting.

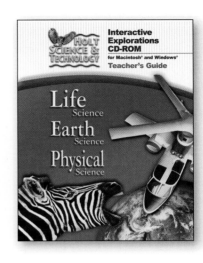

- *One-Stop Planner CD-ROM*® organizes everything you need on one disc, including printable worksheets, customizable lesson plans, a powerful test generator, **PowerPoint**® **LectureNotes, Lab Materials QuickList Software, Holt Calendar Planner, Interactive Teacher Edition,** and more.
- *Science Tutor CD-ROMs* help students practice what they learn with immediate feedback.
- *Lab Videos* make it easier to integrate more experiments into your lessons without the preparation time and costs. Available on DVD and VHS.
- *Brain Food Video Quizzes* are game-show style quizzes that assess students' progress. Available on DVD and VHS.
- *Visual Concepts CD-ROMs* include graphics, animations, and movie clips that demonstrate key chapter concepts.

Science and Math Worksheets

The **Holt Science & Technology** program helps you meet the needs of a wide variety of students, regardless of their skill level. The following pages provide examples of the worksheets available to improve your students' science and math skills whether they already have a strong science and math background or are weak in these areas. Samples of assessment checklists and rubrics are also provided.

In addition to the skills worksheets represented here, **Holt Science & Technology** provides a variety of worksheets that are correlated directly with each chapter of the program. Representations of these worksheets are found at the beginning of each chapter in this *Teacher Edition*.

Many worksheets are also available on the Holt Web site. The address is **go.hrw.com.**

Science Skills Worksheets: Thinking Skills

BEING FLEXIBLE

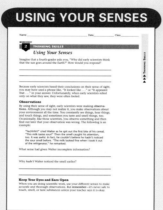

USING YOUR SENSES

THINKING OBJECTIVELY

UNDERSTANDING BIAS

USING LOGIC

BOOSTING YOUR MEMORY

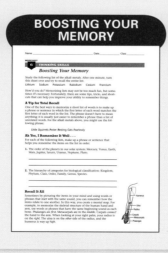

IMPROVING YOUR STUDY HABITS

READING A SCIENCE TEXTBOOK

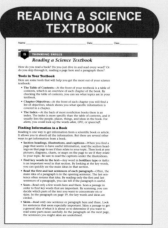

Science Skills Worksheets: Experimenting Skills

SAFETY RULES!

DOING A LAB WRITE-UP

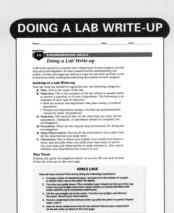

UNDERSTANDING VARIABLES

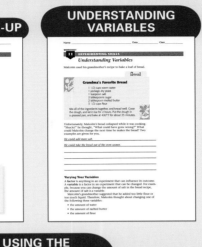

WORKING WITH HYPOTHESES

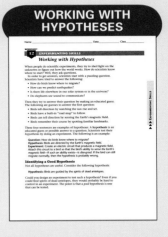

DESIGNING AN EXPERIMENT

USING THE INTERNATIONAL SYSTEM OF UNITS (SI)

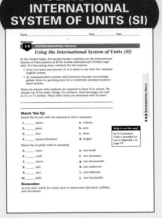

MEASURING

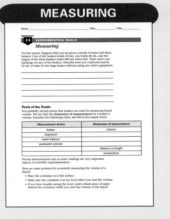

Science Skills Worksheets: Researching Skills

CHOOSING YOUR TOPIC

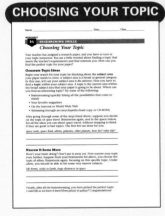

ORGANIZING YOUR RESEARCH

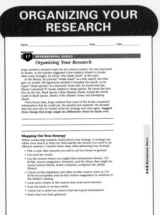

FINDING USEFUL SOURCES

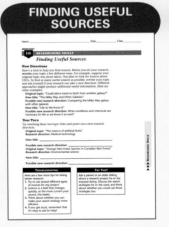

RESEARCHING ON THE WEB

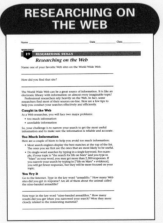

Science Skills Worksheets: Researching Skills (continued)

IDENTIFYING BIAS

TAKING NOTES

Science Skills Worksheets: Communicating Skills

SCIENCE WRITING

SCIENCE DRAWING

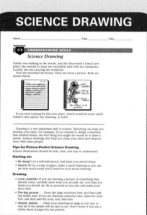

USING MODELS TO COMMUNICATE

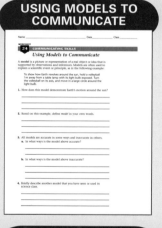

INTRODUCTION TO GRAPHS

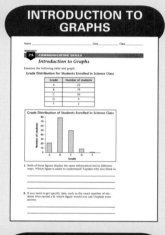

GRASPING GRAPHING

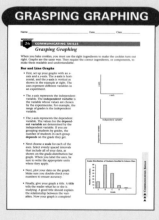

INTERPRETING YOUR DATA

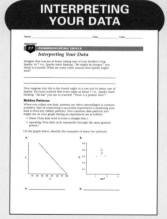

RECOGNIZING BIAS IN GRAPHS

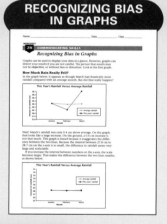

MAKING DATA MEANINGFUL

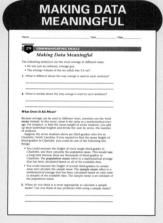

HINTS FOR ORAL PRESENTATIONS

Math Skills for Science

ADDITION AND SUBTRACTION

1 · Addition Review

Addition is used to find the total of two or more quantities. The answer to an addition problem is known as the *sum*.

SAMPLE PROBLEM: Find the sum of 317, 435, and 92.

Step 1: Add the ones. Don't forget to carry your numbers.	Step 2: Add the tens.	Step 3: Add the hundreds.
317 435 + 92 4	317 435 + 92 44	317 435 + 92 844

The sum is **844**.

Add It Up!
1. Find the sum of the following problems.
   a. 348 + 21
   b. 98,125 + 233
   c. 593 + 386
   d. 36,186 + 27,309

2. Your doctor advises you to take 40 mg of vitamin C, 20 mg of niacin, and 15 mg of zinc every day. How many milligrams of nutrients will you take?

3. A chemistry experiment calls for 356 mL of water, 197 mL of saline solution, and 55 mL of vinegar. How much liquid is needed in all?

4. Between 1980 and 1992, the population of San Bernardino County, CA, increased by 639,327 people. If the population in 1980 was 893,016, what was the population in 1992?

5. Halley's comet returns to our solar system every 76 years. Its last visit was in 1986. What year will it appear again?

2 · Subtraction Review

Subtraction is used to take one number from another number. The answer to a subtraction problem is known as the *difference*. The difference is how much larger or smaller one number is than the other.

SAMPLE PROBLEM: Find the difference between 622 and 348.

Step 1: Subtract the ones, borrowing when necessary.	Step 2: Subtract the tens, borrowing when necessary.	Step 3: Subtract the hundreds.

The difference of the two numbers is **274**.

Take It Away!
1. Find the difference in the following problems.
   a. 88 − 36
   b. 1695 − 352
   c. 47,220 − 36,193
   d. 6048 − 3729

2. 571 − 338 =
3. Mars has a diameter of 6790 km. The diameter of Jupiter is 142,984 km. How much larger is the diameter of Jupiter than the diameter of Mars?

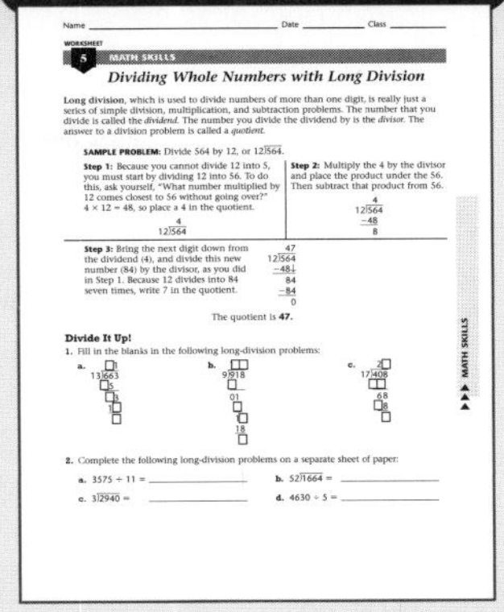

4. A horse is born with a mass of 36 kg. It is expected to have a mass of 495 kg when fully grown. How much mass will it gain?

5. Traveling with the wind, a plane reaches a speed of 212 m/s. On the return trip, the same plane flies into the wind and achieves a speed of only 179 m/s. How much faster does the plane fly with the wind?

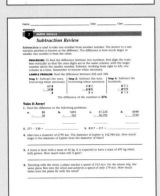

MULTIPLICATION

3 · Multiplying Whole Numbers

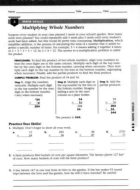

Practice Your Skills!
1. Multiply. Don't forget to show all your work.
   a. 12 × 24
   b. 245 × 36
   c. 46 × 87
   d. 2751 × 11

2. A farm produces 864 bushels of corn per square kilometer. The farmer plants 127 km² of corn. How many bushels of corn will the farm produce?

3. A bee travels 147 m on one way from its hive to the garden. If the bee makes 93 round trips between the hive and the garden, how far will it have traveled? Be careful!

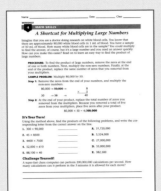

4 · A Shortcut for Multiplying Large Numbers

It's Your Turn!
1. 300 × 90,000 =
2. 45 × 8500 =
3. 4400 × 7500 =
4. 52,000 × 610 =
5. 88,100 × 40 =

A. 31,720,000
B. 3,524,000
C. 27,000,000
D. 33,000,000
E. 382,500

Challenge Yourself!

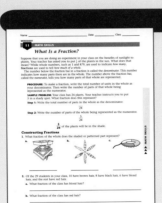

DIVISION

5 · Dividing Whole Numbers with Long Division

Divide It Up!
1. Fill in the blanks in the following long-division problems.

2. Complete the following long-division problems on a separate sheet of paper.
   a. 3575 ÷ 11 =
   b. 527464 =
   c. 172940 =
   d. 4650 ÷ 5 =

6 · Checking Division with Multiplication

Check It Out!
Complete the following divisions, and check your math by multiplying the quotient by your divisor. Are the product and the dividend equal?

1. 15405
2. 147494
3. 12252

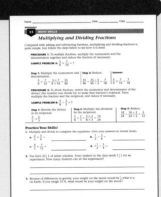

AVERAGES

7 · What Is an Average?

Practice Your Skills!
1. Find the average of each of the following sets of numbers.
   a. 19 m, 11 m, 29 m, 62 m, 14 m
   b. 12 cm, 16 cm, 23 cm, 15 cm
   c. 31°C, 42°C, 35°C, 18°C, 59°C

8 · Average, Mode, and Median

Get in the Mode!
1. Find the mode and median for the following sets of numbers.
   a. 37, 30, 35, 37, 32, 40, 34
   b. 19, 29, 9, 12, 10
   c. 108, 84, 88, 107, 84, 94
   d. 26, 53, 59, 53, 49, 36, 53, 26
   e. 21 m, 24 m, 27 m, 27 m, 49 m, 47 m, 45 m
   f. 98 L, 99 L, 101 L, 111 L, 132 L, 103 L

POSITIVE AND NEGATIVE NUMBERS

9 · Comparing Integers on a Number Line

Practice Your Skills!
1. Locate the following integers on the number line. Then list them in order from smallest to greatest on the line below.
   4, 12, −2, −7, −5, −7, 9, −13

2. Use a number line to correctly place the sign > (greater than) or < (less than) between the numbers in each of the following pairs.
   a. 89 ___ 98
   b. −89 ___ −98
   c. −98 ___ −69

3. This table shows estimates of the mean temperatures on the surface of nine planets. List the planets on the line below in order from hottest to coldest.

Earth	Jupiter	Mars	Mercury	Neptune	Pluto	Saturn	Uranus	Venus
8°C	−150°C	−37°C	179°C	−225°C	−236°C	−185°C	−214°C	453°C

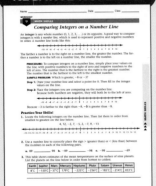

10 · Arithmetic with Positive and Negative Numbers

1. Find the absolute value of the following numbers.
   a. −7
   b. 14
   c. 525,000
   d. −475
   e. 230
   f. −2

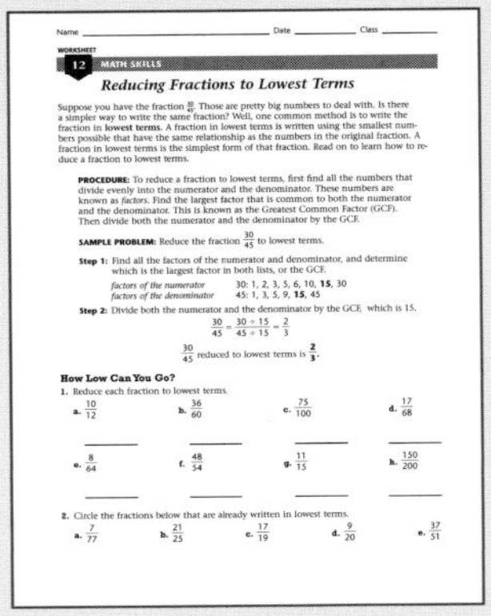

Part 1: Adding Positive and Negative Numbers

Adding same signs	Example −3 + (−5)	Adding opposite signs	Example −8 + 5

Add It Up!
2. Complete the following equations. When finished, go back and check your signs.
   a. 14 + (−17) =
   b. −9 + (−23) =
   c. 8 + (−3) =
   d. −12 + 12 =
   e. 15 + (−4) =
   f. −7 + (−7) =

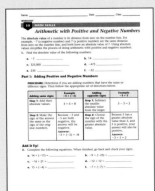

FRACTIONS

13 · Improper Fractions and Mixed Numbers

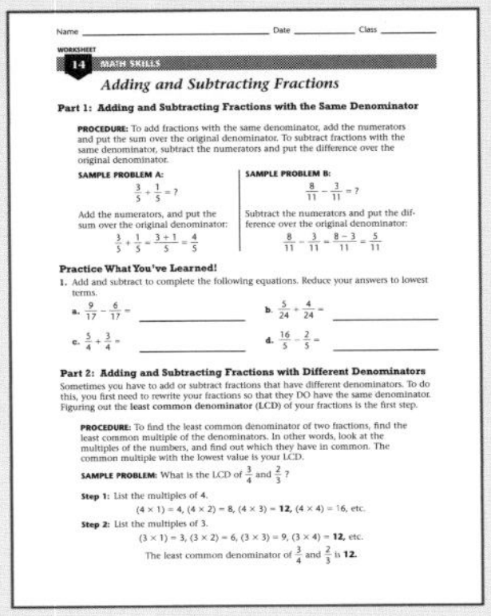

1. Write True or False next to each equation.
   a. 3½ = 9/2
   b. 23/4 = 5¾
   c. 6/5 = 7/2
2. Change each improper fraction to a mixed number, and change each mixed number to an improper fraction.
   a. 16/5
   b. 8/3
   c. 3⅓
   d. 2⅞

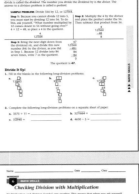

15 · Multiplying and Dividing Fractions

Practice Your Skills!
1. Multiply and divide to complete the equations. Give your answers in lowest terms.

2. You have 23¼ L of saline solution. Every student in the class needs 1¼ L for an experiment. How many students can do the experiment?

3. Because of differences in gravity, your weight on the moon would be ⅙ what it is on Earth. If you weigh 72 N, what would your weight be on the moon?

12 · Reducing Fractions to Lowest Terms

How Low Can You Go?
1. Reduce each fraction to lowest terms.
   a. 10/12
   b. 75/100
   c. 17/51
   d. 48/64
   e. 34/54
   f. 150/200

2. Circle the fractions below that are already written in lowest terms.

14 · Adding and Subtracting Fractions

Part 1: Adding and Subtracting Fractions with the Same Denominator

Practice What You've Learned!
1. Add and subtract to complete the following equations. Reduce your answers to lowest terms.

Part 2: Adding and Subtracting Fractions with Different Denominators

Math Skills for Science (continued)

RATIOS AND PROPORTIONS

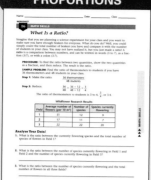

WORKSHEET 16 MATH SKILLS
What Is a Ratio?

Imagine that you are planning a science experiment for your class and you want to make sure you have enough beakers for everyone. What do you do? Well, you could simply count the total number of beakers you have and compare it with the number of students in your class. You may not have realized it, but you just made a ratio! A ratio is a comparison between numbers, and can be written in words (3 to 7), as a fraction (3/7), or with a colon (3:7).

PROCEDURE: To find the ratio between two quantities, show the two quantities as a fraction, and then reduce. The result is the ratio.

SAMPLE PROBLEM: Find the ratio of thermometers to students if you have 36 thermometers and 48 students in your class.

Step 1: Make the ratio.   36 thermometers / 48 students

Step 2: Reduce. $\frac{36}{48} = \frac{36 \div 12}{48 \div 12} = \frac{3}{4}$

The ratio of thermometers to students is 3 to 4, or $\frac{3}{4}$, or 3:4.

Wildflower Research Results

Field	Average number of flowers (per 16 m²)	Number of species	Number of species currently flowering
1	31	12	9
2	17	11	7
3	22	22	20

Analyze Your Data!

1. What is the ratio between the currently flowering species and the total number of species of flowers in Field 1?

2. What is the ratio between the number of species currently flowering in Field 1 and Field 2 and the number of species currently flowering in Field 3?

3. What is the ratio between the number of species currently flowering and the total number of flowers in all three fields?

WORKSHEET 17 MATH SKILLS
Using Proportions and Cross-Multiplication

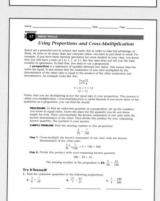

Ratios are a powerful tool in science and math. But in order to take full advantage of them, we have to do more than just calculate ratios—we have to put them to work! For example, if you have three bacteria specimens for every student in your class, you know that you will have a ratio of 3 to 1, or 3:1. But this ratio does not tell you the total number of specimens. To find that, you need to use a proportion.

A **proportion** is a statement of equality between two ratios. This means that the ratios are equal. It also means that the numerator of one ratio multiplied by the denominator of the other ratio is equal to the product of the other numerator and denominator. An example looks like this:

$$\frac{3 \times 4}{6} = \frac{12}{2 \times 6}$$

$$3 \times 4 = 12$$
$$12 = 12$$

Notice that we are multiplying across the equal sign in your proportion. This process is called cross-multiplication. Cross-multiplication is useful because it you know that one of the quantities in a proportion, you can find the fourth.

PROCEDURE: To find an unknown quantity in a proportion, set up the numbers in your proportion in equal ratios. Leave the place for the quantity you do not know empty for now. Then cross-multiply the known numerator of one ratio with the known denominator of the other. Then divide this product by your remaining known quantity. The quotient is your answer.

SAMPLE PROBLEM: Find the missing number in this proportion.

$$\frac{3 \times 7}{5} = 3 \times 100 = 500$$

Step 1: Cross-multiply the known numerator of one ratio with the known denominator of the other ratio.

Step 2: Divide this product with your remaining known quantity.

$$500 \div 5 = 100$$

The missing number in the proportion is 25; $\frac{3}{5} = \frac{25}{100}$

Try It Yourself!

1. Find the unknown quantities in the following proportions:

a. $\frac{3}{8} = \frac{?}{24}$ b. $\frac{15}{21} = \frac{63}{?}$ c. $\frac{?}{3} = \frac{240}{360}$

DECIMALS

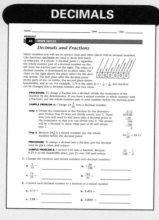

WORKSHEET 18 MATH SKILLS
Decimals and Fractions

Many numbers you will use in science class and other places will be decimal numbers. Like fractions, decimals are used to show how much. Every decimal number is really a fraction—part of a whole, or what part, of a whole. A decimal point (.) separates the whole number part of a decimal number on the left from the fraction part on the right. The value of a decimal number is determined by its place value. The chart on the right shows the place values for the decimal system. The first place after the decimal point shows parts of ten, or tenths, the second place shows hundredths, and so on. For example, 3.74 is the same as $3 + \frac{3}{4} + \frac{4}{100}$. Any fraction can be changed into a decimal number, and vice versa.

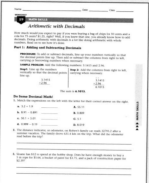

PROCEDURE: To change a fraction into a decimal, divide the numerator of the fraction by the denominator. If you have a mixed number (a whole number with a fraction), put the whole-number part of your number before the decimal point.

SAMPLE PROBLEM: Change $24\frac{3}{20}$ into a decimal number.

Step 1: Divide the numerator of the fraction by the denominator. Notice that 20 does not divide evenly into 3. Therefore, you will need to add zeros after a decimal point in the numerator so that you can divide into it. The answer will be a decimal to show what part of 20 will divide into 3.

Step 2: Because $24\frac{3}{20}$ is a mixed number, put the whole number before the decimal point.

$$24\frac{3}{20} = 24.15$$

PROCEDURE: To change a decimal into a fraction, put the decimal over its place value and reduce.

SAMPLE PROBLEM: Convert 0.25 into a fraction. Because 0.25 is in the hundredths place, put 25 over 100 and reduce.

$$\frac{25}{100} = \frac{1}{4}$$

1. Change the fractions and mixed numbers into decimal numbers.

a. $\frac{3}{8}$ b. $\frac{765}{55}$

c. $\frac{15}{12}$

2. Convert each decimal number to a fraction or a mixed number.

a. 0.13 =   b. 8.405 =

c. 2.98 =   d. 0.0001 =

WORKSHEET 19 MATH SKILLS
Arithmetic with Decimals

How much would you expect to pay if you were buying a bag of chips for 50 cents and a cola for 75 cents? $1.25, right? Well, if you knew that one, you already know how to add decimals. Doing arithmetic with decimals is a lot like doing arithmetic with whole numbers. Read on to see how it's done.

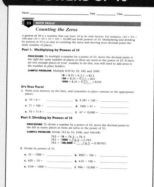

Part 1: Adding and Subtracting Decimals

PROCEDURE: To add or subtract decimals, line up your numbers vertically so that the decimal points line up. Then add or subtract the columns from right to left, carrying or borrowing numbers when necessary.

SAMPLE PROBLEM: Add the following numbers: 3.1415 and 2.96.

Step 1: Line up the numbers vertically so that the decimal points line up.

$$\begin{array}{r} 3.1415 \\ + 2.96 \end{array}$$

Step 2: Add the columns from right to left, carrying when necessary.

$$\begin{array}{r} 3.1415 \\ + 2.96 \\ \hline 6.1015 \end{array}$$

The sum is 6.1015.

Do Some Decimal Math!

1. Match the expressions on the left with their correct answer on the right.

a. 3.2 + 1.9 ___   A. 55.11
b. 8.91 − 0.891 ___   B. 0.809
c. 50.1 − 5.01 ___   C. 5.1
d. 0.999 − 0.19 ___   D. 8.019

2. The distance indicator, or odometer, on Robyn's family car reads 32795.2 after a summer vacation. The family drove 631.4 km on the trip. What did the odometer read before the trip?

3. Seamus has $12 to spend at the hobby shop. Does he have enough money to buy a 5 m rope for $5.64, a bucket of paint for $3.75, and a pack of construction paper for $2.39?

PERCENTAGES

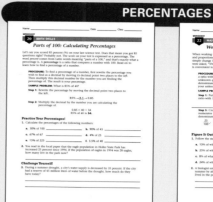

WORKSHEET 20 MATH SKILLS
Parts of 100: Calculating Percentages

Let's say you scored 85 percent (%) on your last science test. Does that mean you got 85 questions right? Probably not. That 85 means it was expressed as a percentage. The word percent comes from Latin words meaning "parts of a 100," and that's exactly what a percentage is. A percentage is a ratio that compares a number with 100. Read on to learn how to find a percentage of a number.

PROCEDURE: To find a percentage of a number, first rewrite the percentage you wish to find as a decimal by moving its decimal point two places to the left. Then multiply the decimal number by the number you are finding the percentage of. The result is your percentage.

SAMPLE PROBLEM: What is 85% of 40?

Step 1: Rewrite the percentage by moving the decimal point two places to the left.

$$85\% \to 85. \to 0.85$$

Step 2: Multiply the decimal by the number you are calculating the percentage of.

$$0.85 \times 40 = 34$$

85% of 40 is **34.**

Practice Your Percentages!

1. Calculate the percentages of the following numbers.

a. 30% of 100 =   b. 90% of 45 =

c. 67% of 67 =   d. 4% of 25 =

e. 13% of 225 =   f. 5.5% of 40 =

2. You read in the local paper that the eagle population in Hollow State Park has increased 25 percent since 1994. If the population of eagles in 1994 was 28 eagles, how many live in the park now?

Challenge Yourself!

3. During a summer drought, a city's water supply is decreased by 35 percent. If the city had a reserve of 43 million liters of water before the drought, how much do they have today?

WORKSHEET 21 MATH SKILLS
Percentages, Fractions, and Decimals

Imagine that your science class is doing a school survey to determine which eye colors are most common. The report from the sixth-grade class says that $\frac{2}{5}$ of the students have brown eyes, 25 percent have blue eyes, and 0.2 have green eyes. The seventh-grade class reports that 0.6 have brown eyes, $\frac{2}{5}$ have blue eyes, and 15 percent have green eyes. The eighth-grade class reports that 0.5 have black or brown eyes, 0.2 have blue or green eyes. Yikes! Each class has a different way of showing its data! So how do you compare the reports? Well, it's not as complicated as it might look. You see, percentages, fractions, and decimals are just different ways of expressing the same information. Each one tells you how much or how many of a certain amount. As you learned on the last page, a percentage can be changed to a decimal. For example, 45 percent is equal to 0.45. Percentages can also be changed into fractions. Likewise, every fraction can be expressed as a decimal or percentage, and so on. When comparing numbers or doing operations with numbers, it is often easier to have all of your numbers in the same form before doing calculations.

PROCEDURE: To change a fraction to a decimal or percentage, divide the numerator of the fraction by the denominator to make a decimal. To change the decimal number into a percentage, move the decimal point two places to the right.

Step 1: Divide the numerator by the denominator.

$$3 \div 5 = 0.6$$

Step 2: To change the decimal into a percentage, move the decimal point two places to the right.

$$0.6 \to 0.6_{\wedge} \to \textbf{60\%}$$

PROCEDURE: To change a decimal number into a fraction or percentage, place the decimal over its place value and reduce. To change a decimal into a percentage, see Step 2 of Procedure 1.

SAMPLE PROBLEM: Express 0.56 as a fraction and a percentage.

Step 1: Because 0.56 is in the hundredths place, put the whole number over 100 and reduce.

$$\frac{56}{100} = \frac{14}{25}$$

Step 2: To change a decimal into a percentage, move the decimal point two places to the right, in to step 2 of procedure 1.

$$0.56 \to 0.56_{\wedge} \to 56\%$$

Practice What You've Learned!

1. Express the following percentages as decimal numbers.

a. 52%   b. 99%

c. 7.8%   d. 0.57%

WORKSHEET 22 MATH SKILLS
Working with Percentages and Proportions

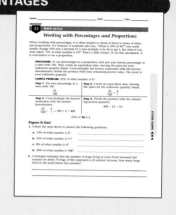

When working with percentages, it is often helpful to think of them in terms of ratios and proportions. For instance, if someone asks you, "What is 10% of 40?" you could simply change 10% into a proportion of 10 to 100. Cross-multiply 10 by 40 to get 4. But what if you were asked, "5% of what number is 10?" That's a little trickier. To do this calculation, it is convenient to use a proportion.

PROCEDURE: To use percentages in a proportion, first put your known percentage in a ratio with 100. Then create an equivalent ratio, leaving the place for your unknown quantity blank. Cross-multiply the known numerator with the known denominator. Divide the product with your remaining known value. The result is your unknown quantity.

SAMPLE PROBLEM: 25% of what number is 4?

Step 1: Put your percentage in a ratio with 100.   **Step 2:** Create an equivalent ratio, leaving the space for the unknown quantity blank.

$$\frac{25}{100}$$

Step 3: Cross-multiply the known numerator with the known denominator.   **Step 4:** Divide the product with the remaining known quantity.

$$\frac{25}{100} = \frac{4}{?} \to 100 \times 4 = 400$$ $$400 \div 25 = 16$$

25% of **16** is 4.

Figure It Out!

1. Follow the steps above to answer the following questions.

a. 15% of what number is 3?

b. 23% of what number is 115?

c. 8% of what number is 4?

d. 24% of what number is 168?

2. A biologist estimates that the total number of frogs living in Lasso Pond increased last summer by about 70 frogs. If this represents a 25 percent increase, how many frogs lived in the pond before last summer?

POWERS OF 10

WORKSHEET 23 MATH SKILLS
Counting the Zeros

A power of 10 is a number that can have 10 as its only factors. For instance, $(10 \times 10) = 100$ and $(10 \times 10 \times 10) = 10,000$ are both powers of 10. Multiplying and dividing by powers of 10 is as easy as counting the zeros and moving your decimal point the same number of places.

Part 1: Multiplying by Powers of 10

PROCEDURE: To multiply by a power of 10, move the decimal point to the right the same number of places as there are zeros in the power of 10. If there are not enough places in your number to do this, you will need to add zeros to the number as place holders.

SAMPLE PROBLEM: Multiply 8.25 by 10, 100, and 1000.

$$10 \times 8.25 = 8.25_{\wedge} = 82.5$$
$$100 \times 8.25 = 8.25_{\wedge\wedge} = 825$$
$$1000 \times 8.25 = 8.250_{\wedge\wedge\wedge} = 8250$$

It's Your Turn!

1. Write your answers on the lines, and remember to place commas in the appropriate places.

a. 10 × 6 =   b. 9.981 × 100 =

c. 710 × 100 =   d. 1000 × 41 =

e. 10 × 11.9 =   f. 67 × 10,000 =

Part 2: Dividing by Powers of 10

PROCEDURE: To divide a number by a power of 10, move the decimal point to the left as many places as there are zeros in the power of 10.

SAMPLE PROBLEM: Divide 763 by 10, 1000, and 100,000.

$$763 \div 10 = 76.3_{\wedge} = 76.3$$
$$763 \div 1000 = {}_{\wedge}7.6.3 = 0.763$$
$$763 \div 100,000 = {}_{\wedge\wedge}7.6.3 = 0.00763$$

2. Divide by powers of 10.

a. 55 ÷ 1000 =   b. 9907 ÷ 100 =

c. 420 ÷ 10 =   d. 4.01 ÷ 100 =

e. 0.04 ÷ 1000 =   f. 996 ÷ 10,000 =

WORKSHEET 24 MATH SKILLS
Creating Exponents

Imagine that you are writing a paper for your science class and need to write many very large numbers, such as 10,000,000,000,000. Your fingers would get pretty tired writing all those zeros. However, there is a simpler way to express these large powers of 10. An exponent is a small number placed above and to the right of a base number to show how many times the base number is multiplied by itself. For example, 100,000 is 10 multiplied by itself five times, or $10 \times 10 \times 10 \times 10 \times 10$. Written in exponential form, 100,000 is 10^5. The exponent number tells you how many zeros are in your power of 10.

PROCEDURE: To change a power of 10 into exponential form, count the number of zeros in your power of 10. This number will be your exponent. Place the exponent above and to the right of the base number 10.

SAMPLE PROBLEM: Write 10,000,000,000,000 in exponential form.

Step 1: Count the zeros in your power of 10.   **Step 2:** Place your exponent above and to the right of the base number 10.

$$10,000,000,000,000 \text{ has } 13 \text{ zeros.}$$ $$10^{13}$$

On Your Own!

1. Convert the following powers of 10 into exponential form.

a. 1000 =   c. 10,000,000 =

b. 1,000,000 =   d. 100,000,000 =

e. 10,000,000,000,000,000,000,000,000,000,000 =

2. Change the following exponent numbers to powers of 10.

a. 10^7 =   b. 10^4 =

c. 10^{12} =   d. 10^2 =

e. 10^{25} =

SCIENTIFIC NOTATION

WORKSHEET 25 MATH SKILLS
What Is Scientific Notation?

Sometimes scientific calculations result in very large numbers, like 918,700,000,000,000, or in very small numbers, such as 0.000000578. Scientific notation is a faster way of representing such numbers without writing out the place-holding zeros. In scientific notation, we write the number as a product of two factors: the first is a number between 1 and 10, and the second is a power of ten, written as 10^{exponent}.

PROCEDURE: To write a number in scientific notation, first identify which digits are not place-holding zeros. Then place the decimal point after the leftmost digit. To find the exponent for the factor of 10, count the number of places that you moved the decimal point. For any number that is greater than 1, the exponent will be positive. If you moved the decimal point to the right, the exponent will be negative.

SAMPLE PROBLEM: Write 653,000,000 in scientific notation.

Step 1: Identify the number without the place-holding zeros.   **Step 2:** Place the decimal point after the leftmost digit.

653   6.53

Step 3: Find the exponent by counting the number of places that you moved the decimal point.   **Step 4:** Write the number in scientific notation.

$$6_{\wedge}5_{\wedge}3_{\wedge}0_{\wedge}0_{\wedge}0_{\wedge}0_{\wedge}0_{\wedge}0 = 6.53$$

The decimal point was moved 8 places to the left. Therefore, the exponent of 10 is positive 8. Remember, if the decimal point had moved to the right, the exponent would be negative. $$6.53 \times 10^8$$

Practice Your Skills!

Original number	Number without place-holding zeros	Power of 10	Number in scientific notation
1. 530,000			
2. 504,180,000			
3. 0.000000617			

4. Express the following data in scientific notation:

a. 13,657 kg   b. 0.000043 L

c. 0.00081 m   d. 1011.9 cm

WORKSHEET 26 MATH SKILLS
Multiplying and Dividing in Scientific Notation

Part 1: Multiplying in Scientific Notation

PROCEDURE: To multiply numbers in scientific notation, multiply the decimal numbers. Then add the exponents of the powers of 10. Place the new power of 10 with the decimal in scientific notation form. If your decimal number is greater than 10, count the number of times the decimal moves to the left, and add this number to the exponent.

SAMPLE PROBLEM: Multiply (2.6×10^3) by (6.3×10^4).

Step 1: Multiply the decimal numbers.   **Step 2:** Add the exponents.

$$2.6 \times 6.3 = 16.38$$ $$3 + 4 = 7$$

Step 3: Put the new decimal number with the new exponent in scientific notation form.   **Step 4:** Because the new decimal number is greater than 10, count the number of places the decimal moves to put the number between 1 and 10. Add this number to the exponent.

$$16.38 \times 10^7$$ $$1.638 \times 10^8$$

The decimal moves one place, so add 1 to the exponent.

Try It Yourself!

1. Follow the steps in the Sample Problem carefully to complete the following equations.

Multiplying with Scientific Notations

Problem	New decimal	New exponent	Answer
Sample problem: $(4.4 \times 10^2) \times (3.9 \times 10^6)$	$4.4 \times 3.9 = 17.16$	$6 + 4 = 10$	1.716×10^{11}
a. $(2.8 \times 10^3) \times (1.9 \times 10^4)$			
b. $(1.3 \times 10^3) \times (4.7 \times 10^2)$			
c. $(2.6 \times 10^3) \times (5.2 \times 10^5)$			
d. $(4.9 \times 10^2) \times (1.4 \times 10^3)$			

2. The mass of one hydrogen atom is 1.67×10^{-27} kg. A cylinder contains 3.01×10^{23} hydrogen atoms. What is the mass of the hydrogen?

SI MEASUREMENT AND CONVERSION

WORKSHEET 27 MATH SKILLS
What Is SI?

To make sharing information easier, most of the world uses the SI system of measurement. SI, which stands for Système Internationale, is a standard for measuring mass, length, volume, and other quantities. It is used by all scientists to avoid the confusion of comparing data that is based on different measuring systems. Three common SI units are in the chart at right. Obviously, these three units are not suitable for all measuring needs. But most quantities can be measured using one of these units with one of the prefixes in the chart below.

Quantity	Unit	Symbol
length	meter	m
volume	liter	L
mass	gram	g

Prefix	Powers of 10	Symbol	Example
kilo-	1000	(10^3)	k	kilogram (kg)
hecto-	100	(10^2)	h	hectoliter (hL)
deca-	10	(10^1)	da	decameter (dam)
—	1			meter (m), gram (g), liter (L)
deci-	0.1	(10^{-1})	d	decigram (dg)
centi-	0.01	(10^{-2})	c	centimeter (cm)
milli-	0.001	(10^{-3})	m	milliliter (mL)

PROCEDURE: To convert between SI units, first find the prefixes of your numbers in the chart above. If you are converting from a smaller prefix to a larger prefix (moving up the chart), divide your number by a power of 10. If you are converting from a larger prefix to a smaller prefix (moving down the chart), multiply your number by a power of 10.

SAMPLE PROBLEM: Convert 500 decimeters (dm) to kilometers (km).

Step 1: Find the prefixes of the numbers.

Step 2: Notice that you will move up the chart four places when converting from deci- to kilo-. Therefore, you will divide your number by $10 \times 10 \times 10 \times 10$, or 10,000.

$$500 \div 10,000 = 2_{\wedge}5 = 0.05 \textbf{ kilometers (km)}$$

SAMPLE PROBLEM: 2.5 centimeters (cm) is how many milliliters (mL)?

Step 1: Find the prefixes.

centiliters to milliliters?

Step 2: Because you move one place when converting from centi- to milli-, multiply your number by 10.

$$2.5 \text{ centimeters (cL)} = \textbf{25 milliliters (mL)}$$

WORKSHEET 28 MATH SKILLS
A Formula for SI Catch-up

Scientists use the SI system all the time. But most people in the United States still use non-SI units. So what do you do if you data are in SI units and you want to convert the data into SI units, or vice versa? Have no fear! Conversion charts, like the one shown below, can help you accomplish the task with ease.

SI Conversion Chart

If you know	Multiply by	To find
inches (in.)	2.54	centimeters (cm)
feet (ft)	30.50	centimeters (cm)
yards (yd)	0.91	meters (m)
miles (mi)	1.61	kilometers (km)
ounces (oz)	28.35	grams (g)
pounds (lb)	0.45	kilograms (kg)
fluid ounces (fl oz)	29.57	milliliters (mL)
cups (c)	0.24	liters (L)
pints (pt)	0.47	liters (L)
quarts (qt)	0.94	liters (L)
gallons (gal)	3.79	liters (L)

PROCEDURE: To convert from non-SI units to SI units, find the prefixes of your numbers in the SI column and multiply it by the number in the center column. The resulting number will be in the SI unit in the right column.

To convert a SI unit into a non-SI unit, find the SI unit in the right column and divide the number in the center column to get the non-SI unit on the left.

SAMPLE PROBLEM: Convert 15 gal into liters (L).

$$15 \times 3.79 = \textbf{56.85 L}$$

Complete the Conversions!

1. Use the conversion chart to do the following conversions.

a. 15 oz =   d. 40 cm =

c. 22 c =   e. 3.2 c =

e. 5.3 gal =   f. 115 lb =

Math Skills for Science (continued)

GEOMETRY

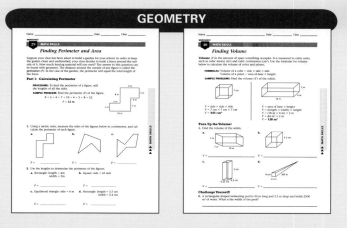

Worksheet 29 — MATH SKILLS: Finding Perimeter and Area

Worksheet 30 — MATH SKILLS: Finding Volume

THE UNIT FACTOR AND DIMENSIONAL ANALYSIS

Worksheet 31 — MATH SKILLS: The Unit Factor and Dimensional Analysis

MATH IN SCIENCE: INTEGRATED SCIENCE

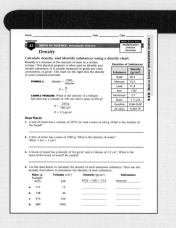

Worksheet 32 — MATH IN SCIENCE: INTEGRATED SCIENCE: Density

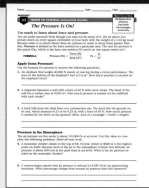

Worksheet 33 — MATH IN SCIENCE: INTEGRATED SCIENCE: The Pressure Is On!

Worksheet 34 — MATH IN SCIENCE: INTEGRATED SCIENCE: Sound Reasoning

Worksheet 35 — MATH IN SCIENCE: INTEGRATED SCIENCE: Using Temperature Scales

Worksheet 36 — MATH IN SCIENCE: INTEGRATED SCIENCE: Radioactive Decay and the Half-life

Worksheet 37 — MATH IN SCIENCE: INTEGRATED SCIENCE: Rain-Forest Math

Math Skills for Science (continued)

MATH IN SCIENCE: LIFE SCIENCE

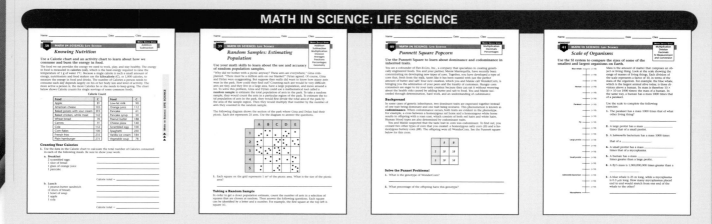

MATH IN SCIENCE: EARTH SCIENCE

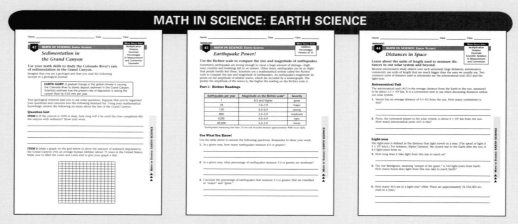

T18

Math Skills for Science (continued)

MATH IN SCIENCE: PHYSICAL SCIENCE

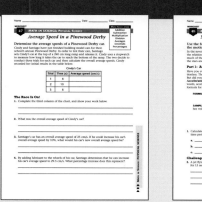

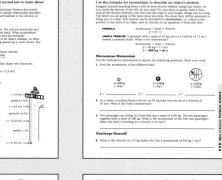
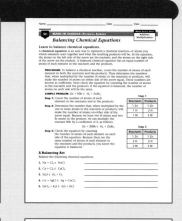

47 Average Speed in a Pinewood Derby

48 Newton: Force and Motion

49 Momentum

50 Balancing Chemical Equations

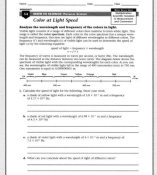

51 Work and Power

52 A Bicycle Trip

53 Mechanical Advantage

54 Color at Light Speed

Assessment Checklist & Rubrics

The following is just a sample of over 50 checklists and rubrics contained in this booklet.

RUBRICS FOR WRITTEN WORK

Basic Rubric for Written Work

RUBRIC FOR EXPERIMENTS

Rubric for Experiments

TEACHER EVALUATION OF COOPERATIVE LEARNING

Teacher Evaluation of Cooperative Group Activity

TEACHER EVALUATION OF STUDENT PROGRESS

Teacher Evaluation of Daily Progress: Homework and Class Participation

National Science Education Standards

The following lists show the chapter correlation of *Holt Science & Technology: Weather and Climate* with the *National Science Education Standards* (grades 5–8).

Unifying Concepts and Processes

Standard	Chapter Correlation	
Evidence, models, and explanation Code: UCP 2	Chapter 1	1.2
	Chapter 2	2.1
	Chapter 3	3.2, 3.4
Change, constancy, and measurement Code: UCP 3	Chapter 2	2.1
	Chapter 3	3.2, 3.4

Science as Inquiry

Standard	Chapter Correlation	
Abilities necessary to do scientific inquiry Code: SAI 1	Chapter 1	1.4
	Chapter 2	2.1, 2.4
	Chapter 3	3.1, 3.2, 3.3, 3.4
Understandings about scientific inquiry Code: SAI 2	Chapter 1	1.2
	Chapter 3	3.2, 3.3, 3.4

Science and Technology

Standard	Chapter Correlation	
Abilities of technological design Code: ST 1	Chapter 2	2.4
	Chapter 3	3.2
Understandings about science and technology Code: ST 2	Chapter 3	3.4

Science in Personal Perspectives

Standard	Chapter Correlation	
Personal health Code: SPSP 1	Chapter 1	1.1
	Chapter 3	3.1, 3.4
Populations, resources, and environments Code: SPSP 2	Chapter 3	3.2, 3.3
Natural hazards Code: SPSP 3	Chapter 1	1.1, 1.2, 1.4
	Chapter 2	2.1, 2.3, 2.4
	Chapter 3	3.1, 3.4
Risks and benefits Code: SPSP 4	Chapter 1	1.1, 1.2, 1.4
	Chapter 2	2.3, 2.4
	Chapter 3	3.4
Science and technology in society Code: SPSP 5	Chapter 3	3.4

History and Nature of Science

Standard	Chapter Correlation	
Science as a human endeavor Code: HNS 1	Chapter 3	3.2, 3.3, 3.4
History of science Code: HNS 3	Chapter 2	2.2
	Chapter 3	3.2, 3.3

Earth Science Content Standards

Structure of the Earth System

Standard	Chapter Correlation	
Water, which covers the majority of the earth's surface, circulates through the crust, oceans, and atmosphere in what is known as the "water cycle." Water evaporates from the earth's surface, rises and cools as it moves to higher elevations, condenses as rain or snow, and falls to the surface where it collects in lakes, oceans soil, and in rocks underground. Code: ES 1f	**Chapter 2** **Chapter 3**	2.1 3.1
The atmosphere is a mixture of nitrogen, oxygen, and trace gases that include water vapor. The atmosphere has different properties at different elevations. Code: ES 1h	**Chapter 1**	1.1
Clouds, formed by the condensation of water vapor, affect weather and climate. Code: ES 1i	**Chapter 2**	2.1, 2.3, 2.4
Global patterns of atmospheric movement influence local weather. Oceans have a major effect on climate, because water in the oceans holds a large amount of heat. Code: ES 1j	**Chapter 1** **Chapter 2** **Chapter 3**	1.3 2.2, 2.3, 2.4 3.3
Living organisms have played many roles in the earth system, including affecting the composition of the atmosphere, producing some types of rocks, and contributing to the weathering of rocks. Code: ES 1k	**Chapter 3**	3.4

Earth's History

Standard	Chapter Correlation	
The earth processes we see today, including erosion, movement of lithospheric plates, and changes in atmospheric composition, are similar to those that occurred in the past. Earth history is also influenced by occasional catastrophes, such as the impact of an asteroid or comet. Code: ES 2a	**Chapter 3**	3.4

Earth in the Solar System

Standard	Chapter Correlation	
The sun is the major source of energy for phenomena on the earth's surface, such as growth of plants, winds, ocean currents, and the water cycle. Seasons result from variations in the amount of the sun's energy hitting the surface, due to the tilt of the earth's rotation on its axis and the length of the day. Code: ES 3d	**Chapter 3**	3.1

HOLT SCIENCE & TECHNOLOGY

Weather and Climate

HOLT, RINEHART AND WINSTON

A Harcourt Education Company

Orlando • **Austin** • New York • San Diego • Toronto • London

Acknowledgments

Contributing Authors

Kathleen Kaska
Former Life and Earth Science Teacher and Science Department Chair

Robert J. Sager, M.S., J.D., L.G.
Coordinator and Professor of Earth Science
Pierce College
Lakewood, Washington

Inclusion Specialist

Karen Clay
Inclusion Specialist Consultant
Boston, Massachusetts

Safety Reviewer

Jack Gerlovich, Ph.D.
Associate Professor
School of Education
Drake University
Des Moines, Iowa

Academic Reviewers

David M. Armstrong, Ph.D.
Professor
Ecology and Evolutionary Biology
University of Colorado
Boulder, Colorado
Institution

John Brockhaus, Ph.D.
Professor of Geospatial Information Science and Director of Geospatial Information Science Program
Department of Geography and Environmental Engineering
United States Military Academy
West Point, New York

Deborah Hanley, Ph.D.
Meteorologist
State of Florida
Department of Agriculture and Consumer Services
Division of Forestry
Tallahassee, Florida

Madeline Micceri Mignone, Ph.D.
Assistant Professor
Natural Science
Dominican College
Orangeburg, New York

Dork Sahagian, Ph.D.
Research Professor
Department of Earth Sciences
Institute for the Study of Earth, Oceans, and Space
University of New Hampshire
Durham, New Hampshire

Teacher Reviewers

Diedre S. Adams
Physical Science Instructor
Science Department
West Vigo Middle School
West Terre Haute, Indiana

Laura Buchanan
Science Teacher and Department Chairperson
Corkran Middle School
Glen Burnie, Maryland

Robin K. Clanton
Science Department Head
Berrien Middle School
Nashville, Georgia

Meredith Hanson
Science Teacher
Westside Middle School
Rocky Face, Georgia

Jennifer L. Lamkie
Science Teacher
Thomas Jefferson Middle School
Edison, New Jersey

Susan H. Robinson
Science Teacher
Oglethorpe County Middle School
Lexington, Georgia

Lab Development

Kenneth E. Creese
Science Teacher
White Mountain Junior High School
Rock Spring, Wyoming

Printed in the United States of America

ISBN 0-03-025574-0

3 4 5 6 7 048 08 07 06 05 04

UNIT 1 Weather and Climate

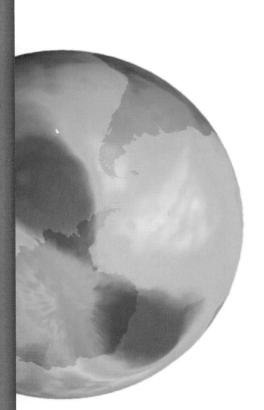

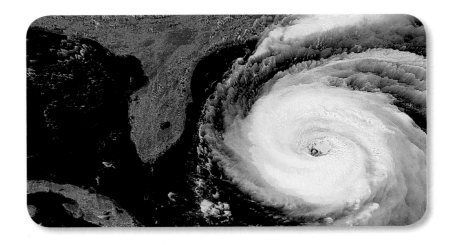

Labs and Activities

How to Use Your Textbook

Your Roadmap for Success with Holt Science and Technology

Reading Warm-Up

A Reading Warm-Up at the beginning of every section provides you with the section's objectives and key terms. The objectives tell you what you'll need to know after you finish reading the section.

Key terms are listed for each section. Learn the definitions of these terms because you will most likely be tested on them. Each key term is highlighted in the text and is defined at point of use and in the margin. You can also use the glossary to locate definitions quickly.

STUDY TIP Reread the objectives and the definitions to the key terms when studying for a test to be sure you know the material.

Get Organized

A Reading Strategy at the beginning of every section provides tips to help you organize and remember the information covered in the section. Keep a science notebook so that you are ready to take notes when your teacher reviews the material in class. Keep your assignments in this notebook so that you can review them when studying for the chapter test.

SECTION 3

Global Winds and Local Winds

If you open the valve on a bicycle tube, the air rushes out. Why? The air inside the tube is at a higher pressure than the air is outside the tube. In effect, letting air out of the tube created a wind.

READING WARM-UP

Objectives
- Explain the relationship between air pressure and wind direction.
- Describe global wind patterns.
- Explain the causes of local wind patterns.

Terms to Learn

wind	westerlies
Coriolis effect	trade winds
polar easterlies	jet stream

READING STRATEGY

Prediction Guide Before reading this section, write the title of each heading in this section. Next, under each heading, write what you think you will learn.

wind the movement of air caused by differences in air pressure

Why Air Moves

The movement of air caused by differences in air pressure is called **wind.** The greater the pressure difference, the faster the wind moves. The devastation shown in **Figure 1** was caused by winds that resulted from extreme differences in air pressure.

Air Rises at the Equator and Sinks at the Poles

Differences in air pressure are generally caused by the unequal heating of the Earth. The equator receives more direct solar energy than other latitudes, so air at the equator is warmer and less dense than the surrounding air. Warm, less dense air rises and creates an area of low pressure. This warm, rising air flows toward the poles. At the poles, the air is colder and denser than the surrounding air, so it sinks. As the cold air sinks, it creates areas of high pressure around the poles. This cold polar air then flows toward the equator.

Figure 1 *In 1992, Hurricane Andrew became the most destructive hurricane in U.S. history. The winds from the hurricane reached 264 km/h.*

458 Chapter 15 The Atmosphere

Be Resourceful — Use the Web

SCiLINKS

Internet Connect boxes in your textbook take you to resources that you can use for science projects, reports, and research papers. Go to scilinks.org, and type in the SciLinks code to get information on a topic.

go.hrw.com

Visit go.hrw.com Find worksheets, Current Science® magazine articles online, and other materials that go with your textbook at **go.hrw.com.** Click on the textbook icon and the table of contents to see all of the resources for each chapter.

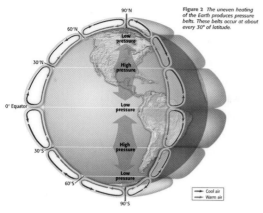

Figure 2 *The uneven heating of the Earth produces pressure belts. These belts occur at about every 30° of latitude.*

- 90°N
- 60°N — Low pressure
- 30°N — High pressure
- 0° Equator — Low pressure
- 30°S — High pressure
- 60°S — Low pressure
- 90°S

→ Cool air
→ Warm air

Pressure Belts Are Found Every 30°

You may imagine that wind moves in one huge, circular pattern from the poles to the equator. In fact, air travels in many large, circular patterns called *convection cells*. Convection cells are separated by *pressure belts*, bands of high pressure and low pressure found about every 30° of latitude, as shown in **Figure 2**. As warm ai... poles, the ai... latitude, som... causes high p... This cool ai... rises again. ... equator. Air ... 60° north an... creates a low...

Reading C... pressure? (Se...

Use the Illustrations and Photos

Art shows complex ideas and processes. Learn to analyze the art so that you better understand the material you read in the text.

Tables and graphs display important information in an organized way to help you see relationships.

A picture is worth a thousand words. Look at the photographs to see relevant examples of science concepts that you are reading about.

Mountain Breezes and Valley Breezes

Mountain and valley breezes are other examples of local winds caused by an area's geography. Campers in mountainous areas may feel a warm afternoon quickly change into a cold night soon after the sun sets. Differences in temperature and elevation cause this effect. The sun warms the valley and the air above it during the day. Then, the warm air rises and blows up the mountain, creating a valley breeze. At night, the mountains cool faster than the valleys. So, the cold air sinks and flows down from the mountains, creating a mountain breeze.

Reading Check Why does the wind tend to blow down from mountains at night?

CONNECTION TO Social Studies

Local Breezes The chinook, the shamal, the sirocco, and the Santa Ana are all local winds. Find out about an interesting local wind, and create a poster-board display that shows how the wind forms and how it affects human cultures.

ACTIVITY

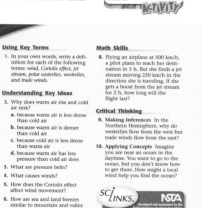

SECTION Review

Summary

- Winds blow from areas of high pressure to areas of low pressure.
- Pressure belts are found approximately every 30° of latitude.
- The Coriolis effect causes wind to appear to curve as it moves across the Earth's surface.
- Global winds include the polar easterlies, the westerlies, and the trade winds.
- Local winds include sea and land breezes and mountain and valley breezes.

Using Key Terms

1. In your own words, write a definition for each of the following terms: *wind, Coriolis effect, jet stream, polar easterlies, westerlies,* and *trade winds.*

Understanding Key Ideas

2. Why does warm air rise and cold air sink?
   a. because warm air is less dense than cold air
   b. because warm air is denser than cold air
   c. because cold air is less dense than warm air
   d. because warm air has less pressure than cold air does

3. What are pressure belts?

4. What causes winds?

5. How does the Coriolis effect affect wind movement?

6. How are sea and land breezes similar to mountain and valley breezes?

7. Would there be winds if the Earth's surface were the same temperature everywhere? Explain your answer.

Math Skills

8. Flying an airplane at 500 km/h, a pilot plans to reach her destination in 5 h. But she finds a jet stream moving 250 km/h in the direction she is traveling. If she gets a boost from the jet stream for 2 h, how long will the flight last?

Critical Thinking

9. **Making Inferences** In the Northern Hemisphere, why do westerlies flow from the west but trade winds flow from the east?

10. **Applying Concepts** Imagine you are near an ocean in the daytime. You want to go to the ocean, but you don't know how to get there. How might a local wind help you find the ocean?

SciLINKS.
Developed and maintained by the National Science Teachers Association

For a variety of links related to this chapter, go to www.scilinks.org

Topic: Atmospheric Pressure and Winds
SciLinks code: HSM0115

463

Answer the Section Reviews

Section Reviews test your knowledge of the main points of the section. Critical Thinking items challenge you to think about the material in greater depth and to find connections that you infer from the text.

STUDY TIP When you can't answer a question, reread the section. The answer is usually there.

Do Your Homework

Your teacher may assign worksheets to help you understand and remember the material in the chapter.

STUDY TIP Don't try to answer the questions without reading the text and reviewing your class notes. A little preparation up front will make your homework assignments a lot easier. Answering the items in the Chapter Review will help prepare you for the chapter test.

Holt Online Learning

Visit Holt Online Learning
If your teacher gives you a special password to log onto the Holt Online Learning site, you'll find your complete textbook on the Web. In addition, you'll find some great learning tools and practice quizzes. You'll be able to see how well you know the material from your textbook.

CNN student News™

Visit CNN Student News
You'll find up-to-date events in science at **cnnstudentnews.com.**

SAFETY FIRST!

Exploring, inventing, and investigating are essential to the study of science. However, these activities can also be dangerous. To make sure that your experiments and explorations are safe, you must be aware of a variety of safety guidelines. You have probably heard of the saying, "It is better to be safe than sorry." This is particularly true in a science classroom where experiments and explorations are being performed. Being uninformed and careless can result in serious injuries. Don't take chances with your own safety or with anyone else's.

The following pages describe important guidelines for staying safe in the science classroom. Your teacher may also have safety guidelines and tips that are specific to your classroom and laboratory. Take the time to be safe.

Safety Rules!

Start Out Right

Always get your teacher's permission before attempting any laboratory exploration. Read the procedures carefully, and pay particular attention to safety information and caution statements. If you are unsure about what a safety symbol means, look it up or ask your teacher. You cannot be too careful when it comes to safety. If an accident does occur, inform your teacher immediately regardless of how minor you think the accident is.

If you are instructed to note the odor of a substance, wave the fumes toward your nose with your hand. Never put your nose close to the source.

Safety Symbols

All of the experiments and investigations in this book and their related worksheets include important safety symbols to alert you to particular safety concerns. Become familiar with these symbols so that when you see them, you will know what they mean and what to do. It is important that you read this entire safety section to learn about specific dangers in the laboratory.

Eye protection

Clothing protection

Hand safety

Heating safety

Electric safety

Chemical safety

Animal safety

Sharp object

Plant safety

x

Eye Safety

Wear safety goggles when working around chemicals, acids, bases, or any type of flame or heating device. Wear safety goggles any time there is even the slightest chance that harm could come to your eyes. If any substance gets into your eyes, notify your teacher immediately and flush your eyes with running water for at least 15 minutes. Treat any unknown chemical as if it were a dangerous chemical. Never look directly into the sun. Doing so could cause permanent blindness.

Avoid wearing contact lenses in a laboratory situation. Even if you are wearing safety goggles, chemicals can get between the contact lenses and your eyes. If your doctor requires that you wear contact lenses instead of glasses, wear eye-cup safety goggles in the lab.

Safety Equipment

Know the locations of the nearest fire alarms and any other safety equipment, such as fire blankets and eyewash fountains, as identified by your teacher, and know the procedures for using the equipment.

Neatness

Keep your work area free of all unnecessary books and papers. Tie back long hair, and secure loose sleeves or other loose articles of clothing, such as ties and bows. Remove dangling jewelry. Don't wear open-toed shoes or sandals in the laboratory. Never eat, drink, or apply cosmetics in a laboratory setting. Food, drink, and cosmetics can easily become contaminated with dangerous materials.

Certain hair products (such as aerosol hair spray) are flammable and should not be worn while working near an open flame. Avoid wearing hair spray or hair gel on lab days.

Sharp/Pointed Objects

Use knives and other sharp instruments with extreme care. Never cut objects while holding them in your hands. Place objects on a suitable work surface for cutting.

Be extra careful when using any glassware. When adding a heavy object to a graduated cylinder, tilt the cylinder so that the object slides slowly to the bottom.

Heat

Wear safety goggles when using a heating device or a flame. Whenever possible, use an electric hot plate as a heat source instead of using an open flame. When heating materials in a test tube, always angle the test tube away from yourself and others. To avoid burns, wear heat-resistant gloves whenever instructed to do so.

Electricity

Be careful with electrical cords. When using a microscope with a lamp, do not place the cord where it could trip someone. Do not let cords hang over a table edge in a way that could cause equipment to fall if the cord is accidentally pulled. Do not use equipment with damaged cords. Be sure that your hands are dry and that the electrical equipment is in the "off" position before plugging it in. Turn off and unplug electrical equipment when you are finished.

Chemicals

Wear safety goggles when handling any potentially dangerous chemicals, acids, or bases. If a chemical is unknown, handle it as you would a dangerous chemical. Wear an apron and protective gloves when you work with acids or bases or whenever you are told to do so. If a spill gets on your skin or clothing, rinse it off immediately with water for at least 5 minutes while calling to your teacher.

Never mix chemicals unless your teacher tells you to do so. Never taste, touch, or smell chemicals unless you are specifically directed to do so. Before working with a flammable liquid or gas, check for the presence of any source of flame, spark, or heat.

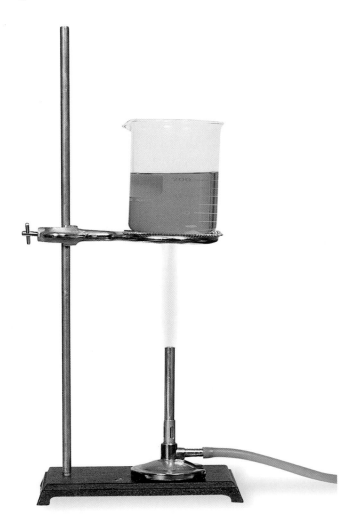

Animal Safety

Always obtain your teacher's permission before bringing any animal into the school building. Handle animals only as your teacher directs. Always treat animals carefully and respectfully. Wash your hands thoroughly after handling any animal.

Plant Safety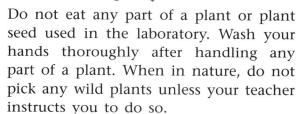

Do not eat any part of a plant or plant seed used in the laboratory. Wash your hands thoroughly after handling any part of a plant. When in nature, do not pick any wild plants unless your teacher instructs you to do so.

Glassware

Examine all glassware before use. Be sure that glassware is clean and free of chips and cracks. Report damaged glassware to your teacher. Glass containers used for heating should be made of heat-resistant glass.

The Atmosphere
Chapter Planning Guide

Compression guide:
To shorten instruction because of time limitations, omit the Chapter Lab.

OBJECTIVES	LABS, DEMONSTRATIONS, AND ACTIVITIES	TECHNOLOGY RESOURCES
PACING • 90 min pp. 2–9 **Chapter Opener**	**SE** Start-up Activity, p. 3 ◆ GENERAL	**OSP** Parent Letter ■ GENERAL **CD** Student Edition on CD-ROM **CD** Guided Reading Audio CD ■ **TR** Chapter Starter Transparency* **VID** Brain Food Video Quiz
Section 1 Characteristics of the Atmosphere • Describe the composition of Earth's atmosphere. • Explain why air pressure changes with altitude. • Explain how air temperature changes with atmospheric composition. • Describe the layers of the atmosphere.	**SE** Connection to Physics Air-Pressure Experiment, p. 5 GENERAL **TE** Group Activity It's a Gas!, p. 5 ◆ ADVANCED **SE** Skills Practice Lab Under Pressure! p. 28 ◆ GENERAL **CRF** Datasheet for Chapter Lab* **LB** Whiz-Bang Demonstrations Blue Sky* ◆ ADVANCED	**CRF** Lesson Plans* **TR** Bellringer Transparency* **TR** Layers of the Atmosphere* **TR** LINK TO LIFE SCIENCE The Connection Between Photosynthesis and Respiration* **VID** Lab Videos for Earth Science
PACING • 90 min pp. 10–13 **Section 2 Atmospheric Heating** • Describe what happens to solar energy that reaches Earth. • Summarize the processes of radiation, conduction, and convection. • Explain the relationship between the greenhouse effect and global warming.	**TE** Activity Popcorn, p. 10 ◆ BASIC **TE** Connection to Environmental Science, p. 11 ◆ GENERAL **TE** Group Activity Model Greenhouses, p. 12 ◆ BASIC **LB** Inquiry Labs Boiling Over!* GENERAL **LB** EcoLabs & Field Activities That Greenhouse Effect!* ◆ GENERAL **LB** Calculator-Based Lab The Greenhouse Effect* ADVANCED **LB** Calculator-Based Lab Heating of Land and Water* ◆ ADVANCED	**CRF** Lesson Plans* **TR** Bellringer Transparency* **TR** Scattering, Absorption, and Reflection* **TR** Radiation, Conduction, and Convection* **TR** The Greenhouse Effect* **CD** Science Tutor
PACING • 45 min pp. 14–19 **Section 3 Global Winds and Local Winds** • Explain the relationship between air pressure and wind direction. • Describe global wind patterns. • Explain the causes of local wind patterns.	**TE** Demonstration Air Movement, p. 14 GENERAL **TE** Activity Coriolis Effect, p. 16 ◆ BASIC **SE** Connection to Social Studies Local Breezes, p. 19 GENERAL **SE** Skills Practice Lab Go Fly a Bike!, p. 106 GENERAL **CRF** Datasheet for LabBook* **SE** Science in Action Math, Social Studies, and Language Arts, pp. 34–35 GENERAL	**CRF** Lesson Plans* **TR** Bellringer Transparency* **TR** Pressure Belts* **TR** The Coriolis Effect* **TR** Global Winds* **TR** Sea and Land Breezes* **SE** Internet Activity, p. 17 GENERAL **CD** Science Tutor
PACING • 45 min pp. 20–27 **Section 4 Air Pollution** • Compare primary and secondary air pollutants. • Identify the major sources of air pollution. • Explain the effects of an ozone hole. • List five effects of air pollution on the human body. • Identify ways to reduce air pollution.	**SE** Connection to Biology Cleaning the Air with Plants, p. 22 GENERAL **TE** Connection Activity Real World, p. 22 GENERAL **SE** Quick Lab Testing for Particulates, p. 23 GENERAL **CRF** Datasheet for Quick Lab* **TE** Demonstration Acid Rain, p. 23 ◆ BASIC **TE** Connection Activity Health, p. 25 GENERAL **SE** School-to-Home Activity Air Pollution Awareness, p. 26 GENERAL **TE** Internet Activity, p. 26 GENERAL **LB** Long-Term Projects & Research Ideas A Breath of Fresh Ether?* ADVANCED	**CRF** Lesson Plans* **TR** Bellringer Transparency* **TR** The Formation of Smog* **TR** Sources of Indoor Air Pollution* **CRF** SciLinks Activity* GENERAL **CD** Interactive Explorations CD-ROM Moose Malady GENERAL **CD** Science Tutor

PACING • 90 min

CHAPTER REVIEW, ASSESSMENT, AND STANDARDIZED TEST PREPARATION

CRF Vocabulary Activity* GENERAL
SE Chapter Review, pp. 30–31 GENERAL
CRF Chapter Review* ■ GENERAL
CRF Chapter Tests A* ■ GENERAL, B* ADVANCED, C* SPECIAL NEEDS
SE Standardized Test Preparation, pp. 32–33 GENERAL
CRF Standardized Test Preparation* GENERAL
CRF Performance-Based Assessment* GENERAL
OSP Test Generator GENERAL
CRF Test Item Listing* GENERAL

Online and Technology Resources

Visit **go.hrw.com** for a variety of free resources related to this textbook. Enter the keyword **HZ5ATM**.

Holt Online Learning

Students can access interactive problem-solving help and active visual concept development with the *Holt Science and Technology* Online Edition available at **www.hrw.com**.

 Guided Reading Audio CD
Also in Spanish

A direct reading of each chapter for auditory learners, reluctant readers, and Spanish-speaking students.

 Science Tutor CD-ROM

Excellent for remediation and test practice.

SKILLS DEVELOPMENT RESOURCES	SECTION REVIEW AND ASSESSMENT	STANDARDS CORRELATIONS
SE Pre-Reading Activity, p. 2 `GENERAL` **OSP** Science Puzzlers, Twisters & Teasers `GENERAL`		National Science Education Standards SAI 1
CRF Directed Reading A* ■ `BASIC`, B* `SPECIAL NEEDS` **CRF** Vocabulary and Section Summary* `GENERAL` **SE** Reading Strategy Mnemonics, p. 4 `GENERAL` **TE** Reading Strategy Reading Organizer, p. 5 `BASIC` **SE** Math Practice Modeling the Atmosphere, p. 6 `GENERAL` **TE** Inclusion Strategies, p. 7 **CRF** Reinforcement Worksheet Earth's Amazing Atmosphere* `BASIC`	**SE** Reading Checks, pp. 4, 6, 8 `GENERAL` **TE** Reteaching, p. 8 `BASIC` **TE** Quiz, p. 8 `GENERAL` **TE** Alternative Assessment, p. 8 `GENERAL` **SE** Section Review,* p. 9 ■ `GENERAL` **CRF** Section Quiz* ■ `GENERAL`	SPSP 1,3,4; ES 1h
CRF Directed Reading A* ■ `BASIC`, B* `SPECIAL NEEDS` **CRF** Vocabulary and Section Summary* `GENERAL` **SE** Reading Strategy Reading Organizer, p. 10 `GENERAL` **TE** Inclusion Strategies, p. 11 ◆	**SE** Reading Checks, pp. 11, 13 `GENERAL` **TE** Reteaching, p. 12 `BASIC` **TE** Quiz, p. 12 `GENERAL` **TE** Alternative Assessment, p. 12 `GENERAL` **SE** Section Review,* p. 13 ■ `GENERAL` **CRF** Section Quiz* ■ `GENERAL`	UCP 2 ; SAI 2; SPSP 3, 4
CRF Directed Reading A* ■ `BASIC`, B* `SPECIAL NEEDS` **CRF** Vocabulary and Section Summary* ■ `GENERAL` **SE** Reading Strategy Prediction Guide, p. 14 `GENERAL`	**SE** Reading Checks, pp. 15, 16, 19 `GENERAL` **TE** Homework, p. 16 `GENERAL` **TE** Reteaching, p. 18 `BASIC` **TE** Quiz, p. 18 `GENERAL` **TE** Alternative Assessment, p. 18 ◆ `GENERAL` **SE** Section Review,* p. 19 ■ `GENERAL` **CRF** Section Quiz* ■ `GENERAL`	ES 1j; *LabBook:* UCP 2; SAI 1; ST 1
CRF Directed Reading A* ■ `BASIC`, B* `SPECIAL NEEDS` **CRF** Vocabulary and Section Summary* ■ `GENERAL` **SE** Reading Strategy Reading Organizer, p. 20 `GENERAL` **CRF** Critical Thinking The Extraordinary GBG5K* `ADVANCED`	**SE** Reading Checks, pp. 20, 23, 24, 26 `GENERAL` **TE** Homework, p. 24 `GENERAL` **TE** Homework, p. 25 `ADVANCED` **TE** Reteaching, p. 26 `BASIC` **TE** Quiz, p. 26 `GENERAL` **TE** Alternative Assessment, p. 26 `BASIC` **SE** Section Review,* p. 27 ■ `GENERAL` **CRF** Section Quiz* ■ `GENERAL`	SAI 1; SPSP 3, 4; *Chapter Lab:* SAI 1

 **One-Stop Planner® CD-ROM**

This convenient CD-ROM includes:
- Lab Materials QuickList Software
- Holt Calendar Planner
- Customizable Lesson Plans
- Printable Worksheets
- ExamView® Test Generator

 **CNN Student News.**

cnnstudentnews.com

Find the latest news, lesson plans, and activities related to important scientific events.

 SCLINKS. NSTA

www.scilinks.org

Maintained by the **National Science Teachers Association.** See Chapter Enrichment pages for a complete list of topics.

 **Current Science®**

Check out *Current Science* articles and activities by visiting the HRW Web site at **go.hrw.com.** Just type in the keyword **HZ5CS15T.**

 **Classroom Videos**

- **Lab Videos** demonstrate the chapter lab.
- **Brain Food Video Quizzes** help students review the chapter material.
- **CNN Videos** bring science into your students' daily life.

Visual Resources

CHAPTER STARTER TRANSPARENCY

This Really Happened!

On August 17, 1998, Steve Fossett was well on his way to making the first around-the-world balloon flight. It was his fourth attempt, and after 10 days and 22,910 km, he had already traveled two-thirds of the way. At the time, this was farther than any other balloonist had traveled in history. But something happened in the dark morning hours that ended Fossett's flight and nearly cost him his life.

While floating over the Pacific Ocean at 8,839 m above sea level, Fossett noticed a row of thunderstorms below. Suddenly his balloon, the *Solo Spirit*, hit an unexpected air disturbance and was sucked downward at a rate of more than 420 km/h. Knowing he was in danger, Fossett climbed out of his bubble hatch

cut loose the heavy tanks of fuel and oxygen to slow the balloon's fall. He then prepared himself for the crash.

When Fossett regained consciousness, his capsule was upside down, half full of water, and on fire. With a satellite radio beacon to give his location and a small life boat, Fossett scrambled out of the capsule to await his rescue.

Fossett experienced firsthand how unpredictable our atmosphere can be. He was fortunate to have survived. The atmosphere can be unpredictable and dangerous, but it also provides us with gases needed for our survival on Earth. In this chapter you will learn how the Earth's atmosphere affects you and how you affect it.

BELLRINGER TRANSPARENCIES

Section: Characteristics of the Atmosphere
List the ways that the atmosphere is different from outer space.

Write your list in your **science journal**.

Section: Atmospheric Heating
How is food heated in an oven? How is food heated on a range top?

Record your response in your **science journal**.

TEACHING TRANSPARENCIES

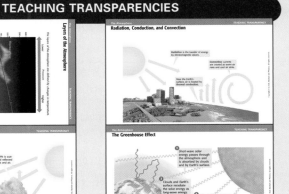

Layers of the Atmosphere

Radiation, Conduction, and Convection

Scattering, Absorption, and Reflection

The Greenhouse Effect

TEACHING TRANSPARENCIES

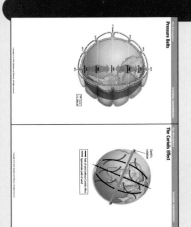

Pressure Belts

The Coriolis Effect

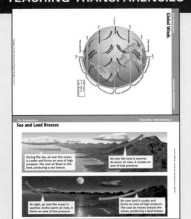

Global Winds

Sea and Land Breezes

During the day, air over the ocean is cooler and forms an area of high pressure. The cool air flows to the land, producing a sea breeze.

Air over the land is warmer. As warm air rises, it creates an area of low pressure.

At night, air over the ocean is warmer. As the warm air rises, it forms an area of low pressure.

Air over land is cooler and forms an area of high pressure. The cool air moves toward the ocean, producing a land breeze.

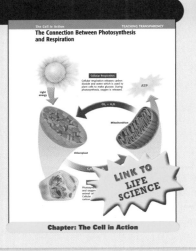

The Cell in Action

The Connection Between Photosynthesis and Respiration

LINK TO LIFE SCIENCE

Chapter: The Cell in Action

CONCEPT MAPPING TRANSPARENCY

Use the following terms to complete the concept map below: radiation, pressure, mesosphere, atmosphere, nitrogen, troposphere, oxygen, thermosphere

Planning Resources

LESSON PLANS

Lesson Plan — SAMPLE

Section: Waves

Pacing
Regular Schedule: with labs(s)2 days — without lab(s)2 days
Block Schedule: with labs(s) 1 1/2 days — without lab(s)1 day

Objectives
1. Relate the seven properties of life to a living organism.
2. Describe seven themes that can help you to organize what you learn about biology.
3. Identify the tiny structures that make up all living organisms.
4. Differentiate between reproduction and heredity and between metabolism and homeostasis.

National Science Education Standards Covered
LSInter: Cells have particular structures that underlie their functions.
LSMat1: Most cell functions involve chemical reactions.
LSBeh1: Cells store and use information to guide their functions.
UCP1: Cell functions are regulated.
SI1: Cells can differentiate and form complete multicellular organisms.
PS1: Species evolve over time.
ESS1: The great diversity of organisms is the result of more than 3.5 billion years of evolution.
ESS2: Natural selection and its evolutionary consequences provide a scientific explanation for the fossil record of ancient life forms as well as for the striking molecular similarities observed among the diverse species of living organisms.
ST1: The millions of different species of plants, animals, and microorganisms that live on Earth today are related by descent from common ancestors.
ST2: The energy for life primarily comes from the sun.
SPSP1: The complexity and organization of organisms accommodates the need for obtaining, transforming, transporting, releasing, and eliminating the matter and energy used to sustain the organism.
SPSP6: As matter and energy flows through different levels of organization of living systems—cells, organs, communities—and between living systems and the physical environment, chemical elements are recombined in different ways.
HNS1: Organisms have behavioral responses to internal changes and to external stimuli.

PARENT LETTER

SAMPLE

Dear Parent,

Your son's or daughter's science class will soon begin exploring the chapter entitled "The World of Physical Science." In this chapter, students will learn about how the scientific method applies to the world of physical science and the role of physical science in the world. By the end of the chapter, students should demonstrate a clear understanding of the chapter's main ideas and will be able to discuss the following topics:

1. physical science is the study of energy and matter (Section 1)
2. the role of physical science in the world around them (Section 1)
3. careers that rely on physical science (Section 1)
4. the steps used in the scientific method (Section 2)
5. examples of technology (Section 2)
6. how the scientific method is used to answer questions and solve problems (Section 2)
7. how our knowledge of science changes over time (Section 2)
8. how models represent real objects or systems (Section 3)
9. examples of different ways models are used in science (Section 3)
10. the importance of the International System of Units (Section 4)
11. the appropriate units to use for particular measurements (Section 4)
12. how area and density are derived quantities (Section 4)

Questions to Ask Along the Way

You can help your son or daughter learn about these topics by asking interesting questions such as the following:

- What are some surprising careers that use physical science?
- What is a characteristic of a good hypothesis?
- When is it a good idea to use a model?
- Why do Americans measure things in terms of inches and yards and meters ?

ALSO IN SPANISH

TEST ITEM LISTING

TEST ITEM LISTING
The World of Earth Science — SAMPLE

MULTIPLE CHOICE

1. A limitation of models is that
   a. they are large enough to see.
   b. they do not act exactly like the things that they model.
   c. they are smaller than the things that they model.
   d. they model unfamiliar things.
   Answer: B   Difficulty: 1   Section: 3   Objective: 2

2. The length 10 m is equal to
   a. 100 cm.   c. 10,000 mm.
   b. 1,000 cm.   d. Both (b) and (c)
   Answer: B   Difficulty: 1   Section: 3   Objective: 2

3. To be valid, a hypothesis must be
   a. testable.   c. made into a law.
   b. supported by evidence.   d. Both (a) and (b)
   Answer: D   Difficulty: 1   Section: 3   Objective: 2   1

4. The statement "Sheila has a stain on her shirt" is an example of a(n)
   a. law.   c. observation.
   b. hypothesis.   d. prediction.
   Answer: B   Difficulty: 1   Section: 3   Objective: 2

5. A hypothesis is often developed out of
   a. observations.   c. laws.
   b. experiments.   d. Both (a) and (b)
   Answer: D   Difficulty: 1   Section: 3   Objective: 2

6. How many milliliters are in 3.5 kL?
   a. 3,500 mL.   c. 3,500,000 mL
   b. 0.0035 mL.   d. 35,000 mL.
   Answer: B   Difficulty: 1   Section: 3   Objective: 2

7. A map of Seattle is an example of a
   a. law.   c. model.
   b. theory.   d. unit.
   Answer: C   Difficulty: 1   Section: 3   Objective: 2

8. A lab has the safety icons shown below. These icons mean that you should wear
   a. only safety goggles.   c. safety goggles and a lab apron.
   b. only a lab apron.   d. safety goggles, a lab apron, and gloves.
   Answer: B   Difficulty: 1   Section: 3   Objective: 2

9. The law of conservation of mass says the total mass before a chemical change is
   a. more than the total mass after the change.
   b. less than the total mass after the change.
   c. the same as the total mass after the change.
   d. not the same as the total mass after the change.
   Answer: C   Difficulty: 1   Section: 3   Objective: 2

10. In which of the following areas might you find a geochemist at work?
    a. studying the chemistry of rocks   c. studying pollution
    b. studying forestry   d. studying the atmosphere
    Answer: D   Difficulty: 1   Section: 3   Objective: 2

One-Stop Planner® CD-ROM

This CD-ROM includes all of the resources shown here and the following time-saving tools:

- *Lab Materials QuickList Software*
- *Customizable lesson plans*
- *Holt Calendar Planner*
- *The powerful ExamView® Test Generator*

Meeting Individual Needs

DIRECTED READING A

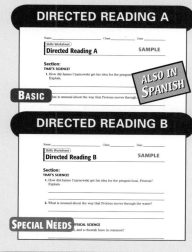

Name ___ Class ___ Date ___
Skills Worksheet
Directed Reading A   SAMPLE

Section:
THAT'S SCIENCE!
1. How did James Czarnowski get his idea for the penguin boat, Proteus? Explain.

ALSO IN SPANISH

BASIC

DIRECTED READING B

Name ___ Class ___ Date ___
Skills Worksheet
Directed Reading B   SAMPLE

Section:
THAT'S SCIENCE!
1. How did James Czarnowski get his idea for the penguin boat, Proteus? Explain.

2. What is unusual about the way that Proteus moves through the water?

SPECIAL NEEDS

VOCABULARY ACTIVITY

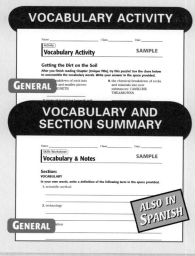

Name ___ Class ___ Date ___
Activity
Vocabulary Activity   SAMPLE

Getting the Dirt on the Soil
After you finish reading Chapter: [Unique Title], try this puzzle! Use the clues below to unscramble the vocabulary words. Write your answer in the space provided.

9. the chemical breakdown of rocks and minerals into new substances: CAMILCHE THEARIGWEN

GENERAL

VOCABULARY AND SECTION SUMMARY

Name ___ Class ___ Date ___
Skills Worksheet
Vocabulary & Notes   SAMPLE

Section:
VOCABULARY
In your own words, write a definition of the following term in the space provided.
1. scientific method

2. technology

ALSO IN SPANISH

GENERAL

REINFORCEMENT

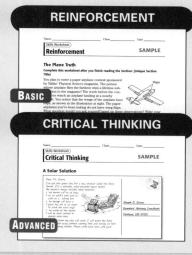

Name ___ Class ___ Date ___
Skills Worksheet
Reinforcement   SAMPLE

The Plane Truth
Complete this worksheet after you finish reading the Section: [Unique Section Title]

You plan to enter a paper airplane contest sponsored by Tailsn' Physical Science magazine. The person whose airplane flies the farthest wins a lifetime subscription to the magazine! The week before the contest, you watch an airplane landing at a nearby

Flaps

BASIC

CRITICAL THINKING

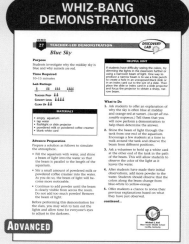

Name ___ Class ___ Date ___
Skills Worksheet
Critical Thinking   SAMPLE

A Solar Solution

ALSO IN SPANISH

ADVANCED

SCILINKS ACTIVITY

Name ___ Class ___ Date ___
Activity
SciLinks Activity   SAMPLE

MARINE ECOSYSTEMS
Go to www.scilinks.com. To find links related to marine ecosystems, type in the keyword HL5490. Then, use the links to answer the questions about marine ecosys-

GENERAL

SCIENCE PUZZLERS, TWISTERS & TEASERS

CHAPTER
15   SCIENCE PUZZLERS, TWISTERS & TEASERS
The Atmosphere

Some Like It Hot
1. Andrea likes school, but she loves the summer even more.

GENERAL

Labs and Activities

ECOLABS & FIELD ACTIVITIES

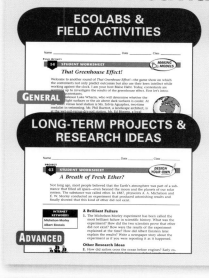

Name ___ Date ___ Class ___
FIELD ACTIVITY
14   STUDENT WORKSHEET
That Greenhouse Effect!

MAKING MODELS

GENERAL

LONG-TERM PROJECTS & RESEARCH IDEAS

Name ___ Date ___ Class ___
PROJECT
43   STUDENT WORKSHEET
A Breath of Fresh Ether?

DESIGN YOUR OWN

INTERNET KEYWORDS
Michelson-Morley
Albert Einstein

A Brilliant Failure
1. The Michelson-Morley experiment has been called the most brilliant failure in scientific history.

Other Research Ideas
2. How did sailors cross the ocean before engines? Early ex-

ADVANCED

WHIZ-BANG DEMONSTRATIONS

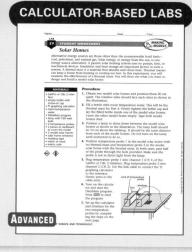

Name ___ Date ___ Class ___
DEMO
27   TEACHER-LED DEMONSTRATION
Blue Sky

DISCOVERY LAB

Purpose
Students investigate why the midday sky is blue and why sunsets are red.

Time Required
10–15 minutes

ADVANCED

CALCULATOR-BASED LABS

Name ___ Date ___ Class ___
LAB
19   STUDENT WORKSHEET
Solar Homes

MAKING MODELS

ADVANCED

DATASHEETS FOR QUICKLABS

Name ___ Class ___ Date ___
TEACHER RESOURCE PAGE
Quick Lab   DATASHEET FOR QUICK LAB
Reaction to Stress   SAMPLE

DATASHEETS FOR CHAPTER LABS

Name ___ Class ___ Date ___
TEACHER RESOURCE PAGE
Skills Practice Lab   DATASHEET FOR CHAPTER LAB
Using Scientific Methods   SAMPLE

Teacher's Notes
TIME REQUIRED
One 45-minute class period.

DATASHEETS FOR LABBOOK

Name ___ Class ___ Date ___
TEACHER RESOURCE PAGE
Skills Practice Lab   DATASHEET FOR LABBOOK LAB
Does It All Add Up?   SAMPLE

Teacher's Notes
TIME REQUIRED
One 45-minute class period.

Review and Assessments

SECTION QUIZ

Name ___ Class ___ Date ___
Assessment
Section Quiz   SAMPLE

Section:
In the space provided, write the letter of the description that best matches the term or phrase.

ALSO IN SPANISH

GENERAL

SECTION REVIEW

Name ___ Class ___ Date ___
Skills Worksheet
Section Review   SAMPLE

Section:
KEY TERMS
1. What do paleontologists study?

2. How does a trace fossil differ from petrified wood?

ALSO IN SPANISH

GENERAL

CHAPTER REVIEW

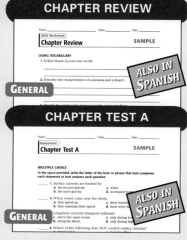

Name ___ Class ___ Date ___
Skills Worksheet
Chapter Review   SAMPLE

USING VOCABULARY
1. Define biome in your own words.

2. Describe the characteristics of a savanna and a desert.

ALSO IN SPANISH

GENERAL

CHAPTER TEST A

Name ___ Class ___ Date ___
Assessment
Chapter Test A   SAMPLE

MULTIPLE CHOICE
In the space provided, write the letter of the term or phrase that best completes each statement or best answers each question.
1. Surface currents are formed by
   a. the moon's gravity.   c. wind.
   b. the sun's gravity.   d. increased water density.
2. When waves come near the shore,
   a. they speed up.   c. their wavel
   b. they maintain their speed.   d. their wave

ALSO IN SPANISH

GENERAL

CHAPTER TEST B

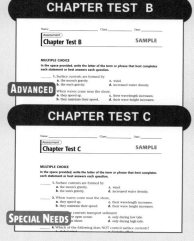

Name ___ Class ___ Date ___
Assessment
Chapter Test B   SAMPLE

MULTIPLE CHOICE
In the space provided, write the letter of the term or phrase that best completes each statement or best answers each question.
1. Surface currents are formed by
   a. the moon's gravity.   c. wind.
   b. the sun's gravity.   d. increased water density.
When waves come near the shore,
   a. they speed up.   c. their wavelength increases.
   b. they maintain their speed.   d. their wave height increases.

ADVANCED

CHAPTER TEST C

Name ___ Class ___ Date ___
Assessment
Chapter Test C   SAMPLE

MULTIPLE CHOICE
In the space provided, write the letter of the term or phrase that best completes each statement or best answers each question.
1. Surface currents are formed by
   a. the moon's gravity.   c. wind.
   b. the sun's gravity.   d. increased water density.
2. When waves come near the shore,
   a. they speed up.   c. their wavelength increases.
   b. they maintain their speed.   d. their wave height increases.

SPECIAL NEEDS

STANDARDIZED TEST PREPARATION

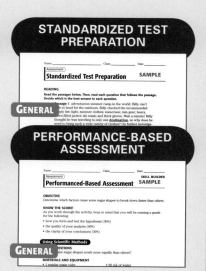

Name ___ Class ___ Date ___
Assessment
Standardized Test Preparation   SAMPLE

READING
Read the passages below. Then, read each question that follows the passage. Decide which is the best answer to each question.

GENERAL

PERFORMANCE-BASED ASSESSMENT

Name ___ Class ___ Date ___
Assessment   SKILL BUILDER
Performanced-Based Assessment   SAMPLE

OBJECTIVE
Determine which factors cause some sugar shapes to break down faster than others.

KNOW THE SCORE!
As you work through the activity, keep in mind that you will be earning a grade for the following:
• how you form and test the hypothesis (30%)
• the quality of your analysis (40%)
• the clarity of your conclusions (30%)

Using Scientific Methods

MATERIALS AND EQUIPMENT
• 1 regular sugar cube   • 90 mL of water

GENERAL

This Chapter Enrichment provides relevant and interesting information to expand and enhance your presentation of the chapter material.

Section 1

Characteristics of the Atmosphere
Take a Deep Breath!

● Near the Earth's surface, the atmosphere consists of 78.08% nitrogen, 20.95% oxygen, 0.93% argon, 0.03% carbon dioxide, and traces of water vapor. Scientists theorize that about 95% of the oxygen present in today's atmosphere formed as a byproduct of photosynthesis.

Is That a Fact!

◆ The Earth's troposphere contains almost 90% of the atmosphere's total mass. In the troposphere, temperature decreases at an average rate of 6.4°C/km as altitude increases.

Section 2

Atmospheric Heating
Specific Heat

● Water has a very high *specific heat,* which means that a great deal of thermal energy is needed to increase the temperature of water. Thus, water heats and cools very slowly. Rock, on the other hand, has a very low specific heat, so it heats and cools more quickly. For this reason, areas of high pressure (anticyclones) form over bodies of water, and areas of low pressure (cyclones) form over landmasses during the summer months. During the winter months, cyclones tend to form over bodies of water, and anticyclones tend to form over landmasses.

Is That a Fact!

◆ The summer monsoon in Asia is caused because central Asia heats up more quickly than the Indian Ocean. As the air above central Asia warms, it rises, creating an area of low pressure that draws moisture-laden air toward central Asia. When this moist air encounters the Himalayas, it cools quickly and releases its moisture in the form of torrential rains.

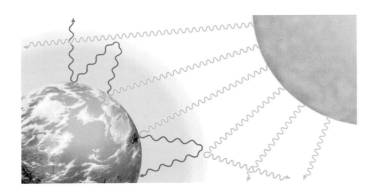

Global Warming—An Idea Before Its Time!

● Since the 1970s, global warming has been a topic of concern. However, a global warming model was proposed as early as 1896 by a Swedish physicist and chemist named Svante Arrhenius. Arrhenius theorized that the carbon dioxide released from burning coal would increase the intensity of Earth's greenhouse effect and lead to global warming. In 1954, it was first suggested that deforestation increases the amount of CO_2 in the atmosphere. Since then, numerous scientific studies have examined the effects of carbon dioxide on the temperature of Earth's atmosphere.

Section 3

Global Winds and Local Winds
Gustave Coriolis

● Gustave Gaspard Coriolis was a French mathematician and engineer who lived and worked in Paris from 1792 to 1843. His most well-known contribution to science is a paper published in 1835 that introduces the Coriolis effect. In "On the Equations of Relative Motion of Systems of Bodies," Coriolis argued that an inertial force (the Coriolis force) acts on a rotating object at a right angle to the object's motion. We now know that the "Coriolis force" is an apparent force.

- The rotation of the Earth causes matter in motion to appear to be deflected from its path. The Coriolis effect influences the general direction of global winds and open-ocean circulation, as well as the rotational movements of weather systems, such as cyclones and anticyclones.

Is That a Fact!

◆ When airplanes fly north or south, pilots have to make corrections to counteract the Coriolis effect.

Convection Cells

- The major convection cells on the Earth's surface have specific names. The cells that circulate between 30° north latitude and 30° south latitude are called *Hadley cells* after an English meteorologist. The cells that circulate between 30° north latitude and 60° north latitude and between 30° south latitude and 60° south latitude are called *Ferrel cells* after an American meteorologist. The cells that circulate between 90° and 60° are called *polar cells* because they are closest to the poles.

Jet Streaks

- Jet streaks are winds within jet streams that flow faster than the adjacent winds. Jet streaks influence storm formation and associated precipitation. Rising jet streaks and the low-pressure area that forms beneath them present favorable conditions for storms to form. Sinking jet streaks inhibit storm formation and precipitation.

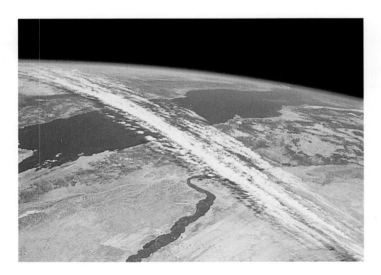

Section 4

Air Pollution
Global Distillation

- Scientists have found high levels of airborne contaminants in the breast milk of Inuit women in Greenland and Arctic Canada. Researchers think the contaminants arrived in these remote areas by a process called global distillation. In this process, contaminants are redistributed around the globe by atmospheric currents. Contaminants tend to concentrate in polar areas for the same reason that water vapor condenses on cold glass: gaseous substances tend to condense at colder temperatures.

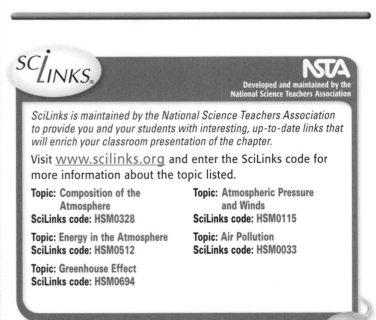

SciLINKS **NSTA**
Developed and maintained by the National Science Teachers Association

SciLinks is maintained by the National Science Teachers Association to provide you and your students with interesting, up-to-date links that will enrich your classroom presentation of the chapter.

Visit www.scilinks.org and enter the SciLinks code for more information about the topic listed.

Topic: Composition of the Atmosphere
SciLinks code: HSM0328

Topic: Atmospheric Pressure and Winds
SciLinks code: HSM0115

Topic: Energy in the Atmosphere
SciLinks code: HSM0512

Topic: Air Pollution
SciLinks code: HSM0033

Topic: Greenhouse Effect
SciLinks code: HSM0694

Overview

Tell students that this chapter will help them learn about the atmosphere. They will study the circulation of energy in the atmosphere and the greenhouse effect. They will also learn about global winds and air pollution.

Assessing Prior Knowledge

Students should be familiar with the following topics:

• changes of state

• radiation, conduction, and convection

Identifying Misconceptions

Because air cannot be seen, students may assume that the atmosphere has no mass and is therefore not subject to the physical laws that affect matter. Point out that air, like water, is a fluid. A *fluid* is any material that can flow and that takes the shape of its container. Students may find it easier to visualize wind if they think of air flowing like water. For example, the Coriolis effect affects the ocean currents as well as the global winds. Similarly, the convection of gases in the atmosphere is similar to the convection of bodies of water in the ocean. Be sure to explain that all fluids move according to specific laws of fluid dynamics.

The Atmosphere

About the PHOTO

Imagine climbing a mountain and taking only one out of three breaths! As altitude increases, the density of the atmosphere decreases. At the heights shown in this picture, the atmosphere is so thin that it contains only 30% of the amount of oxygen found in the atmosphere at sea level. So, most mountaineers carry part of their atmosphere with them—in the form of oxygen tanks.

PRE-READING ACTIVITY

FOLDNOTES **Booklet** Before you read the chapter, create the FoldNote entitled "Booklet" described in the **Study Skills** section of the Appendix. Label each page of the booklet with a main idea from the chapter. As you read the chapter, write what you learn about each main idea on the appropriate page of the booklet.

Standards Correlations

National Science Education Standards

The following codes indicate the National Science Education Standards that correlate to this chapter. The full text of the standards is at the front of the book.

Chapter Opener
SAI 1

Section 1 Characteristics of the Atmosphere
SPSP 1, 3, 4; ES 1h

Section 2 Atmospheric Heating
UCP 2 ; SAI 2; SPSP 3, 4; ES 2a; *LabBook:* SAI 1; ST 1

Section 3 Global Winds and Local Winds
ES 1j, 3d; *LabBook:* UCP 3; SAI 1; ST 1

Section 4 Air Pollution
SAI 1; SPSP 3, 4

Chapter Lab
SAI 1; ST 1

START-UP ACTIVITY
MATERIALS

FOR THE CLASS
- balloon, large (2)
- meterstick
- notebook
- pencil
- pushpins (3)
- safety goggles

Teacher's Note: This activity may work best as a demonstration. You may find it easier to balance the meterstick yourself, or to create a stand on which to balance the meterstick.

Answers

1. Answers may vary. Students should note that the meterstick became unbalanced when the balloon was popped. The reason for this change is that the popped balloon contained air, which has mass.

2. Sample answer: Yes, air has mass. Because air has mass, it is subject to the gravitational attraction of the Earth. The atmosphere is held around the Earth by gravity.

START-UP ACTIVITY

Does Air Have Mass?

In this activity, you will compare an inflated balloon with a deflated balloon to find out if air has mass.

Procedure

1. In a **notebook,** answer the following questions: Does air have mass? Will an inflated balloon weigh more than a deflated balloon?

2. Inflate **two large balloons,** and tie the balloons closed. Attach each balloon to opposite ends of a **meterstick** using identical **pushpins.** Balance the meterstick on a **pencil** held by a volunteer. Check that the meterstick is perfectly balanced.

3. Predict what will happen when you pop one balloon. Record your predictions.

4. Put on **safety goggles,** and carefully pop one of the balloons with a **pushpin.**

5. Record your observations.

Analysis

1. Explain your observations. Was your prediction correct?

2. Based on your results, does air have mass? If air has mass, is the atmosphere affected by Earth's gravity? Explain your answers.

Chapter Review
ES 1h, 1j, 2a, 3d

Science in Action
HNS 1; SPSP 5

This Really Happened!

On August 17, 1998, Steve Fossett was well on his way to making the first around-the-world balloon flight. It was his fourth attempt, and after 10 days and 22,910 km, he had already traveled two-thirds of the way. At the time, this was farther than any other balloonist had traveled in history. But something happened in the dark morning hours that ended Fossett's flight and nearly cost him his life.

While floating over the Pacific Ocean

and cut loose the heavy tanks of fuel and oxygen to slow the balloon's fall. He then prepared himself for the crash.

When Fossett regained consciousness, his capsule was upside down, half full of water, and on fire. With a satellite radio beacon to give his location and a small life boat, Fossett scrambled out of the capsule to await his rescue.

Fossett experienced firsthand how unpredictable our atmosphere can be. He

Chapter Starter Transparency
Use this transparency to help students begin thinking about the atmosphere.

Chapter 1 • The Atmosphere **3**

Focus

Overview

This section defines the atmosphere and explains its basic characteristics. It describes the atmosphere's composition and explains how pressure and temperature are related to altitude. The section also discusses the four layers of the Earth's atmosphere.

Bellringer

Have students list the ways that the atmosphere is different from outer space. Tell students that a little more than a century ago, many scientists believed that the Earth's atmosphere blended with a hypothetical substance called *ether* that filled the entire universe. In 1887, the physicist A. A. Michelson demonstrated that the universe is not filled with ether.

Motivate

Identifying Preconceptions — GENERAL

Atmospheric Composition

Before students read the section, ask them these questions:

• What is the most common gas in the atmosphere? (nitrogen)

• Does air contain anything other than gases? (solids, such as dust, and liquids, such as water)

 Logical

Characteristics of the Atmosphere

If you were lost in the desert, you could survive for a few days without food and water. But you wouldn't last more than five minutes without the atmosphere.

The **atmosphere** is a mixture of gases that surrounds Earth. In addition to containing the oxygen you need to breathe, the atmosphere protects you from the sun's damaging rays. The atmosphere is always changing. Every breath you take, every tree that is planted, and every vehicle you ride in affects the atmosphere's composition.

The Composition of the Atmosphere

As you can see in **Figure 1,** the atmosphere is made up mostly of nitrogen gas. The oxygen you breathe makes up a little more than 20% of the atmosphere. In addition to containing nitrogen and oxygen, the atmosphere contains small particles, such as dust, volcanic ash, sea salt, dirt, and smoke. The next time you turn off the lights at night, shine a flashlight, and you will see some of these tiny particles floating in the air.

Water is also found in the atmosphere. Liquid water (water droplets) and solid water (snow and ice crystals) are found in clouds. But most water in the atmosphere exists as an invisible gas called *water vapor*. When atmospheric conditions change, water vapor can change into solid or liquid water, and rain or snow might fall from the sky.

✓ Reading Check Describe the three physical states of water in the atmosphere. (*See the Appendix for answers to Reading Checks.*)

Figure 1 Composition of the Atmosphere

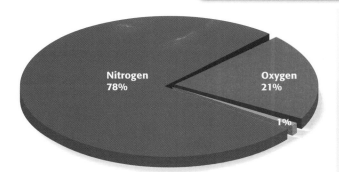

Nitrogen, the most common atmospheric gas, is released when dead plants and dead animals break down and when volcanoes erupt.

Oxygen, the second most common atmospheric gas, is made by phytoplankton and plants.

The remaining 1% of the atmosphere is made up of argon, carbon dioxide, water vapor, and other gases.

Nitrogen 78%

Oxygen 21%

1%

Answer to Reading Check

Water can be liquid (rain), solid (snow or ice), or gas (water vapor).

Atmospheric Pressure and Temperature

What would carrying a column of air that is 700 km high feel like? You may be surprised to learn that you carry this load every day. While air is not very heavy, its weight adds up. At sea level, a square inch of surface area is under almost 15 lb of air. Carrying that much air on such a small surface area is like carrying a large bowling ball on the tip of your finger!

As Altitude Increases, Air Pressure Decreases

The atmosphere is held around the Earth by gravity. Gravity pulls gas molecules in the atmosphere toward the Earth's surface, causing air pressure. **Air pressure** is the measure of the force with which air molecules push on a surface. Air pressure is strongest at the Earth's surface because more air is above you. As you move farther away from the Earth's surface, fewer gas molecules are above you. So, as altitude (distance from sea level) increases, air pressure decreases. Think of air pressure as a human pyramid, as shown in **Figure 2**. The people at the bottom of the pyramid can feel all the weight and pressure of the people on top. Air pressure works in a similar way.

Atmospheric Composition Affects Air Temperature

Air temperature also changes as altitude increases. The temperature differences result mainly from the way solar energy is absorbed as it moves through the atmosphere. Some parts of the atmosphere are warmer because they contain a high percentage of gases that absorb solar energy. Other parts of the atmosphere contain less of these gases and are cooler.

Lower pressure

Higher pressure

Figure 2 As in a human pyramid, air pressure increases closer to the Earth's surface.

WEIRD SCIENCE

An experiment in 1664 demonstrated the force exerted by air pressure. Most of the air was removed from a hollow sphere whose halves had been sealed together with an airtight gasket. Sixteen horses were needed to pull the metal hemispheres apart!

CONNECTION TO Physics

Air-Pressure Experiment
Does air pressure push only downward? Try this experiment to find out. Fill a plastic cup to the brim with water. Firmly hold a piece of cardboard over the mouth of the cup. Quickly invert the glass over a sink, and observe what happens. How do the effects of air pressure explain your observations?

ACTIVITY

atmosphere a mixture of gases that surrounds a planet or moon

air pressure the measure of the force with which air molecules push on a surface

Teach, continued

Using the Figure — BASIC

Atmospheric Layers Have students refer to **Figure 3** to answer these questions:

• Which layer of the atmosphere is closest to Earth? (the troposphere)

• How does temperature change within the stratosphere? (For the first few kilometers, the temperature remains fairly constant. Then, the temperature begins rising steeply and levels off again toward the top of the layer.)

• Which atmospheric layer has the greatest range of temperatures? (the thermosphere)

Students may notice that the iridescent cloud in the thermosphere is an aurora and that the white layer near the top of the stratosphere represents the ozone layer. The space shuttles orbit at an altitude of about 300 km. **LS** Visual

Answer to Reading Check

The troposphere is the layer of turning or change. The stratosphere is the layer in which gases are layered and do not mix vertically. The mesosphere is the middle layer. The thermosphere is the layer in which temperatures are highest.

MATH PRACTICE

Modeling the Atmosphere
In teams, use a metric ruler to create an illustrated scale model of the atmosphere similar to the one shown on this page. Assume that the atmosphere is about 700 km high. If you reduced the height of the atmosphere by a factor of 100,000, your scale model would be 7 m long, and the troposphere would be 16 cm long. Think of a creative way to display your model. You could use sidewalk chalk, stakes and string, poster board, or other materials approved by your teacher. Do some research to add interesting information about each layer.

ACTIVITY

Layers of the Atmosphere

Based on temperature changes, the Earth's atmosphere is divided into four layers, as shown in **Figure 3.** These layers are the *troposphere, stratosphere, mesosphere,* and *thermosphere.* Although these words might sound complicated, the name of each layer gives you clues about its features.

For example, *-sphere* means "ball," which suggests that each layer of the atmosphere surrounds the Earth like a hollow ball. *Tropo-* means "turning" or "change," and the troposphere is the layer where gases turn and mix. *Strato-* means "layer," and the stratosphere is the sphere where gases are layered and do not mix very much. *Meso-* means "middle," and the mesosphere is the middle layer. Finally, *thermo-* means "heat," and the thermosphere is the sphere where temperatures are highest.

Reading Check What does the name of each atmospheric layer mean?

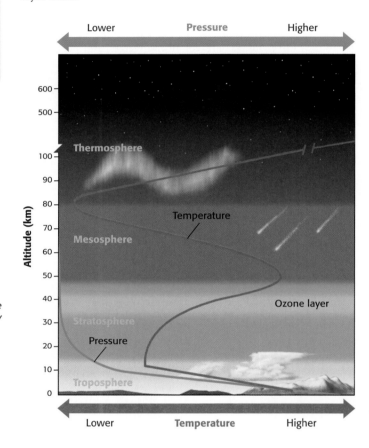

Figure 3 *The layers of the atmosphere are defined by changes in temperature.*

CHAPTER RESOURCES

Technology

 Transparencies
• Layers of the Atmosphere

Is That a Fact!

The oxygen in the Earth's current atmosphere is produced primarily by phytoplankton (tiny, drifting sea plants) and land plants that release oxygen during photosynthesis.

The Troposphere: The Layer in Which We Live

The lowest layer of the atmosphere, which lies next to the Earth's surface, is called the **troposphere.** The troposphere is also the densest atmospheric layer. It contains almost 90% of the atmosphere's total mass! Almost all of the Earth's carbon dioxide, water vapor, clouds, air pollution, weather, and life-forms are in the troposphere. As shown in **Figure 4,** temperatures vary greatly in the troposphere. Differences in air temperature and density cause gases in the troposphere to mix continuously.

The Stratosphere: Home of the Ozone Layer

The atmospheric layer above the troposphere is called the **stratosphere. Figure 5** shows the boundary between the stratosphere and the troposphere. Gases in the stratosphere are layered and do not mix as much as gases in the troposphere. The air is also very thin in the stratosphere and contains little moisture. The lower stratosphere is extremely cold. Its temperature averages –60°C. But temperature rises as altitude increases in the stratosphere. This rise happens because ozone in the stratosphere absorbs ultraviolet radiation from the sun, which warms the air. Almost all of the ozone in the stratosphere is contained in the ozone layer. The *ozone layer* protects life on Earth by absorbing harmful ultraviolet radiation.

The Mesosphere: The Middle Layer

Above the stratosphere is the mesosphere. The **mesosphere** is the middle layer of the atmosphere. It is also the coldest layer. As in the troposphere, the temperature decreases as altitude increases in the mesosphere. Temperatures can be as low as –93°C at the top of the mesosphere.

Figure 4 *As altitude increases in the troposphere, temperature decreases. Snow remains all year on this mountaintop.*

troposphere the lowest layer of the atmosphere, in which temperature decreases at a constant rate as altitude increases

stratosphere the layer of the atmosphere that is above the troposphere and in which temperature increases as altitude increases

mesosphere the layer of the atmosphere between the stratosphere and the thermosphere and in which temperature decreases as altitude increases

Figure 5 *This photograph of Earth's atmosphere was taken from space. The troposphere is the yellow layer; the stratosphere is the white layer.*

Close

Reteaching — BASIC

Describing the Atmosphere

On the board, make a table entitled "The Atmosphere." Include the following headings:

"Layer," "Altitude range," "Temperature range," and "Other features."

Have volunteers contribute information for each section of the table.

[LS] Verbal • English Language Learners

Quiz — GENERAL

1. List the layers of the atmosphere, starting with the one closest to Earth. (troposphere, stratosphere, mesosphere, thermosphere)

2. Explain how density affects the transfer of thermal energy in the air. (The less dense the air is, the less effective it is at transferring thermal energy. Particles must collide with one another to transfer energy. Particles that are farther apart are less likely to collide with other particles.)

Alternative Assessment — GENERAL

Writing **Poetry** Have each student write a poem that creatively yet accurately describes each layer of Earth's atmosphere. Allow time for volunteers to read their poem aloud or to display the poem for others to read on their own.

[LS] Intrapersonal

---

thermosphere the uppermost layer of the atmosphere, in which temperature increases as altitude increases

The Thermosphere: The Edge of the Atmosphere

The uppermost atmospheric layer is called the **thermosphere.** In the thermosphere, temperature again increases with altitude. Atoms of nitrogen and oxygen absorb high-energy solar radiation and release thermal energy, which causes temperatures in the thermosphere to be 1,000°C or higher.

When you think of an area that has high temperatures, you probably think of a place that is very hot. Although the thermosphere has very high temperatures, it does not feel hot. Temperature is different from heat. Temperature is a measure of the average energy of particles in motion. The high temperature of the thermosphere means that particles in that layer are moving very fast. Heat, however, is the transfer of thermal energy between objects of different temperatures. Particles must touch one another to transfer thermal energy. The space between particles in the thermosphere is so great that particles do not transfer much energy. In other words, the density of the thermosphere is so low that particles do not often collide and transfer energy. **Figure 6** shows how air density affects the heating of the troposphere and the thermosphere.

✔ **Reading Check** Why doesn't the thermosphere feel hot?

Figure 6 Temperature in the Troposphere and the Thermosphere

The **thermosphere** is less dense than the troposphere. So, although particles are moving very fast, they do not transfer much thermal energy.

The **troposphere** is denser than the thermosphere. So, although particles in the troposphere are moving much slower than particles in the thermosphere, they can transfer much more thermal energy.

Answer to Reading Check

The thermosphere does not feel hot because air molecules are spaced far apart and cannot collide to transfer much thermal energy.

CONNECTION to Physical Science — BASIC

Thermal Energy Have students imagine a sink full of hot water. Ask them to pretend that they have removed a cup of the hot water from the sink. Students should agree that both volumes of water have the same temperature at this point. Explain that the sink has more thermal energy than the cup because the sink contains more water (and therefore more particles in motion) than the cup. Ask students to help you come up with other examples to explain these ideas.

The Ionosphere: Home of the Auroras

In the upper mesosphere and the lower thermosphere, nitrogen and oxygen atoms absorb harmful solar energy. As a result, the thermosphere's temperature rises, and gas particles become electrically charged. Electrically charged particles are called *ions*. Therefore, this part of the thermosphere is called the *ionosphere*. As shown in **Figure 7,** in polar regions these ions radiate energy as shimmering lights called *auroras*. The ionosphere also reflects AM radio waves. When conditions are right, an AM radio wave can travel around the world by reflecting off the ionosphere. These radio signals bounce off the ionosphere and are sent back to Earth.

Figure 7 *Charged particles in the ionosphere cause auroras, or northern and southern lights.*

SECTION Review

Summary

- Nitrogen and oxygen make up most of Earth's atmosphere.
- Air pressure decreases as altitude increases.
- The composition of atmospheric layers affects their temperature.
- The troposphere is the lowest atmospheric layer. It is the layer in which we live.
- The stratosphere contains the ozone layer, which protects us from harmful UV radiation.
- The mesosphere is the coldest atmospheric layer.
- The thermosphere is the uppermost layer of the atmosphere.

Using Key Terms

1. Use each of the following terms in a separate sentence: *air pressure, atmosphere, troposphere, stratosphere, mesosphere,* and *thermosphere.*

Understanding Key Ideas

2. Why does the temperature of different layers of the atmosphere vary?
   a. because air temperature increases as altitude increases
   b. because the amount of energy radiated from the sun varies
   c. because of interference by humans
   d. because of the composition of gases in each layer

3. Why does air pressure decrease as altitude increases?

4. How can the thermosphere have high temperatures but not feel hot?

5. What determines the temperature of atmospheric layers?

6. What two gases make up most of the atmosphere?

Math Skills

7. If an average cloud has a density of 0.5 g/m³ and has a volume of 1,000,000,000 m³, what is the weight of an average cloud?

Critical Thinking

8. **Applying Concepts** Apply what you know about the relationship between altitude and air pressure to explain why rescue helicopters have a difficult time flying at altitudes above 6,000 m.

9. **Making Inferences** If the upper atmosphere is very thin, why do space vehicles heat up as they enter the atmosphere?

10. **Making Inferences** Explain why gases such as helium can escape Earth's atmosphere.

For a variety of links related to this chapter, go to www.scilinks.org

Topic: Composition of the Atmosphere
SciLinks code: HSM0328

Cultural Awareness `GENERAL`

The Auroras Different cultures have different explanations for the shimmering lights known as *auroras*. Inuit groups thought of the aurora borealis as the torches of spirits that guided souls from Earth to paradise. Have students find out about other myths concerning the auroras. **LS** Intrapersonal

---

Answers to Section Review

1. Sample answer: Air pressure is caused by gravity pulling air molecules in the atmosphere toward the Earth. The atmosphere is a mixture of gases that surrounds the Earth. The troposphere is the layer where most weather occurs. The stratosphere is where the ozone layer is located. The mesosphere is the middle atmospheric layer. The thermosphere is the atmospheric layer with the highest temperatures.

2. d

3. Air pressure decreases as altitude increases because the atmosphere is less dense at higher altitudes.

4. Temperatures in the thermosphere are high because particles are moving quickly in the thermosphere. The thermosphere does not feel hot because it is not very dense, so particles cannot collide to transfer much thermal energy.

5. The temperature of atmospheric layers varies because of the way solar energy is absorbed by different gases.

6. nitrogen and oxygen

7. 0.5 g/m³ × 1,000,000,000 m³ = 500,000,000 g, or 500,000 kg

8. Answers may vary. Students should recognize that air density is lower at higher altitudes. Helicopters need air to provide lift. At altitudes higher than 6,000 m, air density is so low that it is difficult for helicopters to fly.

9. Answers may vary. Space vehicles reenter the atmosphere at a very high rate of speed. Although the atmosphere is not very dense at the altitude that space vehicles reenter, the vehicles are traveling fast enough to compress air in front of them. This layer of air transfers thermal energy to the spacecraft's exterior.

10. Answers may vary. Helium does not have enough mass to be held by the Earth's gravitational attraction.

Overview

This section discusses how the atmosphere is heated by energy from the sun. Thermal energy is transferred by radiation, thermal conduction, and convection. The section concludes with a discussion of the greenhouse effect and global warming.

 Bellringer

Ask students to explain how food is heated in an oven. (The heating coil heats the air in the oven by radiation and thermal conduction. The hot air circulates by convection and heats the food and its container. The hot container heats the food by thermal conduction.)

Motivate

ACTiViTY ──────── BASIC

Popcorn Make some popcorn the "old-fashioned" way—use a hot plate or stove top, a pan with a lid, oil, and popcorn kernels. Have volunteers explain how the processes of convection, conduction, and radiation are involved. Explain that a kernel pops when the water stored inside changes to water vapor and expands suddenly. Share the treat with students if time allows. **LS Kinesthetic**

READING WARM-UP

Objectives

● Describe what happens to solar energy that reaches Earth.
● Summarize the processes of radiation, conduction, and convection.
● Explain the relationship between the greenhouse effect and global warming.

Terms to Learn

radiation
thermal conduction
convection
global warming
greenhouse effect

READING STRATEGY

Reading Organizer As you read this section, make a table comparing radiation, conduction, and convection.

Atmospheric Heating

You are lying in a park. Your eyes are closed, and you feel the warmth of the sun on your face. You may have done this before, but have you ever stopped to think that it takes a little more than eight minutes for the energy that warms your face to travel from a star that is 149,000,000 km away?

Energy in the Atmosphere

In the scenario above, your face was warmed by energy from the sun. Earth and its atmosphere are also warmed by energy from the sun. In this section, you will find out what happens to solar energy as it enters the atmosphere.

Radiation: Energy Transfer by Waves

The Earth receives energy from the sun by radiation. **Radiation** is the transfer of energy as electromagnetic waves. Although the sun radiates a huge amount of energy, Earth receives only about two-billionths of this energy. But this small fraction of energy is enough to drive the weather cycle and make Earth habitable. **Figure 1** shows what happens to solar energy once it enters the atmosphere.

Figure 1 *Energy from the sun is absorbed by the atmosphere, land, and water and is changed into thermal energy.*

About **25%** is scattered and reflected by clouds and air.

About **20%** is absorbed by ozone, clouds, and atmospheric gases.

About **5%** is reflected by Earth's surface.

About **50%** is absorbed by Earth's surface.

CHAPTER RESOURCES

Chapter Resource File

• Lesson Plan
• Directed Reading A **BASIC**
• Directed Reading B **SPECIAL NEEDS**

Technology

Transparencies
• Bellringer
• Scattering, Absorption, and Reflection
• Radiation, Conduction, and Convection

MISCONCEPTION
///ALERT\\\

Thermal Conduction Point out that compared with radiation and convection, thermal conduction plays a relatively minor role in heating the atmosphere. Only the thin layer of air that comes in contact with the Earth's surface is heated by thermal conduction. However, thermal energy that is absorbed and reradiated by the land and oceans play a major role in heating the atmosphere.

Conduction: Energy Transfer by Contact

If you have ever touched something hot, you have experienced the process of conduction. **Thermal conduction** is the transfer of thermal energy through a material. Thermal energy is always transferred from warm to cold areas. When air molecules come into direct contact with the warm surface of Earth, thermal energy is transferred to the atmosphere.

Convection: Energy Transfer by Circulation

If you have ever watched a pot of water boil, you have observed convection. **Convection** is the transfer of thermal energy by the circulation or movement of a liquid or gas. Most thermal energy in the atmosphere is transferred by convection. For example, as air is heated, it becomes less dense and rises. Cool air is denser, so it sinks. As the cool air sinks, it pushes the warm air up. The cool air is eventually heated by the Earth's surface and begins to rise again. This cycle of warm air rising and cool air sinking causes a circular movement of air, called a *convection current,* as shown in **Figure 2.**

✓ **Reading Check** How do differences in air density cause convection currents? (*See the Appendix for answers to Reading Checks.*)

radiation the transfer of energy as electromagnetic waves

thermal conduction the transfer of energy as heat through a material

convection the transfer of thermal energy by the circulation or movement of a liquid or gas

Figure 2 *The processes of radiation, thermal conduction, and convection heat Earth and its atmosphere.*

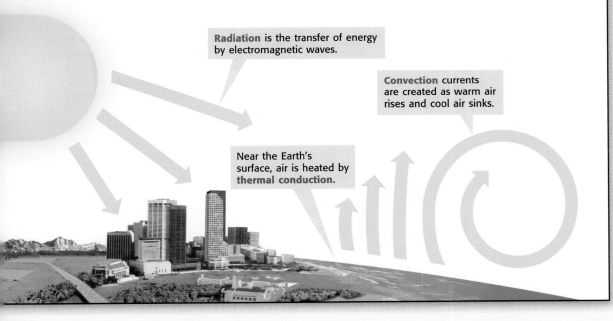

Radiation is the transfer of energy by electromagnetic waves.

Convection currents are created as warm air rises and cool air sinks.

Near the Earth's surface, air is heated by thermal conduction.

CONNECTION ACTIVITY
Environmental Science —— GENERAL

The Heat Island Effect Cities that have few green spaces and a lot of asphalt can have temperatures 10°C higher than surrounding rural areas do. This phenomenon is called the *heat island effect.* The heat island effect occurs because concrete buildings and asphalt absorb solar radiation and reradiate thermal energy, which elevates temperatures and increases the production of smog. The effect is worse in urban areas that have little surface water and few trees because the evaporation of water and plant transpiration cool the air. To counteract the heat island effect, cities have begun to preserve green spaces and plant trees. Some cities are beginning to use construction materials that have a higher reflectivity, such as white rooftops and concrete streets. Have groups of students create a model city in a large box or aquarium. Using two light bulbs and a thermometer, students should test strategies to reduce the heat island effect. **LS Logical**

Reteaching — BASIC

Greenhouse Review Reproduce **Figure 3** on the board, and ask student volunteers to explain how the greenhouse effect works. **LS** Visual/Verbal

Quiz — GENERAL

1. A metal spoon left in a bowl of hot soup feels hot. Which process—radiation, thermal conduction, or convection—is mainly responsible for heating the spoon? (thermal conduction)

2. What is a convection current? (the circular movement of warm and cool particles in a liquid or gas)

3. How does a greenhouse stay warm? (Sunlight passes through the glass. Objects in the structure absorb some of the radiant energy. In turn, the objects radiate this energy as thermal energy. The glass prevents the thermal energy from escaping, which warms the greenhouse.)

Alternative Assessment — GENERAL

Writing

Have students write a two-paragraph essay that explains the concepts in this section. The essay should contain the following terms: *radiation, thermal conduction, convection, greenhouse gas, greenhouse effect, global warming,* and *radiation balance.* Student volunteers can read their essays to the class. **LS** Verbal

Figure 3 The Greenhouse Effect

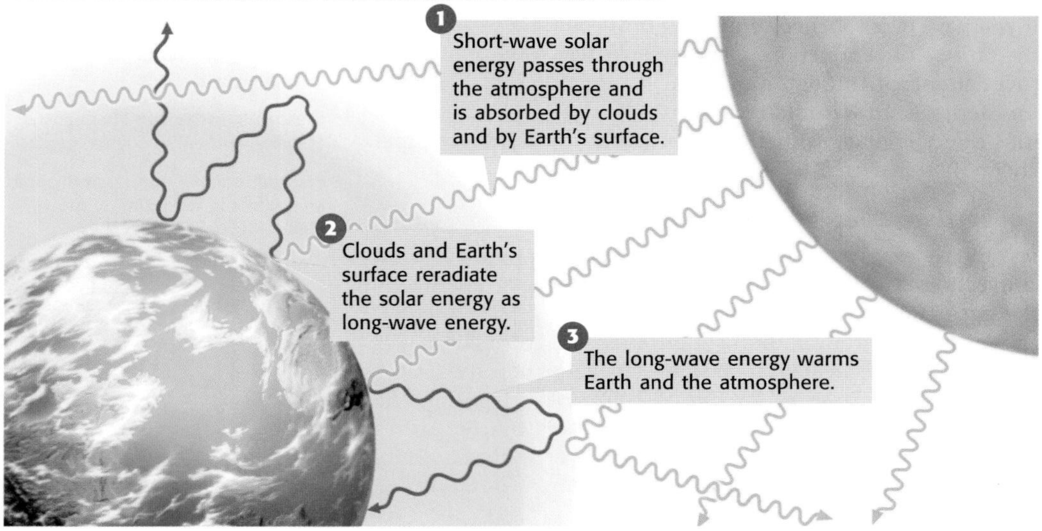

① Short-wave solar energy passes through the atmosphere and is absorbed by clouds and by Earth's surface.

② Clouds and Earth's surface reradiate the solar energy as long-wave energy.

③ The long-wave energy warms Earth and the atmosphere.

greenhouse effect the warming of the surface and lower atmosphere of Earth that occurs when water vapor, carbon dioxide, and other gases absorb and reradiate thermal energy

The Greenhouse Effect and Life on Earth

As you have learned, about 70% of the radiation that enters Earth's atmosphere is absorbed by clouds and by the Earth's surface. This energy is converted into thermal energy that warms the planet. In other words, short-wave visible light is absorbed and reradiated into the atmosphere as long-wave thermal energy. So, why doesn't this thermal energy escape back into space? Most of it does, but the atmosphere is like a warm blanket that traps enough energy to make Earth livable. This process, shown in **Figure 3,** is called the greenhouse effect. The **greenhouse effect** is the process by which gases in the atmosphere, such as water vapor and carbon dioxide, absorb thermal energy and radiate it back to Earth. This process is called the greenhouse effect because the gases function like the glass walls and roof of a greenhouse, which allow solar energy to enter but prevent thermal energy from escaping.

The Radiation Balance: Energy In, Energy Out

For Earth to remain livable, the amount of energy received from the sun and the amount of energy returned to space must be approximately equal. Solar energy that is absorbed by the Earth and its atmosphere is eventually reradiated into space as thermal energy. Every day, the Earth receives more energy from the sun. The balance between incoming energy and outgoing energy is known as the *radiation balance.*

Group ACTiViTY — BASIC

Model Greenhouses Have students work in groups to make model greenhouses by placing a thermometer inside a jar and anchoring the thermometer with modeling clay. Next, have students seal each jar with a lid. Have each group put its model in a different sunny spot. Students should observe and record changes in temperature every day for 1 week. Students can compare the temperatures recorded with the temperatures in a control jar that lacks a lid. Help students infer that solar energy enters a greenhouse and is converted to thermal energy and that the glass prevents most of the thermal energy from escaping. **LS** Kinesthetic   English Language Learners

Greenhouse Gases and Global Warming

Many scientists have become concerned about data that show that average global temperatures have increased in the past 100 years. Such an increase in average global temperatures is called **global warming.** Some scientists have hypothesized that an increase of greenhouse gases in the atmosphere may be the cause of this warming trend. Greenhouse gases are gases that absorb thermal energy in the atmosphere.

Human activity, such as the burning of fossil fuels and deforestation, may be increasing levels of greenhouse gases, such as carbon dioxide, in the atmosphere. If this hypothesis is correct, increasing levels of greenhouse gases may cause average global temperatures to continue to rise. If global warming continues, global climate patterns could be disrupted. Plants and animals that are adapted to live in specific climates would be affected. However, climate models are extremely complex, and scientists continue to debate whether the global warming trend is the result of an increase in greenhouse gases.

global warming a gradual increase in average global temperature

✓ *Reading Check* What is a greenhouse gas?

SECTION Review

Summary

- Energy from the sun is transferred through the atmosphere by radiation, thermal conduction, and convection.

- Radiation is energy transfer by electromagnetic waves. Thermal conduction is energy transfer by direct contact. Convection is energy transfer by circulation.

- The greenhouse effect is Earth's natural heating process. Increasing levels of greenhouse gases could cause global warming.

Using Key Terms

1. Use each of the following terms in a separate sentence: *thermal conduction, radiation, convection, greenhouse effect,* and *global warming.*

Understanding Key Ideas

2. Which of the following is the best example of thermal conduction?
   a. a light bulb warming a lampshade
   b. an egg cooking in a frying pan
   c. water boiling in a pot
   d. gases circulating in the atmosphere

3. Describe three ways that energy is transferred in the atmosphere.

4. What is the difference between the greenhouse effect and global warming?

5. What is the radiation balance?

Math Skills

6. Find the average of the following temperatures: 73.2°F, 71.1°F, 54.6°F, 65.5°F, 78.2°F, 81.9°F, and 82.1°F.

Critical Thinking

7. **Identifying Relationships** How does the process of convection rely on radiation?

8. **Applying Concepts** Describe global warming in terms of the radiation balance.

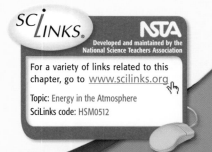

Developed and maintained by the National Science Teachers Association

For a variety of links related to this chapter, go to www.scilinks.org

Topic: Energy in the Atmosphere
SciLinks code: HSM0512

Answer to Reading Check

A greenhouse gas is a gas that absorbs thermal energy in the atmosphere.

CHAPTER RESOURCES

Chapter Resource File

- Section Quiz GENERAL
- Section Review GENERAL
- Vocabulary and Section Summary GENERAL

Technology

Transparencies
- The Greenhouse Effect

Answers to Section Review

1. Sample answer: Thermal conduction is the transfer of thermal energy as heat through a material. Radiation is the transfer of energy by electromagnetic waves. Convection is the transfer of energy by circulation in a fluid. The greenhouse effect is Earth's natural warming process. Global warming is a gradual increase in average global temperature.

2. b

3. Sample answer: Energy from the sun warms the atmosphere by radiation. The Earth reradiates energy from the sun, which warms the atmosphere. The air directly above the Earth's surface is also heated by conduction. Warm air is then circulated through the atmosphere by convection currents.

4. The greenhouse effect is the Earth's natural heating process by which gases in the atmosphere trap reradiated energy, which heats the atmosphere. Global warming is the rise in average global temperature and may be caused by an increase in the greenhouse effect.

5. The radiation balance is the balance between incoming solar energy and thermal energy that the Earth radiates into space.

6. 506.6°F ÷ 7 = 72.4°F

7. Convection in the atmosphere relies on radiation from the sun. If radiation from the sun stopped, air would not be warmed and convection currents would eventually stop circulating.

8. Answers may vary. Global warming occurs when the radiation balance is upset and more energy is coming in than is going out.

SECTION

3

Focus

Overview

This section explains what wind is and describes how differences in atmospheric pressure cause air to move. Students will also learn about global and local winds.

Bellringer

Have students write a poem about moving air. The poem should include an explanation of why air moves.

Motivate

Demonstration —— GENERAL

Air Movement Create an area of high pressure by filling a plastic container with ice. Create an area of low pressure by heating a hot plate. Place the container of ice and the hot plate approximately 30 cm from each other. Make sure the container of ice is slightly higher than the hot plate. Light a splint or long match, and let it burn for a few seconds. Extinguish the splint or match over the ice, and place the smoking end close to the ice. Ask students to observe the movement of the smoke. The smoke should move from the ice to the hot plate (from an area of high pressure to an area of low pressure). **LS** Visual

---

READING WARM-UP

Objectives

● Explain the relationship between air pressure and wind direction.
● Describe global wind patterns.
● Explain the causes of local wind patterns.

Terms to Learn

wind
Coriolis effect
polar easterlies

westerlies
trade winds
jet stream

READING STRATEGY

Prediction Guide Before reading this section, write the title of each heading in this section. Next, under each heading, write what you think you will learn.

---

wind the movement of air caused by differences in air pressure

---

Global Winds and Local Winds

If you open the valve on a bicycle tube, the air rushes out. Why? The air inside the tube is at a higher pressure than the air is outside the tube. In effect, letting air out of the tube created a wind.

Why Air Moves

The movement of air caused by differences in air pressure is called **wind.** The greater the pressure difference, the faster the wind moves. The devastation shown in **Figure 1** was caused by winds that resulted from extreme differences in air pressure.

Air Rises at the Equator and Sinks at the Poles

Differences in air pressure are generally caused by the unequal heating of the Earth. The equator receives more direct solar energy than other latitudes, so air at the equator is warmer and less dense than the surrounding air. Warm, less dense air rises and creates an area of low pressure. This warm, rising air flows toward the poles. At the poles, the air is colder and denser than the surrounding air, so it sinks. As the cold air sinks, it creates areas of high pressure around the poles. This cold polar air then flows toward the equator.

Figure 1 In 1992, Hurricane Andrew became the most destructive hurricane in U.S. history. The winds from the hurricane reached 264 km/h.

CHAPTER RESOURCES

Chapter Resource File

- Lesson Plan
- Directed Reading A **BASIC**
- Directed Reading B **SPECIAL NEEDS**

Technology

Transparencies
- Bellringer
- Pressure Belts

 Cultural Awareness GENERAL

Animals and Air Pressure Changes in atmospheric pressure are often said to affect fish. Egyptian fishers notice that mullet move with the wind to prevent getting stuck in muddy water. According to Caribbean lore, a container of shark oil will grow cloudy when a hurricane is imminent. Have students find out about other organisms that might indicate changes in air pressure and other atmospheric phenomena. **LS** Intrapersonal

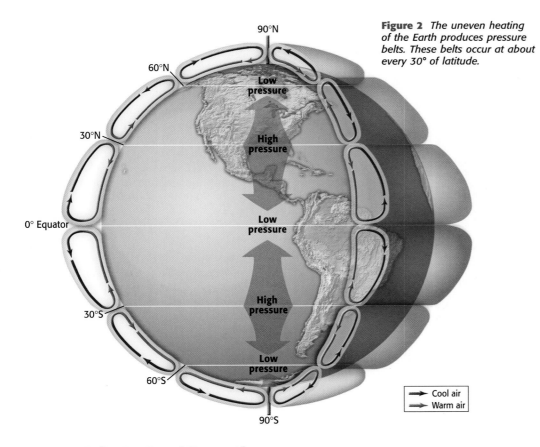

Figure 2 *The uneven heating of the Earth produces pressure belts. These belts occur at about every 30° of latitude.*

90°N
60°N
Low pressure
30°N
High pressure
0° Equator
Low pressure
30°S
High pressure
60°S
Low pressure
90°S

→ Cool air
→ Warm air

Teach

MISCONCEPTION ALERT

What Causes Wind? Make sure students understand that air circulates because of temperature differences that cause pressure differences in the atmosphere. The sun heats the Earth, which heats the air above it by radiation and conduction. This warm air is less dense than the colder air above it, so the warm air rises, while the cold, denser air sinks. Air is colder near the poles because less solar energy reaches the ground at the poles than at the equator. Because air is warmer and less dense at the equator, air tends to rise and circulate toward the poles.

Answer to Reading Check

Sinking air causes areas of high pressure because sinking air presses down on the air beneath it.

Pressure Belts Are Found Every 30°

You may imagine that wind moves in one huge, circular pattern from the poles to the equator. In fact, air travels in many large, circular patterns called *convection cells*. Convection cells are separated by *pressure belts,* bands of high pressure and low pressure found about every 30° of latitude, as shown in **Figure 2.** As warm air rises over the equator and moves toward the poles, the air begins to cool. At about 30° north and 30° south latitude, some of the cool air begins to sink. Cool, sinking air causes high pressure belts near 30° north and 30° south latitude. This cool air flows back to the equator, where it warms and rises again. At the poles, cold air sinks and moves toward the equator. Air warms as it moves away from the poles. Around 60° north and 60° south latitude, the warmer air rises, which creates a low pressure belt. This air flows back to the poles.

✓ Reading Check Why does sinking air cause areas of high pressure? (*See the Appendix for answers to Reading Checks.*)

CONNECTION to Physical Science ──── **ADVANCED**

Katabatic Winds A katabatic wind is the movement of air due to the influence of gravity. This flow can range from a gentle breeze to gale-force winds. The world's strongest katabatic winds occur in Antarctica because there is plenty of cold air and the highest spot is near the center of the continent. Because the continent is basically cone shaped, winds radiate from the South Pole, accelerating like a car rolling down a hill. Cold, dense air rushes down mountainsides, tumbles across the ice sheets, and spills out over the ocean. The winds can blow for months, and they sometimes reach speeds as fast as 320 km/h! Use dry ice and a modeling-clay mountain to demonstrate this phenomenon. **LS Kinesthetic**

Coriolis Effect Try the following activity to help students who have problems understanding the Coriolis effect. You will need a globe, some flour, an eyedropper, red food coloring, and water. Mix a few drops of food coloring with water, and fill the eyedropper with the solution. Dust the globe thoroughly with flour. If the flour doesn't stick, mist the globe lightly with water, and sprinkle the flour over the globe. Enlist a volunteer to slowly spin the globe counterclockwise to simulate Earth's rotation. Have another volunteer slowly drop water from the dropper at the top of the globe, at the North Pole. Students will observe that the water is deflected westward in the Northern Hemisphere.

English Language Learners

LS Kinesthetic

Answer to Reading Check

the westerlies

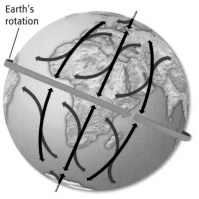

Earth's rotation

——▶ Path of wind without Coriolis effect
——▶ Approximate path of wind

Figure 3 *The Coriolis effect in the Northern Hemisphere causes winds traveling north to appear to curve to the east and winds traveling south to appear to curve to the west.*

Coriolis effect the apparent curving of the path of a moving object from an otherwise straight path due to the Earth's rotation

polar easterlies prevailing winds that blow from east to west between 60° and 90° latitude in both hemispheres

westerlies prevailing winds that blow from west to east between 30° and 60° latitude in both hemispheres

trade winds prevailing winds that blow northeast from 30° north latitude to the equator and that blow southeast from 30° south latitude to the equator

The Coriolis Effect

As you have learned, pressure differences cause air to move between the equator and the poles. But try spinning a globe and using a piece of chalk to trace a straight line from the equator to the North Pole. The chalk line curves because the globe was spinning. Like the chalk line, winds do not travel directly north or south, because the Earth is rotating. The apparent curving of the path of winds and ocean currents due to the Earth's rotation is called the **Coriolis effect.** Because of the Coriolis effect in the Northern Hemisphere, winds traveling north curve to the east, and winds traveling south curve to the west, as shown in **Figure 3.**

Global Winds

The combination of convection cells found at every 30° of latitude and the Coriolis effect produces patterns of air circulation called *global winds*. **Figure 4** shows the major global wind systems: polar easterlies, westerlies, and trade winds. Winds such as easterlies and westerlies are named for the direction from which they blow.

Polar Easterlies

The wind belts that extend from the poles to 60° latitude in both hemispheres are called the **polar easterlies.** The polar easterlies are formed as cold, sinking air moves from the poles toward 60° north and 60° south latitude. In the Northern Hemisphere, polar easterlies can carry cold arctic air over the United States, producing snow and freezing weather.

Westerlies

The wind belts found between 30° and 60° latitude in both hemispheres are called the **westerlies.** The westerlies flow toward the poles from west to east. The westerlies can carry moist air over the United States, producing rain and snow.

Trade Winds

In both hemispheres, the winds that blow from 30° latitude almost to the equator are called **trade winds.** The Coriolis effect causes the trade winds to curve to the west in the Northern Hemisphere and to the east in the Southern Hemisphere. Early traders used the trade winds to sail from Europe to the Americas. As a result, the winds became known as "trade winds."

✓ **Reading Check** If the trade winds carried traders from Europe to the Americas, what wind system carried traders back to Europe?

Homework ——————— **GENERAL**

The Coriolis Effect Many people often assume that the Coriolis effect affects the direction that water drains from sink basins or toilet bowls. Challenge students to devise an experiment to test this assumption. Students should record their data and present their data to the class. If time allows, graph the class results, and discuss any trends that appear.

LS Intrapersonal

CHAPTER RESOURCES
Technology
Transparencies
• The Coriolis Effect
• Global Winds

The Doldrums

The trade winds of the Northern and Southern Hemispheres meet in an area around the equator called the *doldrums*. In the doldrums, there is very little wind because the warm, rising air creates an area of low pressure. The name *doldrums* means "dull" or "sluggish."

The Horse Latitudes

At about 30° north and 30° south latitude, sinking air creates an area of high pressure. The winds at these locations are weak. These areas are called the *horse latitudes*. According to legend, this name was given to these areas when sailing ships carried horses from Europe to the Americas. When the ships were stuck in this windless area, horses were sometimes thrown overboard to save drinking water for the sailors. Most of the world's deserts are located in the horse latitudes because the sinking air is very dry.

INTERNET ACTIVITY

For another activity related to this chapter, go to **go.hrw.com** and type in the keyword **HZ5ATMW.**

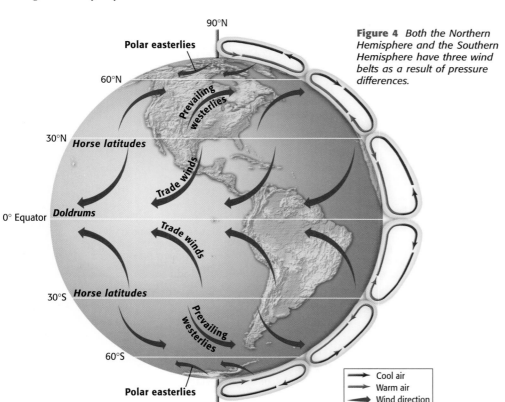

Figure 4 *Both the Northern Hemisphere and the Southern Hemisphere have three wind belts as a result of pressure differences.*

Using the Figure — BASIC

Wind Systems Have students use **Figure 4** to answer the following questions:

- Where are the trade winds? (The trade winds blow from 30° north and south latitudes to the equator.)

- Describe the motion of the trade winds in the Southern Hemisphere. (They move from the southeast to the northwest.)

- How do the westerlies flow in the Northern Hemisphere? (The westerlies flow from the southwest to the northeast.)

LS Logical

MISCONCEPTION ALERT

The Coriolis "Force" The Coriolis effect is not a force. When an object appears to be deflected from its path, it is not the object that is deflected but the Earth that has moved. Because the Earth is rotating, the Earth moves out from under the object that is passing over the surface. The change of the Earth's position gives the path traveled by the object the appearance of being curved. However, the Coriolis "force" can be used in mathematical equations to predict the movement of objects.

Science Bloopers

The Coriolis Effect During a World War I naval engagement off the Falkland Islands, British gunners were astonished to see that their artillery shells were landing 100 yd to the left of German ships. The gunners had made corrections for the Coriolis effect at 50° north latitude, not 50° south of the equator. Consequently, their shells fell at a distance from the target equal to twice the Coriolis deflection!

Is That a Fact!

Because the air descending over the horse latitudes has lost most of its moisture, the land around these latitudes receives very little precipitation. In fact, the Earth's largest deserts are in these areas.

Reteaching ——— BASIC

Concept Mapping Have students create a concept map using the vocabulary and concepts in this section. **LS** Visual

Quiz ——————— GENERAL

1. How does air temperature over landmasses and adjacent bodies of water change between day and night? (During the day, the air is cooler over water. At night, the air is cooler over land.)

2. List two kinds of breezes that result from local topography. (mountain and valley breezes)

Alternative Assessment ——— GENERAL

Modeling Sea and Land Breezes
Give each group two baking pans—one filled with sand and the other filled with ice. Groups should carefully warm the sand in an oven until the sand is very warm. Have the groups place the pans side by side. Then, they should fold a cardboard wind screen in three places so that it surrounds both pans. As they hold a burning splint at the boundary between the pans, students should see smoke travel toward the hot sand in the same way that the wind blows toward the beach during the daytime. Ask them to explain their observations and try to simulate a land breeze. (They could simulate a land breeze by letting the sand cool and replacing the ice with warm water.) **LS** Kinesthetic

Figure 5 *The jet stream forms this band of clouds as it flows above the Earth.*

jet stream a narrow belt of strong winds that blow in the upper troposphere

Jet Streams: Atmospheric Conveyor Belts

The flight from Seattle to Boston can be 30 minutes faster than the flight from Boston to Seattle. Why? Pilots take advantage of a jet stream similar to the one shown in **Figure 5.** The **jet streams** are narrow belts of high-speed winds that blow in the upper troposphere and lower stratosphere. These winds can reach maximum speeds of 400 km/h. Unlike other global winds, the jet streams do not follow regular paths around the Earth. Knowing the path of a jet stream is important not only to pilots but also to meteorologists. Because jet streams affect the movement of storms, meteorologists can track a storm if they know the location of a jet stream.

Local Winds

Local winds generally move short distances and can blow from any direction. Local geographic features, such as a shoreline or a mountain, can produce temperature differences that cause local winds. For example, the formation of sea and land breezes is shown in **Figure 6.** During the day, the land heats up faster than the water, so the air above the land becomes warmer than the air above the ocean. The warm land air rises, and the cold ocean air flows in to replace it. At night, the land cools faster than water, so the wind blows toward the ocean.

Figure 6 **Sea and Land Breezes**

During the day, air over the ocean is cooler and forms an area of high pressure. The cool air flows to the land, producing a sea breeze.

Air over the land is warmer. As warm air rises, it creates an area of low pressure.

At night, air over the ocean is warmer. As the warm air rises, it forms an area of low pressure.

Air over land is cooler and forms an area of high pressure. The cool air moves toward the ocean, producing a land breeze.

CONNECTION to Life Science ——— GENERAL

High-Altitude Highway Migrating birds use jet streams and local winds as aerial highways to reach their destinations. Insects and spiders also take advantage of wind currents. Glider plane pilots have reported seeing air so thick with spiders that it looked like snow, and ships 800 km out at sea have been deluged with spiders falling from the sky! Dangling from the end of long, silk streamers, spiders ride updrafts until they reach a wind current. They occasionally reach altitudes of 4 km. There they can travel for weeks, rolling in their streamers and dropping from the sky after covering up to 300 km. Students might enjoy finding radar entomology Internet sites for people who track traveling insects.

Mountain Breezes and Valley Breezes

Mountain and valley breezes are other examples of local winds caused by an area's geography. Campers in mountainous areas may feel a warm afternoon quickly change into a cold night soon after the sun sets. During the day, the sun warms the air along the mountain slopes. This warm air rises up the mountain slopes, creating a valley breeze. At nightfall, the air along the mountain slopes cools. This cool air moves down the slopes into the valley, producing a mountain breeze.

✓ Reading Check Why does the wind tend to blow down from mountains at night?

CONNECTION TO Social Studies

Local Breezes The chinook, the shamal, the sirocco, and the Santa Ana are all local winds. Find out about an interesting local wind, and create a poster-board display that shows how the wind forms and how it affects human cultures.

ACTIVITY

SECTION Review

Summary

- Winds blow from areas of high pressure to areas of low pressure.
- Pressure belts are found approximately every 30° of latitude.
- The Coriolis effect causes wind to appear to curve as it moves across the Earth's surface.
- Global winds include the polar easterlies, the westerlies, and the trade winds.
- Local winds include sea and land breezes and mountain and valley breezes.

Using Key Terms

1. In your own words, write a definition for each of the following terms: *wind, Coriolis effect, jet stream, polar easterlies, westerlies,* and *trade winds*.

Understanding Key Ideas

2. Why does warm air rise and cold air sink?
   a. because warm air is less dense than cold air
   b. because warm air is denser than cold air
   c. because cold air is less dense than warm air
   d. because warm air has less pressure than cold air does

3. What are pressure belts?

4. What causes winds?

5. How does the Coriolis effect affect wind movement?

6. How are sea and land breezes similar to mountain and valley breezes?

7. Would there be winds if the Earth's surface were the same temperature everywhere? Explain your answer.

Math Skills

8. Flying an airplane at 500 km/h, a pilot plans to reach her destination in 5 h. But she finds a jet stream moving 250 km/h in the direction she is traveling. If she gets a boost from the jet stream for 2 h, how long will the flight last?

Critical Thinking

9. **Making Inferences** In the Northern Hemisphere, why do westerlies flow from the west but trade winds flow from the east?

10. **Applying Concepts** Imagine you are near an ocean in the daytime. You want to go to the ocean, but you don't know how to get there. How might a local wind help you find the ocean?

SCI LINKS Developed and maintained by the National Science Teachers Association

For a variety of links related to this chapter, go to www.scilinks.org

Topic: Atmospheric Pressure and Winds
SciLinks code: HSM0115

Answers to Section Review

1. Sample answer: Wind is the movement of air from areas of high pressure to areas of low pressure. The Coriolis effect is the apparent deflection of a moving object due to Earth's rotation. Jet streams are high altitude belts of strong winds. Polar easterlies are global winds that blow from the poles toward 60° north and 60° south latitude. Westerlies are global winds that blow between 30° and 60° latitude in both hemispheres. Trade winds are global winds that blow between 30° latitude and the equator in both hemispheres.

CHAPTER RESOURCES

Chapter Resource File
- Section Quiz **GENERAL**
- Section Review **GENERAL**
- Vocabulary and Section Summary **GENERAL**

Technology
Transparencies
- Sea and Land Breezes

2. a

3. Pressure belts are bands of high and low pressure that are found about every 30° of latitude.

4. Winds are caused by the unequal heating of the Earth's surface, which causes pressure differences.

5. The Coriolis effect causes winds to appear to be deflected to the east or west depending on the direction that the winds are traveling in each hemisphere. Because of the Coriolis effect, winds in the Northern Hemisphere appear to curve to the right, and winds in the Southern Hemisphere appear to curve to the left.

6. Both types of breezes result from pressure differences caused by unequal heating of materials.

7. Because unequal heating of the Earth's surface causes winds, there would probably not be winds near Earth's surface if Earth's surface were the same temperature everywhere.

8. 500 km/h $\times$ 5 h = 2,500 km
(500 km/h + 250 km/h) $\times$ 2 h = 1,500 km
2,500 km − 1,500 km = 1,000 km
1,000 km ÷ 500 km = 2 h
2 h + 2 h = 4 h

9. Both winds are affected by the Coriolis effect. In the Northern Hemisphere, the westerlies travel in a northerly direction. They appear to be deflected to the northeast by the Coriolis effect. In contrast, in the Northern Hemisphere, the trade winds blow in a southerly direction, so they appear to be deflected to the southwest.

10. During the day, a sea breeze is caused by cooler air over the water moving toward the land. Walking toward the sea breeze would lead you to the ocean.

Answer to Reading Check

At night, the air along the mountain slopes cools. This cool air moves down the slopes into the valley and produces a mountain breeze.

Focus

Overview

This section discusses the causes and effects of air pollution. Students learn the difference between primary and secondary pollutants and about acid precipitation and the ozone hole. The section concludes with a discussion about reducing air pollution.

Bellringer

Bring a filter mask to class. Have each student make a list of three situations in which one might wear such a mask. For example, surgeons wear such masks to prevent the transfer of disease-causing microbes, and sandblasters wear masks to avoid inhaling dust and paint chips. Tell students that some people living in areas with heavily polluted air wear such masks to protect themselves from impurities in the air they breathe.

READING WARM-UP

Objectives

- Compare primary and secondary air pollutants.
- Identify the major sources of air pollution.
- Explain the effects of an ozone hole.
- List five effects of air pollution on the human body.
- Identify ways to reduce air pollution.

Terms to Learn

air pollution
acid precipitation

READING STRATEGY

Reading Organizer As you read this section, make a table that identifies major sources of air pollution and that suggests ways to reduce pollution from each source.

 air pollution the contamination of the atmosphere by the introduction of pollutants from human and natural sources

---

Air Pollution

In December 1952, one of London's dreaded "pea souper" fogs settled on the city. But this was no ordinary fog—it was thick with coal smoke and air pollution. It burned people's lungs, and the sky grew so dark that people could not see their hands in front of their faces. When the fog lifted four days later, thousands of people were dead!

London's killer fog shocked the world and caused major changes in England's air-pollution laws. People began to think that air pollution was not simply a part of urban life that had to be endured. Air pollution had to be reduced. Although this event is an extreme example, air pollution is common in many parts of the world. However, nations are taking major steps to reduce air pollution. But what is air pollution? **Air pollution** is the contamination of the atmosphere by the introduction of pollutants from human and natural sources. Air pollutants are classified according to their source as either primary pollutants or secondary pollutants.

Primary Pollutants

Pollutants that are put directly into the air by human or natural activity are *primary pollutants*. Primary pollutants from natural sources include dust, sea salt, volcanic gases and ash, smoke from forest fires, and pollen. Primary pollutants from human sources include carbon monoxide, dust, smoke, and chemicals from paint and other substances. In urban areas, vehicle exhaust is a common source of primary pollutants. Examples of primary pollutants are shown in **Figure 1**.

✓ **Reading Check** List three primary pollutants from natural sources. (*See the Appendix for answers to Reading Checks.*)

Figure 1 **Examples of Primary Pollutants**

Industrial emissions   **Vehicle exhaust**   **Volcanic ash**

CHAPTER RESOURCES

Chapter Resource File

- **Lesson Plan**
- **Directed Reading A** BASIC
- **Directed Reading B** SPECIAL NEEDS

Technology

Transparencies
- Bellringer
- The Formation of Smog

Answer to Reading Check

Sample answer: smoke, dust, and sea salt

Secondary Pollutants

Pollutants that form when primary pollutants react with other primary pollutants or with naturally occurring substances, such as water vapor, are *secondary pollutants*. Ozone and smog are examples of secondary pollutants. Ozone is produced when sunlight reacts with vehicle exhaust and air. You may have heard of "Ozone Action Day" warnings in your community. When such a warning is issued, people are discouraged from outdoor physical activity because ozone can damage their lungs. In the stratosphere, ozone forms a protective layer that absorbs harmful radiation from the sun. Near the Earth's surface, however, ozone is a dangerous pollutant that negatively affects the health of organisms.

The Formation of Smog

Smog forms when ozone and vehicle exhaust react with sunlight, as shown in **Figure 2.** Local geography and weather patterns can also contribute to smog formation. Los Angeles, shown in **Figure 3,** is almost completely surrounded by mountains that trap pollutants and contribute to smog formation. Although pollution controls have reduced levels of smog in Los Angeles, smog remains a problem for Los Angeles and many other large cities.

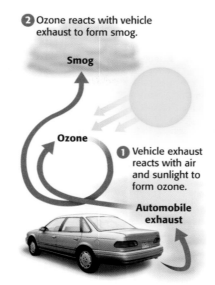

2 Ozone reacts with vehicle exhaust to form smog.

Smog

Ozone

1 Vehicle exhaust reacts with air and sunlight to form ozone.

Automobile exhaust

Figure 2 *Smog forms when sunlight reacts with ozone and vehicle exhaust.*

Figure 3 *Smog levels in Los Angeles can vary dramatically. During summer, a layer of warm air can trap smog near the ground. However, in the winter, a storm can quickly clear the air.*

Answer to Connection to Biology Activity

Plants that are effective at removing indoor air pollutants include: philodendrons, spider plants, golden pothos, gerbera daisies, chrysanthemums, corn plant, peace lily, and English ivy.

CONNECTION to
Physical Science—GENERAL

Incomplete Combustion

Explain to students that much of the human-caused air pollution results from incomplete combustion. Combustion, another word for burning, is the process by which substances combine with oxygen rapidly, producing thermal energy. Byproducts are produced when a substance does not burn completely, as in an automobile engine. Many of these byproducts, such as carbon monoxide, are harmful to living organisms.

CONNECTION TO
Biology

Cleaning the Air with Plants Did you know that common houseplants can help fight indoor air pollution? Some houseplants are so effective at removing air pollutants that NASA might use them as part of the life-support system in future space stations. Back on Earth, you can use plants to clean the air in your school or home. Research the top 10 air-cleaning houseplants, and find out if you can grow any of them in your classroom or home. **ACTIVITY**

Figure 4 *There are many sources of indoor air pollution. Indoor air pollution can be difficult to detect because it is often invisible.*

Sources of Human-Caused Air Pollution

Human-caused air pollution comes from a variety of sources. A major source of air pollution today is transportation. Cars contribute about 10% to 20% of the human-caused air pollution in the United States. Vehicle exhaust contains nitrogen oxide, which contributes to smog formation and acid precipitation. However, pollution controls and cleaner gasoline have greatly reduced air pollution from vehicles.

Industrial Air Pollution

Many industrial plants and electric power plants burn fossil fuels, such as coal, to produce energy. Burning some types of coal without pollution controls can release large amounts of air pollutants. Some industries also produce chemicals that can pollute the air. Oil refineries, chemical manufacturing plants, dry-cleaning businesses, furniture refinishers, and auto body shops are all potential sources of air pollution.

Indoor Air Pollution

Sometimes, the air inside a building can be more polluted than the air outside. Some sources of indoor air pollution are shown in **Figure 4.** *Ventilation,* or the mixing of indoor air with outdoor air, can reduce indoor air pollution. Another way to reduce indoor air pollution is to limit the use of chemical solvents and cleaners.

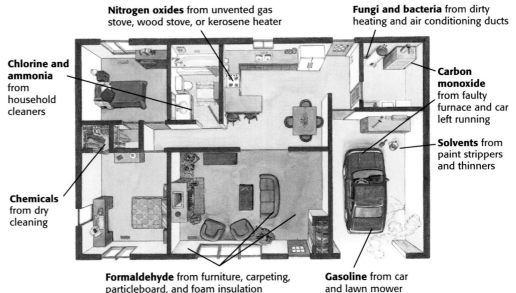

Nitrogen oxides from unvented gas stove, wood stove, or kerosene heater

Fungi and bacteria from dirty heating and air conditioning ducts

Chlorine and ammonia from household cleaners

Carbon monoxide from faulty furnace and car left running

Solvents from paint strippers and thinners

Chemicals from dry cleaning

Formaldehyde from furniture, carpeting, particleboard, and foam insulation

Gasoline from car and lawn mower

CHAPTER RESOURCES
Technology

 Transparencies
• Sources of Indoor Air Pollution

CONNECTION ACTIVITY
Real World——GENERAL

Local Air Pollution and Weather Air quality varies greatly from place to place. Even in one location, air quality can change seasonally or from day to day. Have students research the air quality where they live. Ask students to consider the following questions: "What are the sources of air pollution where you live? What are the weather conditions that lead to the worst and best air quality in your area?" **LS Interpersonal**

Acid Precipitation

Precipitation such as rain, sleet, or snow that contains acids from air pollution is called **acid precipitation.** When fossil fuels are burned, they can release sulfur dioxide and nitrogen oxide into the atmosphere. When these pollutants combine with water in the atmosphere, they form sulfuric acid and nitric acid. Precipitation is naturally acidic, but sulfuric acid and nitric acid can make it so acidic that it can negatively affect the environment. In most areas of the world, pollution controls have helped reduce acid precipitation.

Acid Precipitation and Plants

Plant communities have adapted over long periods of time to the natural acidity of the soil in which they grow. Acid precipitation can cause the acidity of soil to increase. This process, called *acidification*, changes the balance of a soil's chemistry in several ways. When the acidity of soil increases, some nutrients are dissolved. Nutrients that plants need for growth get washed away by rainwater. Increased acidity also causes aluminum and other toxic metals to be released. Some of these toxic metals are absorbed by the roots of plants.

Reading Check How does acid precipitation affect plants?

The Effects of Acid Precipitation on Forests

Forest ecology is complex. Scientists are still trying to fully understand the long-term effects of acid precipitation on groups of plants and their habitats. In some areas of the world, however, acid precipitation has damaged large areas of forest. The effects of acid precipitation are most noticeable in Eastern Europe, as shown in **Figure 5.** Forests in the northeastern United States and in eastern Canada have also been affected by acid precipitation.

acid precipitation rain, sleet, or snow that contains a high concentration of acids

Testing for Particulates

1. Particulates are pollutants such as dust that are extremely small. In this lab, you will measure the amount of particulates in the air. Begin by covering **ten 5 in. × 7 in. index cards** with a thin coat of **petroleum jelly.**

2. Hang the cards in various locations inside and outside your school.

3. One day later, use a **magnifying lens** to count the number of particles on the cards. Which location had the fewest number of particulates? Which location had the highest number of particulates? Hypothesize why.

Figure 5 *This forest in Poland was damaged by acid precipitation.*

Is That a Fact!

Ozone can form during thunderstorms. Lightning provides the energy to change O_2 to O_3. In fact, the distinct smell that people notice after an intense thunderstorm is probably the smell of ozone.

Answer to Reading Check

Answers may vary. Acid precipitation may decrease the soil nutrients that are available to plants.

Homework — GENERAL

Writing **The Ozone Holes**
Remind students that there are two ozone holes—the large Antarctic ozone hole and the smaller Arctic ozone hole. Although the Arctic ozone hole is smaller, it has a more direct effect on North America. Have interested students find out how the ozone holes have changed since they were first measured. Have students graph the values on both a yearly and seasonal basis, and have them describe any trends they see. Have them compile their findings into a short report. **LS** Intrapersonal

Acid Precipitation and Aquatic Ecosystems

Aquatic organisms have adapted to live in water with a particular range of acidity. If acid precipitation increases the acidity of a lake or stream, aquatic plants, fish, and other aquatic organisms may die. The effects of acid precipitation on lakes and rivers are worst in the spring, when the acidic snow that built up in the winter melts and acidic water flows into lakes and rivers. A rapid change in a body of water's acidity is called *acid shock*. Acid shock can cause large numbers of fish to die. Acid shock can also affect the delicate eggs of fish and amphibians.

To reduce the effects of acid precipitation on aquatic ecosystems, some communities spray powdered lime on acidified lakes in the spring, which reduces the acidity of the lakes. Lime, a base, neutralizes the acid in the water. Unfortunately, lime cannot be spread to offset all acid damage to lakes.

✓ *Reading Check* Why is powdered lime sprayed on lakes in the spring instead of the fall?

Figure 6 *Polar weather conditions cause the size of the ozone hole (shown in blue) to vary. In the 2001 image, the ozone hole is larger than North America. One year later, it was 40% smaller.*

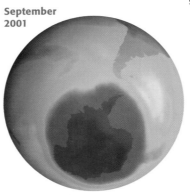

September 2001

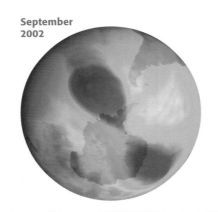

September 2002

The Ozone Hole

In 1985, scientists reported an alarming discovery about the Earth's protective ozone layer. Over the Antarctic regions, the ozone layer was thinning, particularly during the spring. This change was also noted over the Arctic. Chemicals called *CFCs* were causing ozone to break down into oxygen, which does not block the sun's harmful ultraviolet (UV) rays. The thinning of the ozone layer creates an ozone hole, shown in **Figure 6.** The ozone hole allows more UV radiation to reach the Earth's surface. UV radiation is dangerous to organisms because it damages genes and can cause skin cancer.

Cooperation to Reduce the Ozone Hole

In 1987, a group of nations met in Canada and agreed to take action against ozone depletion. Agreements were made to reduce and eventually ban CFC use, and CFC alternatives were quickly developed. Because many countries agreed to take swift action to control CFC use, and because a technological solution was quickly found, many people consider ozone protection an environmental success story. The battle to protect the ozone layer is not over, however. CFC molecules can remain active in the stratosphere for 60 to 120 years. So, CFCs released 30 years ago are still destroying ozone today. Thus, it will take many years for the ozone layer to completely recover.

WEIRD SCIENCE

Ice core samples from Greenland show large-scale lead pollution in the atmosphere more than 2,000 years ago. The pollution can be traced to Roman silver mines in southern Spain. Large amounts of lead were released into the atmosphere during the smelting of silver ore.

Answer to Reading Check

Powdered lime is used to counteract the effects of acidic snowmelt from snow that accumulated during the winter.

Air Pollution and Human Health

Daily exposure to small amounts of air pollution can cause serious health problems. Children, elderly people, and people with asthma, allergies, lung problems, and heart problems are especially vulnerable to the effects of air pollution. **Table 1** shows some of the effects of air pollution on the human body. The short-term effects of air pollution are immediately noticeable. Coughing, headaches, and increase in asthma-related problems are only a few short-term effects. The long-term effects of air pollution, such as lung cancer, are more dangerous because they may not be noticed until many years after an individual has been exposed to pollutants.

Cleaning Up Air Pollution

Much progress has been made in reducing air pollution. For example, in the United States the Clean Air Act was passed by Congress in 1970. The Clean Air Act is a law that gives the Environmental Protection Agency (EPA) the authority to control the amount of air pollutants that can be released from any source, such as cars and factories. The EPA also checks air quality. If air quality worsens, the EPA can set stricter standards. The Clean Air Act was strengthened in 1990.

Controlling Air Pollution from Industry

The Clean Air Act requires many industries to use pollution-control devices such as scrubbers. A *scrubber* is a device that is used to remove some pollutants before they are released by smokestacks. Scrubbers in coal-burning power plants remove particles such as ash from the smoke. Other industrial plants, such as the power plant shown in **Figure 7,** focus on burning fuel more efficiently so that fewer pollutants are released.

Table 1	Effects of Air Pollution on Human Health
Short-term effects	headache; nausea; irritation of eyes, nose, and throat; coughing; upper respiratory infections; worsening of asthma and emphysema
Long-term effects	emphysema; lung cancer; permanent lung damage; heart disease

Figure 7 *This power plant in Florida is leading the way in clean-coal technology. The plant turns coal into a gas before it is burned, so fewer pollutants are released.*

Homework ——— ADVANCED

Radon Radon is a naturally occurring gas that results from the decay of uranium, particularly in igneous rocks such as granite. Have students use the Internet to research the health problems associated with radon. Have students assess the potential for significant radon concentrations in your community and write a short informative essay based on their findings.
LS Intrapersonal

Close

Pollution Terms Have students use each of the following terms in a sentence that correctly conveys the meaning of the term: *scrubber, smog, acid precipitation, industrial pollutants, ozone hole,* and *air quality.* **LS** Visual

Quiz — GENERAL

1. Classify each of the following as either a primary or secondary air pollutant: smog, tobacco smoke, chalk dust, and acid rain. (Sample answer: Tobacco smoke and chalk dust are primary pollutants. Smog and acid rain are secondary pollutants.)

2. What are two health problems that can result from breathing polluted air? (Sample answer: dizziness; headaches; burning, itchy eyes; runny nose; coughing; shortness of breath; sore throat; lung cancer and other respiratory diseases; chest pain; colds; and allergies)

Alternative Assessment — BASIC

Writing **Critical Reading** Have students find an article about air pollution in a popular periodical or newspaper. Students should photocopy the article on 11 × 17 paper. Then, ask students to critique the article's strengths and weaknesses and write comments on the margin of the paper. **LS** Verbal

SCHOOL to HOME

Air Pollution Awareness

Work at home with a parent to develop a presentation for an "Air Pollution Awareness Day" at school. Develop a unique way to educate the public about air pollution, but have your presentation approved by your teacher before working on it. On "Air Pollution Awareness Day," your teacher might decide to invite students from another grade or a parent to come see the exhibits.

ACTIVITY

The Allowance Trading System

The Allowance Trading System is another initiative to reduce air pollution. In this program, the EPA establishes allowances for the amount of a pollutant that companies can release. If a company exceeds their allowance, they must pay a fine. A company that releases less than its allowance can sell some of its allowance to a company that releases more. Allowances are also available for the public to buy. So, organizations seeking to reduce air pollution can buy an allowance of 1,000 tons of sulfur dioxide, thus reducing the total amount of sulfur dioxide released by industries.

Reading Check How does the Allowance Trading System work?

Reducing Air Pollution from Vehicles

A large percentage of air pollution in the United States comes from the vehicles we drive. To reduce air pollution from vehicles, the EPA requires car makers to meet a certain standard for vehicle exhaust. Devices such as catalytic converters remove many pollutants from exhaust and help cars meet this standard. Cleaner fuels and more-efficent engines have also helped reduce air pollution from vehicles. Car manufacturers are also making cars that run on fuels other than gasoline. Some of these cars run on hydrogen or natural gas. Hybrid cars, which are becoming more common, use gasoline and electric power to reduce emissions. Another way to reduce air pollution is to carpool, use public transportation, or bike or walk to your destination, as shown in **Figure 8.**

Figure 8 *In Copenhagen, Denmark, companies loan free bicycles in exchange for publicity. The program helps reduce air pollution and auto traffic.*

Answer to Reading Check

Allowance trading establishes allowances for a certain type of pollutant. Companies are permitted to release their allowance of the pollutant, but if they exceed the allowance, they must buy additional allowances or pay a fine.

INTERNET ACTIVITY
Short Story — GENERAL

For an internet activity related to this chapter, have students go to **go.hrw.com** and type in the keyword **HZ5ATMW.**

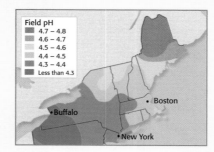

Summary

- Primary pollutants are pollutants that are put directly into the air by human or natural activity.
- Secondary pollutants are pollutants that form when primary pollutants react with other primary pollutants or with naturally occurring substances.
- Transportation, industry, and natural sources are the main sources of air pollution.
- Air pollution can be reduced by legislation, such as the Clean Air Act; by technology, such as scrubbers; and by changes in lifestyle.

Using Key Terms

The statements below are false. For each statement, replace the underlined term to make a true statement.

1. Air pollution is a sudden change in the acidity of a stream or lake.

2. Smog is rain, sleet, or snow that has a high concentration of acid.

Understanding Key Ideas

3. Which of the following results in the formation of smog?
   a. Acids in the air react with ozone.
   b. Ozone reacts with vehicle exhaust.
   c. Vehicle exhaust reacts with sunlight and ozone.
   d. Water vapor reacts with sunlight and ozone.

4. What is the difference between primary and secondary pollutants?

5. Describe five sources of indoor air pollution. Is all air pollution caused by humans? Explain.

6. What is the ozone hole, and why does it form?

7. Describe five effects of air pollution on human health. How can air pollution be reduced?

Critical Thinking

8. **Expressing Opinions** How do you think that nations should resolve air-pollution problems that cross national boundaries?

9. **Making Inferences** Why might establishing a direct link between air pollution and health problems be difficult?

Interpreting Graphics

The map below shows the pH of precipitation measured at field stations in the northeastern U.S. On the pH scale, lower numbers indicate solutions that are more acidic than solutions with higher numbers. Use the map to answer the questions below.

Field pH
4.7 – 4.8
4.6 – 4.7
4.5 – 4.6
4.4 – 4.5
4.3 – 4.4
Less than 4.3

• Boston

• Buffalo

• New York

10. Which areas have the most acidic precipitation? Hypothesize why.

11. Boston is a larger city than Buffalo is, but the precipitation measured in Buffalo is more acidic than the precipitation in Boston. Explain why.

SCiLINKS®
Developed and maintained by the National Science Teachers Association

For a variety of links related to this chapter, go to www.scilinks.org

Topic: Air Pollution
SciLinks code: HSM0033

Answers to Section Review

1. Acid shock
2. Acid precipitation
3. c
4. Primary pollutants are pollutants that are put into the air directly by human or natural activity. Secondary pollutants form when primary pollutants react with other substances.

CHAPTER RESOURCES

Chapter Resource File

- Section Quiz GENERAL
- Section Review GENERAL
- Vocabulary and Section Summary GENERAL
- Critical Thinking ADVANCED
- SciLinks Activity GENERAL
- Datasheet for Quick Lab

Technology

- **Interactive Explorations CD-ROM**
  - Moose Malady GENERAL

5. Answers may vary. Household cleaners, paint products, dirty air heating and air conditioning vents, furniture and carpeting, heaters, and stoves can all be sources of indoor air pollution. There are many natural sources of air pollution, including dust, ash from volcanoes, pollen, and smoke.

6. The ozone hole is a thinning of the ozone layer in polar regions, particularly the Antarctic. Levels of ozone vary seasonally, but the ozone hole is caused primarily by CFCs that were released into the atmosphere by human activity.

7. Answers may vary. Accept any of the effects of air pollution on human health mentioned in this section. There are many ways that air pollution can be reduced. Legislation, such as the Clean Air Act, gives the Environmental Protection Agency the power to control the amount of air pollutants released from most sources. In addition, new technology has helped create cars that release fewer pollutants and devices, such as scrubbers, that reduce industrial air pollution.

8. Answers may vary. Cooperation is important to reducing air pollution problems that cross national boundaries.

9. Answers may vary. Students should note that it can take a long time before the effects of air pollution on an individual's health can be observed.

10. western New York and Pennsylvania; Answers may vary. Students may suggest that the prevailing winds concentrate the pollutants that contribute to acid precipitation on the Eastern seaboard.

11. Students may note that the prevailing winds and topographic features such as the Adirondack mountains concentrate acid precipitation over Buffalo.

Under Pressure!

Teacher's Notes

Time Required

One 45-minute class period plus 15 minutes each day for 3 or 4 days

Lab Ratings

EASY ——————→ HARD

Teacher Prep 🧪🧪
Student Set-Up 🧪🧪🧪🧪
Concept Level 🧪🧪
Clean Up 🧪🧪

MATERIALS

The materials listed on the student page are enough for a group of 2–4 students.

Safety Caution

Remind students to review all safety cautions and icons before beginning this lab activity.

Preparation Notes

A week before the activity, have students bring in large coffee cans. Jars can substitute for coffee cans in this experiment. For more-accurate results, make sure students place their barometers in a shaded area. As students work on this lab in class, have them collect newspaper clippings of daily weather reports.

Under Pressure!

Imagine that you are planning a picnic with your friends, so you look in the newspaper for the weather forecast. The temperature this afternoon should be in the low 80s. This temperature sounds quite comfortable! But you notice that the newspaper's forecast also includes the barometer reading. What's a barometer? And what does the reading tell you? In this activity, you will build your own barometer and will discover what this tool can tell you.

OBJECTIVES

Predict how changes in air pressure affect a barometer.

Build a barometer to test your hypothesis.

MATERIALS

- balloon
- can, coffee, large, empty, 10 cm in diameter
- card, index
- scissors
- straw, drinking
- tape, masking, or rubber band

SAFETY

Ask a Question

1. How can I use a barometer to detect changes in air pressure?

Form a Hypothesis

2. Write a few sentences that answer the question above.

Test the Hypothesis

3. Stretch the balloon a few times. Then, blow up the balloon, and let the air out. This step will make your barometer more sensitive to changes in atmospheric pressure.

4. Cut off the open end of the balloon. Next, stretch the balloon over the open end of the coffee can. Then, attach the balloon to the can with masking tape or a rubber band.

Terry J. Rakes
Elmwood Jr. High
Rogers, Arkansas

CLASSROOM TESTED & APPROVED

CHAPTER RESOURCES

Chapter Resource File

- **Datasheet for Chapter Lab**
- **Lab Notes and Answers**

Technology
📀 **Classroom Videos**
- Lab Video

LabBook
- Go Fly a Bike!

⑤ Cut one end of the straw at an angle to make a pointer.

⑥ Place the straw on the stretched balloon so that the pointer is directed away from the center of the balloon. Five centimeters of the end of the straw should hang over the edge of the can. Tape the straw to the balloon as shown in the illustration at right.

⑦ Tape the index card to the side of the can as shown in the illustration at right. Congratulations! You have just made a barometer!

⑧ Now, use your barometer to collect and record information about air pressure. Place the barometer outside for 3 or 4 days. On each day, mark on the index card where the tip of the straw points.

Analyze the Results

① **Explaining Events** What atmospheric factors affect how your barometer works? Explain your answer.

② **Recognizing Patterns** What does it mean when the straw moves up?

③ **Recognizing Patterns** What does it mean when the straw moves down?

Draw Conclusions

④ **Applying Conclusions** Compare your results with the barometric pressures listed in your local newspaper. What kind of weather is associated with high pressure? What kind of weather is associated with low pressure?

⑤ **Evaluating Results** Does the barometer you built support your hypothesis? Explain your answer.

Applying Your Data

Now, you can use your barometer to measure the actual air pressure! Get the weather section from your local newspaper for the same 3 or 4 days that you were testing your barometer. Find the barometer reading in the newspaper for each day, and record the reading beside that day's mark on your index card. Use these markings on your card to create a scale with marks at regular intervals. Transfer this scale to a new card and attach it to your barometer.

Analyze the Results

1. A change in air pressure will affect how the barometer works. Temperature changes may also affect the barometer.

2. An upward movement of the straw indicates that the atmospheric pressure is increasing. Air pressure is pushing on the balloon, which causes the pointer to rise.

3. A downward movement of the straw indicates that the atmospheric pressure is decreasing. Less air pressure causes the pointer to dip downward.

Draw Conclusions

4. Clear, dry days are associated with high pressure. Cloudy, rainy, or humid days are associated with low pressure. A sudden drop in air pressure usually indicates that a storm is on the way.

5. Answers will vary depending on the hypothesis. Students should explain how their barometer was affected by atmospheric pressure and why the experiment supported or disproved their hypothesis.

Applying Your Data

Make sure students are aware that barometric pressure changes throughout the day. Students should try to get recorded pressures for the same time of day that they were testing their barometer. Some Internet sites provide weather reports that are updated hourly. Be sure to tell students that their barometric measurements will be approximate.

Chapter Review

Assignment Guide

Section	Questions
1	2, 6, 7–9, 11, 17–19, 21
2	3, 4, 12, 13, 22, 24
3	5, 14, 23, 25, 26
4	15, 16, 20
1 and 3	1

ANSWERS

Using Key Terms

1. Sample answer: Air pressure is the measure of the force with which air molecules are pushing on a surface. Wind is the movement of air caused by differences in air pressure.

2. Sample answer: The troposphere is the lowest layer of the Earth's atmosphere. The thermosphere is the uppermost layer of the Earth's atmosphere.

3. Sample answer: The greenhouse effect is the Earth's natural heating process, by which gases in the atmosphere absorb and reradiate thermal energy. Global warming is a rise in average global temperature.

4. Sample answer: Convection is the transfer of thermal energy by the circulation of a liquid or gas. Thermal conduction is the transfer of thermal energy through a material.

USING KEY TERMS

For each pair of terms, explain how the meanings of the terms differ.

1. *air pressure* and *wind*

2. *troposphere* and *thermosphere*

3. *greenhouse effect* and *global warming*

4. *convection* and *thermal conduction*

5. *global wind* and *local wind*

6. *stratosphere* and *mesosphere*

UNDERSTANDING KEY IDEAS

Multiple Choice

7. What is the most abundant gas in the atmosphere?
   a. oxygen
   b. hydrogen
   c. nitrogen
   d. carbon dioxide

8. A major source of oxygen for the Earth's atmosphere is
   a. sea water.
   b. the sun.
   c. plants.
   d. animals.

9. The bottom layer of the atmosphere, where almost all weather occurs, is the
   a. stratosphere.
   b. troposphere.
   c. thermosphere.
   d. mesosphere.

10. What percentage of the solar energy that reaches the outer atmosphere is absorbed at the Earth's surface?
    a. 20%   c. 50%
    b. 30%   d. 70%

11. The ozone layer is located in the
    a. stratosphere.
    b. troposphere.
    c. thermosphere.
    d. mesosphere.

12. By which method does most thermal energy in the atmosphere circulate?
    a. conduction
    b. convection
    c. advection
    d. radiation

13. The balance between incoming and outgoing energy is called
    a. the convection balance.
    b. the conduction balance.
    c. the greenhouse effect.
    d. the radiation balance.

14. In which wind belt is most of the United States located?
    a. westerlies
    b. northeast trade winds
    c. southeast trade winds
    d. doldrums

15. Which of the following pollutants is NOT a primary pollutant?
    a. car exhaust
    b. acid precipitation
    c. smoke from a factory
    d. fumes from burning plastic

5. Sample answer: A global wind is a large-scale pattern of air circulation in the atmosphere. A local wind generally flows short distances and can blow from any direction.

6. Sample answer: The stratosphere is the atmospheric layer above the troposphere, where temperature rises with altitude. The mesosphere is between the stratosphere and thermosphere, where temperature decreases with increasing altitude.

Understanding Key Ideas

7. c	**12.** b
8. c	**13.** d
9. b	**14.** a
10. c	**15.** b
11. a	**16.** d

16 The Clean Air Act

   a. controls the amount of air pollutants that can be released from many sources.

   b. requires cars to run on fuels other than gasoline.

   c. requires many industries to use scrubbers.

   d. Both (a) and (c)

Short Answer

17 Why does the atmosphere become less dense as altitude increases?

18 Explain why air rises when it is heated.

19 What is the main cause of temperature changes in the atmosphere?

20 What are secondary pollutants, and how do they form? Give an example of a secondary pollutant.

CRITICAL THINKING

21 **Concept Mapping** Use the following terms to create a concept map: *mesosphere, stratosphere, layers, temperature, troposphere,* and *atmosphere.*

22 **Identifying Relationships** What is the relationship between the greenhouse effect and global warming?

23 **Applying Concepts** How do you think the Coriolis effect would change if the Earth rotated twice as fast as it does? Explain.

24 **Making Inferences** The atmosphere of Venus has a very high level of carbon dioxide. How might this fact influence the greenhouse effect on Venus?

INTERPRETING GRAPHICS

Use the diagram below to answer the questions that follow. When answering the questions that follow, assume that ocean currents do not affect the path of the boats.

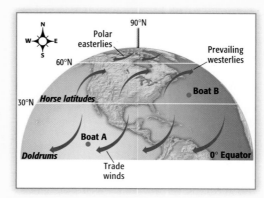

25 If Boat A traveled to 50°N, from which direction would the prevailing winds blow?

26 If Boat B sailed with the prevailing westerlies in the Northern Hemisphere, in which direction would the boat be traveling?

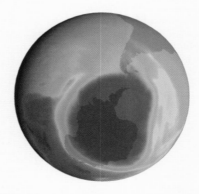

17. As altitude increases, there are fewer gas molecules. Gravity pulls most of the atmosphere's gas molecules close to the Earth's surface, which makes the lower layers more dense than the upper layers.

18. Air rises as it is heated because it becomes less dense.

19. The temperature differences in the atmosphere result mainly from the way solar energy is absorbed. Some layers are warmer because they contain gases that absorb solar energy.

20. Secondary pollutants form when primary pollutants react with other primary pollutants or with other naturally occurring substances. Acid rain is an example of a secondary pollutant.

Critical Thinking

21. 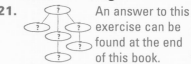 An answer to this exercise can be found at the end of this book.

22. Sample answer: Global warming is a gradual rise in Earth's average temperature. It is possibly caused by an increase in the greenhouse effect.

23. The Coriolis effect would be greater if the Earth rotated twice as fast. The apparent deflection of winds is caused by the Earth's rotation.

24. Answers may vary. The greater concentration of carbon dioxide in Venus's atmosphere causes the greenhouse effect to be more extreme on Venus than on Earth.

Interpreting Graphics

25. The prevailing winds would be blowing east.

26. The boat would be traveling northeast.

Teacher's Note

To provide practice under more realistic testing conditions, give students 20 minutes to answer all of the questions in this Standardized Test Preparation.

Answers to the standardized test preparation can help you identify student misconceptions and misunderstandings.

READING

Passage 1

1. D
2. F

 **TEST DOCTOR**

Question 2: All of the answer options may appear similar. Remind students that they must read the passage carefully to discover the correct answer choice.

READING

Read each of the passages below. Then, answer the questions that follow each passage.

Passage 1 An important part of the EPA's Acid Rain Program is the allowance trading system, which is designed to reduce sulfur dioxide emissions. In this system, 1 ton of sulfur dioxide (SO_2) emission is equivalent to one <u>allowance</u>. A limited number of allowances are allocated for each year. Companies purchase the allowances from the EPA and are allowed to produce as many tons of SO_2 as they have allowances for the year. Companies can buy, sell, or trade allowances, but if they exceed their allowances, they must pay a fine. The system allows a company to determine the most cost-effective ways to comply with the Clean Air Act. A company can reduce emissions by using technology that conserves energy, using renewable energy sources, or updating its pollution-control devices and using low-sulfur fuels.

1. According to the passage, which of the following methods can a company use to reduce emissions?

   A preserving wildlife habitat
   B lobbying Congress
   C using high-sulfur fuels
   D using technology that conserves energy

2. In the passage, what does *allowance* mean?

   F an allotment for a pollutant
   G an allocation of money for reducing pollution
   H an alleviation of pollution
   I an allegation of pollution

Passage 2 The chinook, or "snow eater," is a dry wind that blows down the eastern side of the Rocky Mountains from New Mexico to Alaska. Arapaho Indians gave the chinook its name because of its ability to melt large amounts of snow very quickly. Chinooks form when moist air is forced over a mountain range. The air cools as it rises. As the air cools, it releases moisture by raining or snowing. As the dry air flows over the mountaintop, it compresses and heats the air below. The warm, dry wind that results is worthy of the name "snow eater" because it melts a half meter of snow in a few hours! The temperature change caused when a chinook rushes down a mountainside can also be dramatic. In 1943 in Spearfish, South Dakota, the temperature at 7:30 in the morning was −4°F. But two minutes later, a chinook caused the temperature to soar 49° to 45°F.

1. Which of the following descriptions best explains why the chinook is called "the snow eater"?

   A The chinook is so cold that it prevents the formation of snow in the atmosphere.
   B The chinook is so warm that it prevents the formation of snow in the atmosphere.
   C The chinook is a warm wind that has high humidity.
   D The chinook is a warm wind that has low humidity.

2. According to the passage, at what time did the temperature reach 45°F in Spearfish, South Dakota?

   F 7:30 P.M.
   G 7:32 P.M.
   H 7:30 A.M.
   I 7:32 A.M.

Passage 2

1. D
2. I

 **TEST DOCTOR**

Question 2: Students may see the time *7:30* in the text and conclude that H is the answer to Question 2. Remind students to read the passage thoroughly. The most obvious answer is not always the correct choice.

Use the illustration below to answer the questions that follow.

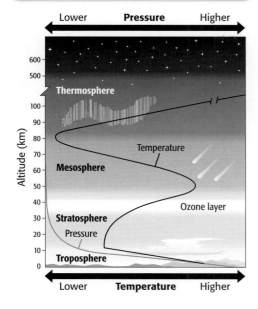

Lower — **Pressure** — Higher

Altitude (km)

Thermosphere

Mesosphere

Temperature

Ozone layer

Stratosphere

Pressure

Troposphere

Lower — **Temperature** — Higher

1. Which of the following statements describes how temperature changes in the mesosphere?

A Temperature increases as altitude increases.

B Temperature decreases as altitude increases.

C Temperature decreases as pressure increases.

D Temperature does not change as pressure increases.

2. In which layers does temperature decrease as pressure decreases?

F the troposphere and the mesosphere

G the troposphere and the stratosphere

H the ozone layer and the troposphere

I the ozone layer and the thermosphere

3. A research balloon took measurements at 23 km, 35 km, 52 km, 73 km, 86 km, 92 km, 101 km, and 110 km. Which measurements were taken in the mesosphere?

A measurements at 23 km and 35 km

B measurements at 52 km and 73 km

C measurements at 86 km and 92 km

D measurements at 101 km and 110 km

Read each question below, and choose the best answer.

1. An airplane is flying at a speed of 500 km/h when it encounters a jet stream moving in the same direction at 150 km/h. If the plane flies with the jet stream, how much farther will the plane travel in 1.5 h?

A 950 km

B 525 km

C 225 km

D 150 km

2. Today's wind speed was measured at 18 km/h. What was the wind speed in meters per hour?

F 1.8 m/h

G 180 m/h

H 1,800 m/h

I 18,000 m/h

3. Rockport received 24.1 cm of rain on Monday, 12.5 cm of rain on Tuesday, and 5.8 cm of rain on Thursday. The rest of the week, it did not rain. How much rain did Rockport receive during the week?

A 18.3 cm

B 36.6 cm

C 42.4 cm

D 45.7 cm

4. A weather station recorded the following temperatures during a 5 h period: 15°C, 18°C, 13°C, 15°C, and 20°C. What was the average temperature during this period?

F 14.2°C

G 15.2°C

H 16.2°C

I 20.2°C

5. The temperature in Waterford, Virginia, increased 1.3°C every hour for 5 h. If the temperature in the morning was –4°C, what was the temperature 4 h later?

A 2.5°C

B 2.3°C

C 1.3°C

D 1.2°C

Standardized Test Preparation

1. B

2. F

3. B

 TEST DOCTOR

Question 1: This is a complex graphic that may appear intimidating to students at first. The illustration synthesizes three types of data: altitude, temperature, and pressure. To help students answer this question, have them analyze each statement and eliminate the incorrect statements until they are left with the correct choice.

1. C

2. I

3. C

4. H

5. D

 TEST DOCTOR

Question 4: Students may choose answer choice I if they divide the total temperature by 4 instead of 5. Remind students to always double-check the number of numbers that they are asked to average. If scrap paper is available during the test, it is a good strategy to write down all of the numbers given in a test question before solving a problem.

CHAPTER RESOURCES

Chapter Resource File

• Standardized Test Preparation GENERAL

State Resources

For specific resources for your state, visit **go.hrw.com** and type in the keyword **HSMSTR.**

Science, Technology, and Society

ACTIVITY — BASIC

The HyperSoar jet looks like a giant paper airplane. This design makes the jet more aerodynamic, so it is able to glide for long distances. Organize students into small groups, and have them design and test paper airplanes for gliding ability. Have a contest, and give a prize for the best glider.

Weird Science

ACTIVITY — GENERAL

Students can learn a lot about NEXRAD radar and animal migrations by visiting the Clemson University Radar Ornithology Web Site. The Web Site has NEXRAD images of bird, bat, and insect migrations. Images of bat migrations are especially interesting. When bats leave their roosts in the evening, they usually fly in a spiral pattern. This pattern is shown as a crescent shape in the radar images. Insects are indicated by a dotted pattern that is similar to the pattern that birds make but insects have a lower reflectivity because they are less dense.

Science in Action

Science, Technology, and Society

The HyperSoar Jet

Imagine traveling from Chicago to Tokyo in 72 minutes. If the HyperSoar jet becomes a reality, you may be able to travel to the other side of the world in less time than it takes to watch a movie! To accomplish this amazing feat, the jet would "skip" across the upper stratosphere. To begin skipping, the jet would climb above the stratosphere, turn off its engines, and glide for about 60 km. Then, gravity would pull the jet down to where the air is denser. The denser air would cause the jet to soar upward. In this way, the jet would skip across a layer of dense air until it was ready to land. Each 2-minute skip would cover about 450 km, and the HyperSoar would be able to fly at Mach 10—a speed of 3 km/s!

Math ACTIVITY

A trip on the HyperSoar from Chicago to Tokyo would require about 18 "skips." Each skip is 450 km. If the trip is 10,123 km, how many kilometers will the jet travel when it is not skipping?

Weird Science

Radar Zoology

"For tonight's forecast, expect a light shower of mayflies. A wave of warblers will approach from the south. Tomorrow will be cloudy, and a band of free-tailed bats will move to the south in the early evening." Such a forecast may not make the evening news, but it is a familiar scenario for radar zoologists. Radar zoologists use a type of radar called *NEXRAD* to track migrating birds, bands of bats, and swarms of insects. NEXRAD tracks animals in the atmosphere in the same way that it tracks storms. The system sends out a microwave signal. If the signal hits an object, some of the energy reflects back to a receiver. NEXRAD has been especially useful to scientists who study bird migration. Birds tend to migrate at night, when the atmosphere is more stable, so until now, nighttime bird migration has been difficult to observe. NEXRAD has also helped identify important bird migration routes and critical stopovers. For example, scientists have discovered that many birds migrate over the Gulf of Mexico instead of around it.

Social Studies ACTIVITY

Geography plays an important role in bird migration. Many birds ride the "thermals" produced by mountain ranges. Find out what thermals are, and create a map of bird migration routes over North America.

Answer to Math Activity
10,123 km − (18 skips × 450 km) = 2023 km

Answer to Social Studies Activity
Thermals are strong updrafts created by rising columns of warm air. When warm air encounters a mountain or ridge, it may rise sharply upward. Birds take advantage of thermals to conserve energy. Maps of bird migration routes are available on the Internet. The four major migratory routes in North America are the Central Flyway, the Mississippi Flyway, the Atlantic Flyway, and the Pacific Flyway.

Ellen Paneok

Bush Pilot For Ellen Paneok, understanding weather patterns is a matter of life and death. As a bush pilot, she flies mail, supplies, and people to remote villages in Alaska that can be reached only by plane. Bad weather is one of the most serious challenges Paneok faces. "It's beautiful up here," she says, "but it can also be harsh." One dangerous situation is landing a plane in mountainous regions. "On top of a mountain you can't tell which way the wind is blowing," Paneok says. In this case, she flies in a rectangular pattern to determine the wind direction. Landing a plane on the frozen Arctic Ocean is also dangerous. In white-out conditions, the horizon can't be seen because the sky and the ground are the same color. "It's like flying in a milk bottle full of milk," Paneok says. In these conditions, she fills black plastic garbage bags and drops them from the plane to help guide her landing.

Paneok had to overcome many challenges to become a pilot. As a child, she lived in seven foster homes before being placed in an all-girls' home at the age of 14. In the girls' home, she read a magazine about careers in aviation and decided then and there that she wanted to become a pilot. At first, she faced a lot of opposition from people telling her that she wouldn't be able to become a pilot. Now, she encourages young people to pursue their goals. "If you decide you want to go for it, go for it. There may be obstacles in your way, but you've just got to find a way to go over them, get around them, or dig under them," she says.

Ellen Paneok is shown at right with two of her Inupiat passengers.

Language Arts ACTIVITY

Beryl Markham lived an exciting life as a bush pilot delivering mail and supplies to remote areas of Africa. Read about her life or the life of Bessie Coleman, one of the most famous African American women in the history of flying.

go.hrw.com

To learn more about these Science in Action topics, visit go.hrw.com and type in the keyword **HZ5ATMF**.

Current Science

Check out Current Science® articles related to this chapter by visiting go.hrw.com. Just type in the keyword **HZ5CS15**.

SCIENCE HUMOR

Ellen Paneok has had many exciting adventures during her years of flying in Alaska. When the weather turns bad, she sometimes has to spend the night in small villages where the only available bed is in the jail house. Once, she had to chase two polar bears off the runway before she could land. After she landed, Paneok was starting to unload the plane when she realized that she didn't know exactly where the polar bears had gone. "You've never seen anyone unload a thousand pounds off an airplane so fast," she laughs.

Understanding Weather
Chapter Planning Guide

Compression guide:
To shorten instruction because of time limitations, omit thge Chapter Lab.

OBJECTIVES	LABS, DEMONSTRATIONS, AND ACTIVITIES	TECHNOLOGY RESOURCES
PACING • 90 min pp. 36–45 **Chapter Opener**	SE **Start-up Activity**, p. 37 ◆ GENERAL	OSP **Parent Letter** ■ GENERAL CD **Student Edition on CD-ROM** CD **Guided Reading Audio CD** ■ TR **Chapter Starter Transparency*** VID **Brain Food Video Quiz**
Section 1 Water in the Air • Explain how water moves through the water cycle. • Describe how relative humidity is affected by temperature and levels of water vapor. • Describe the relationship between dew point and condensation. • List three types of cloud forms. • Identify four kinds of precipitation.	TE **Group Activity** Air Molecules, p. 38 GENERAL TE **Demonstration** Water in Air, p. 39 ◆ BASIC TE **Activity** Sentence Completion, p. 40 GENERAL SE **Quick Lab** Out of Thin Air, p. 41 GENERAL SE **Connection to Language Arts** Cloud Clues, p. 42 GENERAL TE **Activity** Naming Clouds, p. 43 BASIC TE **Connection Activity** Language Arts, p. 43 GENERAL SE **Inquiry Lab** Boiling Over!, p. 64 ◆ GENERAL SE **Skills Practice Lab** Let It Snow!, p. 111 GENERAL LB **Whiz-Bang Demonstrations** It's Raining Again* ◆ GENERAL LB **Calculator-Based Lab** Relative Humidity* ◆ GENERAL	CRF **Lesson Plans*** TR **Bellringer Transparency*** TR The Water Cycle* TR Cloud Types Based on Form and Altitude* SE **Internet Activity**, p. 40 GENERAL CRF **SciLinks Activity** GENERAL VID **Lab Videos for Earth Science** CD **Science Tutor**
PACING • 45 min pp. 46–51 **Section 2 Air Masses and Fronts** • Identify the four kinds of air masses that influence weather in the United States. • Describe the four major types of fronts. • Explain how fronts cause weather changes. • Explain how cyclones and anticyclones affect the weather.	TE **Demonstration** Density, p. 47 ◆ GENERAL TE **Activity** Using Maps, p. 49 BASIC LB **Whiz-Bang Demonstrations** When Air Bags Collide* ◆ GENERAL LB **Long-Term Projects & Research Ideas** A Storm on the Horizon* ADVANCED SE **Science in Action** Math, Social Studies, and Language Arts Activities, pp. 70–71	CRF **Lesson Plans*** TR **Bellringer Transparency*** TR Cold and Warm Fronts* TR Occluded and Stationary Fronts* CD **Science Tutor**
PACING • 45 min pp. 52–59 **Section 3 Severe Weather** • Describe how lightning forms. • Describe the formation of thunderstorms, tornadoes, and hurricanes. • Describe the characteristics of thunderstorms, tornadoes, and hurricanes. • Explain how to stay safe during severe weather.	TE **Demonstration** Modeling Thunder, p. 52 ◆ GENERAL TE **Connection Activity** Math, p. 53 GENERAL TE **Connection Activity** Real World, p. 54 GENERAL TE **Activity** Weather and Energy, p. 56 GENERAL TE **Group Activity** Hurricane Newscast, p. 56 GENERAL SE **School-to-Home Activity** Natural Disaster Plan, p. 57 GENERAL TE **Connection Activity** Meteorology, p. 57 ADVANCED LB **Inquiry Labs** When Disaster Strikes* BASIC	CRF **Lesson Plans*** TR **Bellringer Transparency*** CRF **SciLinks Activity*** GENERAL TR *LINK TO PHYSICAL SCIENCE* How Lightning Forms CD **Science Tutor**
PACING • 45 min pp. 60–63 **Section 4 Forecasting the Weather** • Describe the different types of instruments used to take weather measurements. • Explain how radar and weather satellites help meteorologists forecast the weather. • Explain how to interpret a weather map.	TE **Demonstration** Air Pressure and Barometers, p. 60 ◆ GENERAL TE **Connection Activity** Real World, p. 61 GENERAL TE **Connection Activity** Math, p. 62 GENERAL SE **Skills Practice Lab** Watching the Weather, p. 108 GENERAL SE **Model-Making Lab** Gone With the Wind, p. 112 ◆ GENERAL LB **EcoLabs & Field Activities** Rain Maker or Rain Faker?* ◆ ADVANCED	CRF **Lesson Plans*** TR **Bellringer Transparency*** CD **Science Tutor**

PACING • 90 min

CHAPTER REVIEW, ASSESSMENT, AND STANDARDIZED TEST PREPARATION

CRF **Vocabulary Activity*** GENERAL
SE **Chapter Review**, pp. 66–67 GENERAL
CRF **Chapter Review*** ■ GENERAL
CRF **Chapter Tests A*** ■ GENERAL, **B*** ADVANCED, **C*** SPECIAL NEEDS
SE **Standardized Test Preparation**, pp. 68–69 GENERAL
CRF **Standardized Test Preparation*** GENERAL
CRF **Performance-Based Assessment*** GENERAL
OSP **Test Generator** GENERAL
CRF **Test Item Listing*** GENERAL

Online and Technology Resources

Visit **go.hrw.com** for a variety of free resources related to this textbook. Enter the keyword **HZ5WEA**.

Holt Online Learning

Students can access interactive problem-solving help and active visual concept development with the *Holt Science and Technology* Online Edition available at **www.hrw.com**.

 Guided Reading Audio CD
Also in Spanish

A direct reading of each chapter for auditory learners, reluctant readers, and Spanish-speaking students.

 Science Tutor
CD-ROM

Excellent for remediation and test practice.

SKILLS DEVELOPMENT RESOURCES	SECTION REVIEW AND ASSESSMENT	STANDARDS CORRELATIONS
SE Pre-Reading Activity, p. 36 `GENERAL` **OSP** Science Puzzlers, Twisters & Teasers* `GENERAL`		National Science Education Standards UCP 2; SAI 1; SPSP 3, 4; ES 1f, 1i, 1j
CRF Directed Reading A* ■ `BASIC`, B* `SPECIAL NEEDS` **CRF** Vocabulary and Section Summary* ■ `GENERAL` **SE** Reading Strategy Paired Summarizing, p. 38 `GENERAL` **SE** Math Practice Relative Humidity, p. 39 `GENERAL` **TE** Inclusion Strategies, p. 40 ◆ **TE** Reading Strategy Sequencing, p. 42 `GENERAL`	**SE** Reading Checks, pp. 38, 40, 41, 43 `GENERAL` **TE** Homework, p. 42 `BASIC` **TE** Reteaching, p. 44 `BASIC` **TE** Quiz, p. 44 `GENERAL` **TE** Alternative Assessment, p. 44 `ADVANCED` **TE** Homework, p. 44 `ADVANCED` **SE** Section Review,* p. 45 ■ `GENERAL` **CRF** Section Quiz* ■ `GENERAL`	UCP 2, 3; SAI 1; SPSP 3; ES 1f, 1i; *Chapter Lab:* UCP 2, 3; SAI 1, 2; ST 1; HNS 2; *LabBook:* UCP 3; SAI 1
CRF Directed Reading A* ■ `BASIC`, B* `SPECIAL NEEDS` **CRF** Vocabulary and Section Summary* ■ `GENERAL` **SE** Reading Strategy Reading Organizer, p. 46 `GENERAL`	**SE** Reading Checks, pp. 47, 49, 51 `GENERAL` **TE** Homework, p. 46 `GENERAL` **TE** Reteaching, p. 50 `BASIC` **TE** Quiz, p. 50 `GENERAL` **TE** Alternative Assessment, p. 50 `GENERAL` **SE** Section Review,* p. 51 ■ `GENERAL` **CRF** Section Quiz* ■ `GENERAL`	HNS 3; ES 1j
CRF Directed Reading A* ■ `BASIC`, B* `SPECIAL NEEDS` **CRF** Vocabulary and Section Summary* ■ `GENERAL` **SE** Reading Strategy Reading Organizer, p. 52 `GENERAL` **TE** Inclusion Strategies, p. 54 ◆ **CRF** Reinforcement Worksheet Precipitation Situations* `BASIC`	**SE** Reading Checks, pp. 53, 55, 56 `GENERAL` **TE** Homework, p. 55 `ADVANCED` **TE** Reteaching, p. 58 `BASIC` **TE** Quiz, p. 58 `GENERAL` **TE** Alternative Assessment, p. 58 `GENERAL` **SE** Section Review,* p. 59 ■ `GENERAL` **CRF** Section Quiz* ■ `GENERAL`	SPSP 3, 4; ES 1i, 1j
CRF Directed Reading A* ■ `BASIC`, B* `SPECIAL NEEDS` **CRF** Vocabulary and Section Summary* ■ `GENERAL` **SE** Reading Strategy Reading Organizer, p. 60 `GENERAL` **MS** Math Skills for Science Using Temperature Scales* ■ `GENERAL` **CRF** Critical Thinking Commanding the Sky* `ADVANCED`	**SE** Reading Checks, p. 60 `GENERAL` **TE** Reteaching, p. 62 `BASIC` **TE** Quiz, p. 62 `GENERAL` **TE** Alternative Assessment, p. 62 `GENERAL` **SE** Section Review,* p. 63 ■ `GENERAL` **CRF** Section Quiz* ■ `GENERAL`	SPSP 3, 4; ES 1i, 1j; *LabBook:* SAI 1; ST 1

One-Stop Planner® CD-ROM

This convenient CD-ROM includes:
- Lab Materials QuickList Software
- Holt Calendar Planner
- Customizable Lesson Plans
- Printable Worksheets
- ExamView® Test Generator

cnnstudentnews.com

Find the latest news, lesson plans, and activities related to important scientific events.

www.scilinks.org

Maintained by the **National Science Teachers Association.** See Chapter Enrichment pages for a complete list of topics.

Current Science®

Check out *Current Science* articles and activities by visiting the HRW Web site at **go.hrw.com.** Just type in the keyword **HZ5CS16T** .

 Classroom Videos

- **Lab Videos** demonstrate the chapter lab.
- **Brain Food Video Quizzes** help students review the chapter material.
- **CNN Videos** bring science into your students' daily life.

Visual Resources

CHAPTER STARTER TRANSPARENCY

Understanding Weather · CHAPTER STARTER

Would You Believe

In May of 1997, a springtime tornado wreaked havoc on Jarrell, Texas. The Jarrell tornado was one of the rarest and most powerful tornadoes, with winds estimated at more than 410 km/h. Its twister peeled the asphalt from paved roads, stripped fields of corn bare, and destroyed an entire neighborhood.

North America experiences more tornadoes than any other continent—averaging about 700 per year. Most of these tornadoes hit an area in the central United States called Tornado Alley. Tornado Alley covers most of the Great Plains, extending from Texas across Oklahoma, Kansas, southern Nebraska, Iowa, and South Dakota. But what causes these tornadoes, and why is the Great Plains area so vulnerable?

In the spring and early summer, cold, dry air from the North Pole clashes with warm, moist air from the Tropics. This clash forces the warm air to rise and become unstable. When there is a large contrast between the two clashing air masses, the chances that a tornado will form are increased.

Tornado Alley experiences more tornadoes than any other area because its flatness and location on the Earth's surface make it possible for warm and cold air masses to collide with one another.

In this chapter you will learn about what causes weather, the different types of air masses, and how weather can suddenly turn violent.

BELLRINGER TRANSPARENCIES

Understanding Weather · BELLRINGER TRANSPARENCY

Section: Water in the Air
Observe two glasses of water. One filled with ice water, and one filled with warm water. Why do water droplets form on the outside of the cold glass? Where do the water beads come from? Why don't the water beads form on the warm glass? Have you seen this happen before on other containers? On your soda can? On a coffee cup or a soup bowl?

Write your answers in your **science journal.**

Section: Air Masses and Fronts
How would you describe the air you are breathing right now? Is it warm or cool? Humid or dry? Is it stale, sweet, or salty? The air you are breathing right now was hundreds of miles away yesterday. Do you know how or why air moves from one place to another?

Write your response in your **science journal.**

TEACHING TRANSPARENCIES

The Water Cycle

Cloud Types Based on Form and Altitude

Cumulus clouds look like piles of cotton balls.

Stratus clouds are not as tall as cumulus clouds, but they cover more area.

Cirrus clouds are made of ice crystals.

TEACHING TRANSPARENCIES

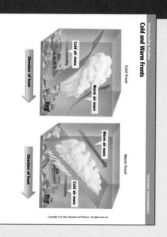

Cold and Warm Fronts

Cold air mass / Warm air mass / Cold Front / Warm Front / Direction of front

Occluded and Stationary Fronts

Cold air mass / Warm air mass / Occluded Front / Stationary Front / Direction of front

How Lightning Forms

Chapter: Introduction to Electricity

LINK TO PHYSICAL SCIENCE

CONCEPT MAPPING TRANSPARENCY

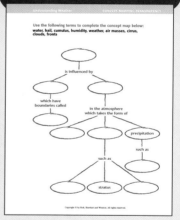

Understanding Weather · CONCEPT MAPPING TRANSPARENCY

Use the following terms to complete the concept map below:
water, hail, cumulus, humidity, weather, air masses, cirrus, clouds, fronts

is influenced by / which have boundaries called / in the atmosphere / which takes the form of / precipitation / such as / stratus

Planning Resources

LESSON PLANS

Lesson Plan SAMPLE

Section: Waves

Pacing
Regular Schedule: with lab(s):2 days without lab(s)2 days
Block Schedule: with lab(s):1 1/2 days without lab(s)1 day

Objectives
1. Relate the seven properties of life to a living organism.
2. Describe seven themes that can help you to organize what you learn about biology.
3. Identify the tiny structures that make up all living organisms.
4. Differentiate between reproduction and heredity and between metabolism and homeostasis.

National Science Education Standards Covered
LSInter6:Cells have particular structures that underlie their functions.
LSMat1: Most cell functions involve chemical reactions.
LSBeh1:Cells store and use information to guide their functions.
UCP1:Cell functions are regulated.
SI1: Cells can differentiate and form complete multicellular organisms.
PS1: Species evolve over time.
ESS1: The great diversity of organisms is the result of more than 3.5 billion years of evolution.
ESS2: Natural selection and its evolutionary consequences provide a scientific explanation for the fossil record of ancient life forms as well as for the striking molecular similarities observed among the diverse species of living organisms.
ST1: The millions of different species of plants, animals, and microorganisms that live on Earth today are related by descent from common ancestors.
ST2: The energy for life primarily comes from the sun.
SPSP1: The complexity and organization of organisms accommodates the need for obtaining, transforming, transporting, releasing, and eliminating the matter and energy used to sustain the organism.
SPSP6: As matter and energy flows through different levels of organization of living systems—cells, organs, communities—and between living systems and the physical environment, chemical elements are recombined in different ways.
HNS1: Organisms have behavioral responses to internal changes and to external stimuli.

PARENT LETTER

SAMPLE

Dear Parent,

Your son's or daughter's science class will soon begin exploring the chapter entitled "The World of Physical Science." In this chapter, students will learn about how the scientific method applies to the world of physical science and the role of physical science in the world. By the end of the chapter, students should demonstrate a clear understanding of the chapter's main ideas and be able to discuss the following topics:

1. physical science is the study of energy and matter (Section 1)
2. the role of physical science in the world around them (Section 1)
3. careers that rely on physical science (Section 1)
4. the steps used in the scientific method (Section 2)
5. examples of technology (Section 2)
6. how the scientific method is used to answer questions and solve problems (Section 2)
7. how our knowledge of science changes over time (Section 2)
8. how models represent real objects or systems (Section 3)
9. examples of different ways models are used in science (Section 3)
10. the importance of the International System of Units (Section 4)
11. the appropriate units to use for particular measurements (Section 4)
12. how area and density are derived quantities (Section 4)

Questions to Ask Along the Way

You can help your son or daughter learn about these topics by asking interesting questions such as the following:

• What are some surprising careers that use physical science?
• What is a characteristic of a good hypothesis?
• When is it a good idea to use a model?
• Why do Americans measure things in terms of inches and yards and meters?

ALSO IN SPANISH

TEST ITEM LISTING

TEST ITEM LISTING SAMPLE
The World of Earth Science

MULTIPLE CHOICE

1. A limitation of models is that
   a. they are large enough to see.
   b. they do not exactly like the things that they model.
   c. they are smaller than the things that they model.
   d. they model unfamiliar things.
   Answer: B   Difficulty: 1   Section: 3   Objective: 2
2. The length 10 m is equal to
   a. 100 cm.   c. 10,000 mm.
   b. 1,000 cm.   d. Both (b) and (c)
   Answer: B   Difficulty: 1   Section: 3   Objective: 2
3. To be valid, a hypothesis must be
   a. testable.   c. made into a law.
   b. supported by evidence. d. Both (a) and (b)
   Answer: B   Difficulty: 1   Section: 3   Objective: 2 1
4. The statement "Sheila has a stain on her shirt" is an example of a(n)
   a. law.   c. observation.
   b. hypothesis.   d. prediction.
   Answer: B   Difficulty: 1   Section: 3   Objective: 2
5. A hypothesis is often developed out of
   a. observations.   c. laws.
   b. experiments.   d. Both (a) and (b)
   Answer: B   Difficulty: 1   Section: 3   Objective: 2
6. How many milliliters are in 3.5 kL?
   a. 3,500 mL   c. 3,500,000 mL.
   b. 0.0035 mL   d. 35,000 mL.
   Answer: B   Difficulty: 1   Section: 3   Objective: 2
7. A map of Seattle is an example of a
   a. law.   c. model.
   b. theory.   d. unit.
   Answer: B   Difficulty: 1   Section: 3   Objective: 2
8. A lab has the safety icons above below. These icons mean that you should wear
   a. only safety goggles.   c. safety goggles and a lab apron.
   b. only a lab apron.   d. safety goggles, a lab apron, and gloves.
   Answer: B   Difficulty: 1   Section: 3   Objective: 2
9. The law of conservation of mass says the tot al mass before a chemical change is
   a. more than the total mass after the change.
   b. less than the total mass after the change.
   c. the same as the total mass after the change.
   d. not the same as the total mass after the change.
   Answer: B   Difficulty: 1   Section: 3   Objective: 2
10. In which of the following areas might you find a geochemist at work?
    a. studying the chemistry of rocks   c. studying forestry
    b. studying forestry   d. studying the atmosphere
    Answer: B   Difficulty: 1   Section: 3   Objective: 2

One-Stop Planner® CD-ROM

This CD-ROM includes all of the resources shown here and the following time-saving tools:

• Lab Materials QuickList Software
• Customizable lesson plans
• Holt Calendar Planner
• The powerful ExamView® Test Generator

Meeting Individual Needs

DIRECTED READING A

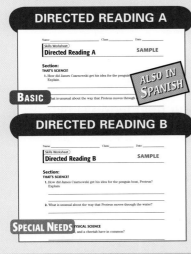

BASIC

DIRECTED READING B

SPECIAL NEEDS

VOCABULARY ACTIVITY

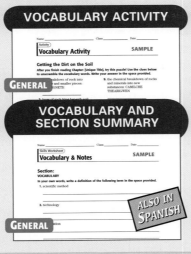

GENERAL

VOCABULARY AND SECTION SUMMARY

GENERAL

REINFORCEMENT

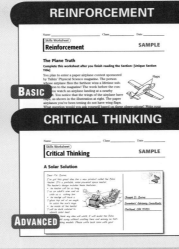

BASIC

CRITICAL THINKING

ADVANCED

SCILINKS ACTIVITY

GENERAL

SCIENCE PUZZLERS, TWISTERS & TEASERS

GENERAL

Labs and Activities

ECOLABS & FIELD ACTIVITIES

GENERAL

LONG-TERM PROJECTS & RESEARCH IDEAS

ADVANCED

WHIZ-BANG DEMONSTRATIONS

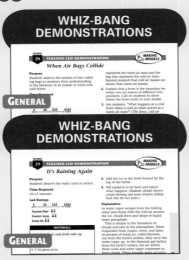

GENERAL

WHIZ-BANG DEMONSTRATIONS

GENERAL

INQUIRY LABS

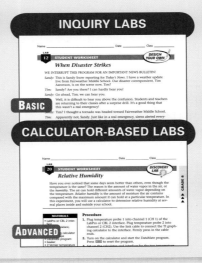

BASIC

CALCULATOR-BASED LABS

ADVANCED

DATASHEETS FOR QUICKLABS

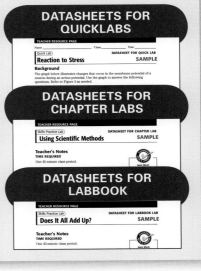

DATASHEETS FOR CHAPTER LABS

DATASHEETS FOR LABBOOK

Review and Assessments

SECTION QUIZ

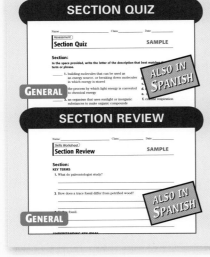

GENERAL

SECTION REVIEW

GENERAL

CHAPTER REVIEW

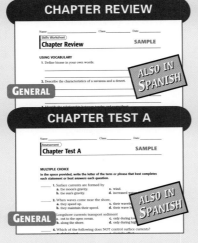

GENERAL

CHAPTER TEST A

GENERAL

CHAPTER TEST B

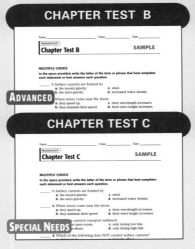

ADVANCED

CHAPTER TEST C

SPECIAL NEEDS

STANDARDIZED TEST PREPARATION

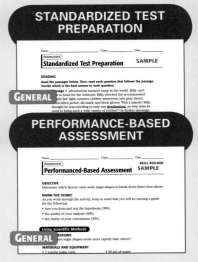

GENERAL

PERFORMANCE-BASED ASSESSMENT

GENERAL

This Chapter Enrichment provides relevant and interesting information to expand and enhance your presentation of the chapter material.

Section 1

Water in the Air

Earth's Water Cycle

- The atmosphere contains only about 0.001% of the total volume of water on the planet (about 1.46×10^9 km^3).
- The rate at which water evaporates into Earth's atmosphere is about 5.1×10^{17} L per year.
- About 78% of all precipitation falls over Earth's oceans. Of the 22% that falls on land, about 65% returns to the air by evaporation.

Clouds

- Clouds may be composed of water droplets, ice crystals, or a combination of the two. For example, cirrus clouds are made of only ice crystals; stratus clouds are made of only water droplets; and altostratus clouds are mixtures of ice and liquid water. Cumulonimbus clouds, which produce snowflakes and hail, consist of water droplets near the bottom of the clouds and ice crystals in the upper parts of the clouds.

Is That a Fact!
- The largest hailstone ever recorded fell on Coffeyville, Kansas, on September 3, 1970. The hailstone was the size of a softball and weighed 0.75 kg.

Precipitation

- Due to differences in condensation rates within the cloud, not all of the millions of droplets of water that make up a cloud are the same size. Larger drops collide and merge with smaller drops to form raindrops.

Section 2

Air Masses and Fronts

Fronts

- As a warm front approaches, the first clouds to appear in the sky are the high clouds: cirrus, cirrostratus, and cirrocumulus. As the warm front moves closer, medium-height clouds, then low clouds appear. As the warm front arrives, the temperature and air pressure drop. In the Northern Hemisphere, winds generally blow from the northeast. Nimbostratus clouds bring drizzly precipitation, which may fall within 24 hours of the first cloud sighting.

- When a cold front enters an area, cumulonimbus clouds can produce thunderstorms, heavy rain, or snow along the front. After the cold front passes through an area, winds change direction and barometric pressure rises. Behind the cold front, temperatures usually fall, which brings cool, clear weather to the area.

Section 3

Severe Weather

Tornadoes

- Meteorologists rate tornado intensity using the Fujita Tornado Intensity Scale. An F0 tornado is a relatively weak storm that may damage chimneys, tree branches, and billboard signs. An F1 tornado is a moderate storm that can peel the surfaces off roofs, overturn mobile homes, and push moving cars off roads. F2 and F3 tornadoes cause considerable to severe damage by tearing roofs off houses, overturning railroad cars, and uprooting mature trees. An F4 tornado is a devastating storm that levels houses and other buildings and tosses cars into the air. The most severe tornado is an F5 tornado, which can lift houses off their foundations and carry them great distances. An F5 tornado can also carry cars over 100 m and strip the bark off trees.

Hurricanes

- On the Saffir-Simpson Scale, hurricanes fall into five categories. Category 1 hurricanes have sustained winds between 74 and 95 km/h and usually cause relatively minimal damage. Category 2 hurricanes cause moderate damage with winds ranging between 96 and 110 km/h. Category 3 hurricanes cause extensive damage with winds that blow between 111 and 130 km/h. Category 4 hurricanes have sustained winds between 131 and 155 km/h. Category 5 hurricanes, like Hurricane Andrew, which struck Florida in 1992, have sustained winds of more than 155 km/h. Category 5 hurricanes are classified as catastrophic storms.

Is That a Fact!

◆ A hurricane is called a *willy-willy* in Australia, a *taino* in Haiti, a *baguio* in the Philippines, and a *cordonazo* in western Mexico.

Section 4

Forecasting the Weather
Weather-Prediction Methods

- One of the simplest methods of weather prediction, the *persistence method,* assumes that the atmospheric conditions at the time of a weather forecast will not change in the near future. This method is fairly accurate in areas where weather patterns change very slowly, such as in southern California, where summer weather typically changes very little from day to day. Other methods are described below.

- The *trends method* involves determining high- and low-pressure areas, gauging the velocity of weather fronts, and locating areas of clouds and precipitation. A forecaster then uses these data to predict where these weather phenomena will be in the future. This method of weather prediction works well only when weather systems maintain constant velocities for a long period of time.

- The *climatology method* involves averaging weather data that have accumulated over many years to make a forecast. This method is accurate when weather patterns are similar to those expected for a given time of year.

- The *numerical weather-prediction (NWP)* method uses complex computer programs to generate models of probable air temperature, barometric pressure, wind velocity, and precipitation. A meteorologist then analyzes how he or she thinks the features predicted by the computer will interact to produce the day's weather. Despite its flaws, the NWP method is one of the most reliable methods available.

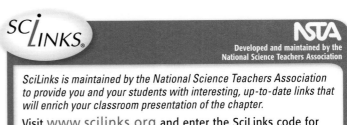

SCiLINKS
NSTA
Developed and maintained by the National Science Teachers Association

SciLinks is maintained by the National Science Teachers Association to provide you and your students with interesting, up-to-date links that will enrich your classroom presentation of the chapter.

Visit www.scilinks.org and enter the SciLinks code for more information about the topic listed.

Topic: The Water Cycle
SciLinks code: HSM1626

Topic: Severe Weather
SciLinks code: HSM1383

Topic: Air Masses and Fronts
SciLinks code: HSM0032

Topic: Forecasting the Weather
SciLinks code: HSM0606

Overview

This chapter introduces some fundamental principles of meteorology and weather forecasting. Students learn about relative humidity, clouds, air masses and fronts, severe weather, and weather forecasting.

Assessing Prior Knowledge

Students should be familiar with the following topics:

• the water cycle
• characteristics of the atmosphere

Identifying Misconceptions

Students may think that weather forecasting is extremely complicated. Point out that the science of meteorology relies on a few simple concepts, such as relative humidity, simple gas laws, and the movement of air masses. The tools needed to forecast weather are inexpensive and easy to use. If students become familiar with these tools and concepts, they will understand the basic science of meteorology. As you teach this chapter, work as a class every day to forecast the next day's weather. Review the predictions at the beginning of each class. Forecasts should improve as students learn more about weather.

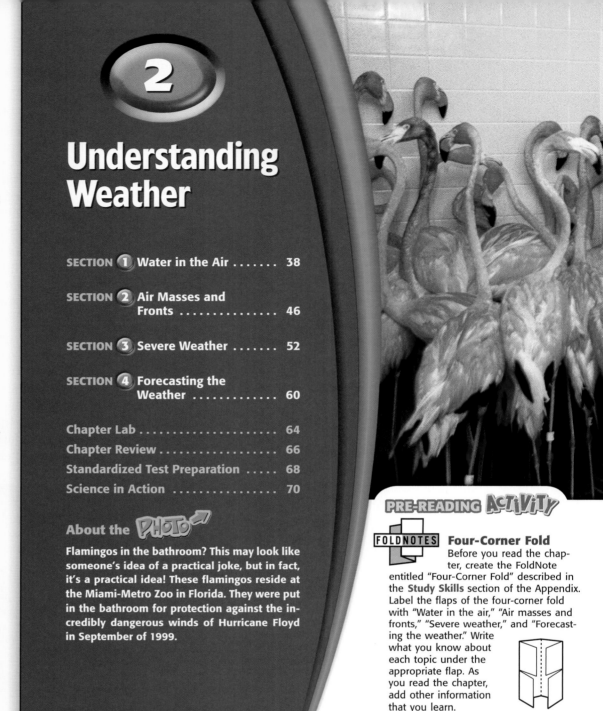

2
Understanding Weather

About the PHOTO

Flamingos in the bathroom? This may look like someone's idea of a practical joke, but in fact, it's a practical idea! These flamingos reside at the Miami-Metro Zoo in Florida. They were put in the bathroom for protection against the incredibly dangerous winds of Hurricane Floyd in September of 1999.

PRE-READING ACTIVITY

FOLDNOTES **Four-Corner Fold**
Before you read the chapter, create the FoldNote entitled "Four-Corner Fold" described in the **Study Skills** section of the Appendix. Label the flaps of the four-corner fold with "Water in the air," "Air masses and fronts," "Severe weather," and "Forecasting the weather." Write what you know about each topic under the appropriate flap. As you read the chapter, add other information that you learn.

Standards Correlations

National Science Education Standards

The following codes indicate the National Science Education Standards that correlate to this chapter. The full text of the standards is at the front of the book.

Chapter Opener
UCP 2; SAI 1; SPSP 3, 4; ES 1f, 1i, 1j

Section 1 Water in the Air
UCP 2, 3; SAI 1; SPSP 3; ES 1f, 1i; *LabBook:* UCP 3; SAI 1

Section 2 Air Masses and Fronts
HNS 3; ES 1j

Section 3 Severe Weather
SPSP 3, 4; ES 1i, 1j

Section 4 Forecasting the Weather
SPSP 3, 4; ES 1i, 1j; *LabBook:* SAI 1; ST 1

Chapter Lab
UCP 2, 3; SAI 1, 2; ST 1; HNS 2

Chapter Review
UCP 1; ST 2; SPSP 3, 4, 5; ES 1f, 1i, 1j

Science in Action
ST 2; SPSP 3, 5; HNS 1, 3

START-UP ACTIVITY

MATERIALS

FOR EACH GROUP
- beaker (2)
- container, clear plastic
- cooking oil (500 mL)
- water (500 mL)

Teacher's Notes: Students should be able to distinguish the oil from the water when the two liquids are poured together. If not, try the experiment again using water with food coloring.

Answers

1. The oil rises to the top and sits on the surface of the water.
2. Answers may vary.
3. Sample answer: The warm air mass would be pushed up by the cold air mass.

START-UP ACTIVITY

Meeting of the Masses

In this activity, you will model what happens when two air masses that have different temperature characteristics meet.

Procedure

1. Pour **500 mL of water** into a **beaker.** Pour **500 mL of cooking oil** into a **second beaker.** The water represents a dense cold air mass. The cooking oil represents a less dense warm air mass.
2. Predict what would happen to the two liquids if you tried to mix them.
3. Pour the contents of both beakers into a **clear, plastic, rectangular container** at the same time from opposite ends of the container.

4. Observe the interaction of the oil and water.

Analysis

1. What happens when the liquids meet?
2. Does the prediction that you made in step 2 of the Procedure match your results?
3. Using your results, hypothesize what would happen if a cold air mass met a warm air mass.

Chapter Starter Transparency
Use this transparency to help students begin thinking about the types of conditions that produce tornadoes.

CHAPTER RESOURCES

Technology

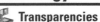

Transparencies
- Chapter Starter Transparency

READING
SKILLS

Student Edition on CD-ROM

Guided Reading Audio CD
- English or Spanish

Classroom Videos
- Brain Food Video Quiz

Workbooks

Science Puzzlers, Twisters & Teasers
- Understanding Weather GENERAL

Focus

Overview

This section discusses the water cycle, relative humidity, types of clouds, and forms of precipitation.

 **Bellringer**

Place a glass of ice water and a glass of warm water on your desk. Ask students: "Why do water drops form on the cold glass? Where does the water come from? Why are there no water drops on the warm glass?"

Motivate

Group ACTiViTy — GENERAL

Air Molecules Divide the class in half. Half of the students will pretend to be air molecules; half will pretend to be water molecules. Ask the "air molecules" to stand four feet apart in a square grid. Then, have the "water molecules" stand between the air molecules without touching anyone. Tell students that they are modeling a warm air mass. Cool the air mass by moving the air molecules closer together so that eventually they are holding hands. As the temperature drops, the water molecules will be expelled as "precipitation." Finally, ask the air molecules to stand with their shoulders touching to show how a cold air mass expels the water molecules. **LS Kinesthetic**

READING WARM-UP

Objectives

- Explain how water moves through the water cycle.
- Describe how relative humidity is affected by temperature and levels of water vapor.
- Describe the relationship between dew point and condensation.
- List three types of cloud forms.
- Identify four kinds of precipitation.

Terms to Learn

weather
humidity
relative humidity
condensation
cloud
precipitation

READING STRATEGY

Paired Summarizing Read this section silently. In pairs, take turns summarizing the material. Stop to discuss ideas that seem confusing.

CHAPTER RESOURCES

Chapter Resource File

- Lesson Plan
- Directed Reading A **BASIC**
- Directed Reading B **SPECIAL NEEDS**

Technology

Transparencies
- Bellringer
- The Water Cycle

Water in the Air

What will the weather be this weekend? Depending on what you have planned, knowing the answer to this question could be important. A picnic in the rain can be a mess!

Have you ever wondered what weather is? **Weather** is the condition of the atmosphere at a certain time and place. The condition of the atmosphere is affected by the amount of water in the air. So, to understand weather, you need to understand how water cycles through Earth's atmosphere.

The Water Cycle

Water in liquid, solid, and gaseous states is constantly being recycled through the water cycle. The *water cycle* is the continuous movement of water from sources on Earth's surface—such as lakes, oceans, and plants—into the air, onto and over land, into the ground, and back to the surface. The movement of water through the water cycle is shown in **Figure 1**.

✓ **Reading Check** What is the water cycle? (*See the Appendix for answers to Reading Checks.*)

Figure 1 The Water Cycle

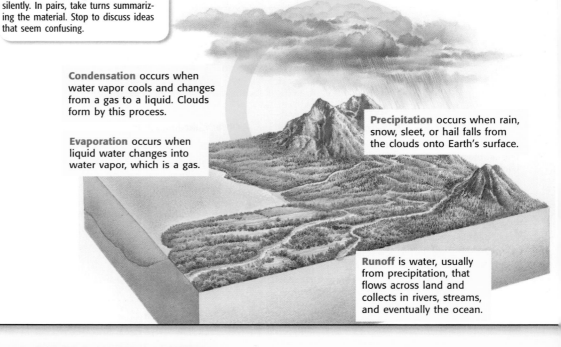

Condensation occurs when water vapor cools and changes from a gas to a liquid. Clouds form by this process.

Evaporation occurs when liquid water changes into water vapor, which is a gas.

Precipitation occurs when rain, snow, sleet, or hail falls from the clouds onto Earth's surface.

Runoff is water, usually from precipitation, that flows across land and collects in rivers, streams, and eventually the ocean.

Answer to Reading Check

The water cycle is the continuous movement of water from Earth's oceans and rivers into the atmosphere, into the ground, and back into the oceans and rivers.

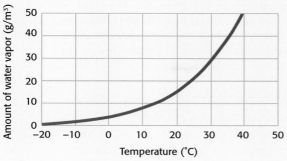

Amount of Water Vapor Air Can Hold at Various Temperatures

y-axis: Amount of water vapor (g/m³)
x-axis: Temperature (°C)

Figure 2 *This graph shows that as air gets warmer, the amount of water vapor that the air can hold increases.*

Humidity

As water evaporates from lakes, oceans, and plants, it becomes *water vapor*, or moisture in the air. Water vapor is invisible. The amount of water vapor in the air is called **humidity.** As water evaporates and becomes water vapor, the humidity of the air increases. The air's ability to hold water vapor changes as the temperature of the air changes. **Figure 2** shows that as the temperature of the air increases, the air's ability to hold water vapor also increases.

Relative Humidity

One way to express humidity is through relative humidity. **Relative humidity** is the amount of water vapor in the air compared with the maximum amount of water vapor that the air can hold at a certain temperature. So, relative humidity is given as a percentage. When air holds all of the water that it can at a given temperature, it is said to be *saturated*. Saturated air has a relative humidity of 100%. But how do you find the relative humidity of air that is not saturated? If you know the maximum amount of water vapor that air can hold at a given temperature and the actual amount of water vapor in the air, you can calculate the relative humidity.

Suppose that 1 m³ of air at a certain temperature can hold 24 g of water vapor. However, you know that the air actually contains 18 g of water vapor. You can calculate the relative humidity by using the following formula:

$$\frac{actual\ water\ vapor\ content\ (g/m^3)}{saturation\ water\ vapor\ content\ (g/m^3)} \times 100 = relative\ humidity\ (\%)$$

$$\frac{18\ g/m^3}{24\ g/m^3} = 75\%$$

weather the short-term state of the atmosphere, including temperature, humidity, precipitation, wind, and visibility

humidity the amount of water vapor in the air

relative humidity the ratio of the amount of water vapor in the air to the maximum amount of water vapor the air can hold at a set temperature

Relative Humidity

Assume that 1 m³ of air at 25°C contains 11 g of water vapor. At this temperature, the air can hold 24 g/m³ of water vapor. Calculate the relative humidity of the air.

CONNECTION to
Life Science —— ADVANCED

Hair Hygrometer   When the air is humid, hair becomes frizzy. Hair is made of a protein called *keratin*. Each hair fiber has a scaly outer cuticle, which you can feel by running your fingers up and down a single hair. The scales allow moisture to enter the inner part of the hair fiber. When the air is humid, hair absorbs moisture and becomes longer and frizzy. Hair dries out and becomes shorter when the air is dry. Because humidity can cause hair length to change by as much as 2.5%, a device called a *hair hygrometer* can very accurately measure changes in humidity. Have students design and build their own hair hygrometers. Plans for making a hair hygrometer are available on the Internet. Note: This project will not work on very short hair. **LS** Kinesthetic

Sentence Completion After students have read this page, have them complete the following sentences:

- If the humidity is low, a _____ amount of water will evaporate from a wet-bulb thermometer and the _____ between the wet-bulb reading and the dry-bulb reading of the psychrometer will be high. (large, temperature difference)

- If the dry bulb reads 10°C, and the difference between the thermometers is 8°C, the relative humidity is _____. (15%)

LS Verbal

Cultural Awareness — GENERAL

Hopi Rainmakers Have students research the rainmakers in Hopi Indian culture. Students might find out about *Leenangkatsina*, whose flute brings rain; *Qaleetaqa*, who carries lightning and a bull-roarer to bring rain; and *Si'o Sa'lakwmana* or *Pawtiwa*, both of whom bring rain and mist to villages. **LS** Interpersonal

---

Answer to Reading Check

A psychrometer is used to measure relative humidity.

INTERNET ACTIVITY

For another activity related to this chapter, go to **go.hrw.com** and type in the keyword **HZ5WEAW**.

Factors Affecting Relative Humidity

Two factors that affect relative humidity are amount of water vapor and temperature. At constant temperature and pressure, as the amount of water vapor in air changes, the relative humidity changes. The more water vapor there is in the air, the higher the relative humidity is. If the amount of water vapor in the air stays the same but the temperature changes, the relative humidity changes. The relative humidity decreases as the temperature rises and increases as the temperature drops.

Measuring Relative Humidity

A *psychrometer* (sie KRAHM uht uhr) is an instrument that is used to measure relative humidity. A psychrometer consists of two thermometers, one of which is a wet-bulb thermometer. The bulb of a wet-bulb thermometer is covered with a damp cloth. The other thermometer is a dry-bulb thermometer.

The difference in temperature readings between the thermometers indicates the amount of water vapor in the air. The larger the difference between the two readings is, the less water vapor the air contains and thus the lower the humidity is. **Figure 3** shows how to use a table of differences between wet-bulb and dry-bulb readings to determine relative humidity.

✓ **Reading Check** What tool is used to measure relative humidity?

Figure 3 Determining Relative Humidity

Find the relative humidity by locating the column head that is equal to the difference between the wet-bulb and dry-bulb readings. Then, locate the row head that equals the temperature reading on the dry-bulb thermometer. The value that lies where the column and row intersect equals the relative humidity. You can see a psychrometer below.

Relative Humidity (%)								
Dry-bulb reading (°C)	Difference between wet-bulb reading and dry-bulb reading (°C)							
	1	2	3	4	5	6	7	8
0	81	64	46	29	13			
2	84	68	52	37	22	7		
4	85	71	57	43	29	16		
6	86	73	60	48	35	24	11	
8	87	75	63	51	40	29	19	8
10	88	77	66	55	44	34	24	15
12	89	78	68	58	48	39	29	21
14	90	79	70	60	51	42	34	26
16	90	81	71	63	54	46	38	30
18	91	82	73	65	57	49	41	34
20	91	83	74	66	59	51	44	37

INCLUSION Strategies

- **Learning Disabled**   - **Attention Deficit Disorder**

Have student groups make a pyschrometer. Give each group two identical thermometers, gauze, tape, water, a rubber band, and an 8 1/2 in. × 11 in. piece of cardboard. Ask each group to wrap the gauze around the bulb of a thermometer and attach it firmly with the rubber band. Next, have students wet the gauze. Then, have students place the thermometers side by side with the bulbs hanging over the edge of a desk. Students should tape the thermometers securely to the desk. Have students use the cardboard to carefully fan the thermometers until the temperature of the wet-bulb thermometer stops decreasing. Have students subtract the wet-bulb temperature from the dry-bulb temperature and record the difference. Then, have students determine the relative humidity of the air in the classroom using **Figure 3**. **LS** Kinesthetic

How a Wet-Bulb Thermometer Works

A wet-bulb thermometer works differently than a dry-bulb thermometer, which measures only air temperature. As air passes over the wet-bulb thermometer, the water in the cloth evaporates. As the water evaporates, the cloth cools. If the humidity is low, the water will evaporate more quickly and the temperature reading on the wet-bulb thermometer will drop. If the humidity is high, only a small amount of water will evaporate from the cloth of the wet-bulb thermometer and the change in temperature will be small.

 **Reading Check** Explain how a wet-bulb thermometer works.

Condensation

You have probably seen water droplets form on the outside of a glass of ice water, as shown in **Figure 4.** Where did those water drops come from? The water came from the surrounding air, and droplets formed as a result of condensation. **Condensation** is the process by which a gas, such as water vapor, becomes a liquid. Before condensation can occur, the air must be saturated, which means that the air must have a relative humidity of 100%. Condensation occurs when saturated air cools.

Dew Point

Air can become saturated when water vapor is added to the air through evaporation. Air can also become saturated when it cools to its dew point. The *dew point* is the temperature at which a gas condenses into a liquid. At its dew point, air is saturated. The ice in the glass of water causes the air surrounding the glass to cool to its dew point.

Before water vapor can condense, though, it must have a surface to condense on. In the case of the glass of ice water, water vapor condenses on the outside of the glass.

Figure 4 *Condensation occurred when the air next to the glass cooled to its dew point.*

condensation the change of state from a gas to a liquid

Out of Thin Air

1. Pour **room-temperature water** into a **plastic container,** such as a drinking cup, until the water level is near the top of the cup.
2. Observe the outside of the container, and record your observations.
3. Add **one or two ice cubes** to the container of water.
4. Watch the outside of the container for any changes.
5. What happened to the outside of the container?
6. What is the liquid on the container?
7. Where did the liquid come from? Explain your answer.

Cultural Awareness GENERAL

Chinese Meteorology Dating back to 1216 BCE, Chinese meteorological records have helped modern climatologists determine long-term global climate patterns. To measure humidity, Chinese meteorologists dried pieces of charcoal in an oven and weighed them. The charcoal was then left outside to absorb moisture from the atmosphere and weighed again. The difference between the two weights accurately indicated the humidity. Have students test this method with a balance and some pieces of charcoal. Students can also design their own experiment to measure humidity and share the experiment with the class. **LS Kinesthetic**

Discussion ——— GENERAL

What Dew You Think Have students decide if the following statements are true or false:

• Condensation is the process in which a liquid changes to a gas. (false)

• Dew point is the temperature to which air must cool before it becomes saturated. (true)

• The dew you observe on grass forms on hot, cloudy, windless nights. (false)

LS Verbal

Answer to Reading Check

The bulb of a wet-bulb thermometer is covered with moistened material. The bulb cools as water evaporates from the material. If the air is dry, more water will evaporate from the material, and the temperature recorded by the thermometer will be low. If the air is humid, less water will evaporate from the material, and the temperature recorded by the thermometer will be higher.

Answers to Quick Lab

5. Liquid droplets formed on the outside of the container.
6. The liquid is water.
7. The air next to the cup cooled to below its dew point, and water vapor condensed on the cup.

READING STRATEGY — GENERAL

Sequencing After students read this page, have them arrange the following steps in a logical order:

- Water vapor condenses on smoke, dust, salt, and other small particles suspended in the air. (4)

- The relative humidity of the air increases. (2)

- Warm air rises and cools. (1)

- Air eventually becomes saturated. (3)

- Millions of tiny drops of liquid water collect to form a cloud. (5)

LS Logical

Debate — ADVANCED

Cloud Seeding Meteorologists sometimes use a technique known as *cloud seeding* to try to cause or increase precipitation. Have groups of students research this technique and write a position paper about it. After students have gathered their information, have small groups debate the pros and cons of artificially stimulating precipitation. **LS** Verbal

---

Figure 5 Three Forms of Clouds

Cumulus clouds look like piles of cotton balls.

Stratus clouds are not as tall as cumulus clouds, but they cover more area.

Cirrus clouds are made of ice crystals.

cloud a collection of small water droplets or ice crystals suspended in the air, which forms when the air is cooled and condensation occurs

CONNECTION TO Language Arts

Cloud Clues Did you know that the name of a cloud actually describes the characteristics of the cloud? For example, the word *cumulus* comes from the Latin word meaning "heap." A cumulus cloud is a puffy, white cloud, which could be described as a "heap" of clouds. Use a dictionary or the Internet to find the word origins of the names of the other cloud types you learn about in this section.

Clouds

Have you ever wondered what clouds are and how they form? A **cloud** is a collection of millions of tiny water droplets or ice crystals. Clouds form as warm air rises and cools. As the rising air cools, it becomes saturated. When the air is saturated, the water vapor changes to a liquid or a solid, depending on the air temperature. At temperatures above freezing, water vapor condenses on small particles in the air and forms tiny water droplets. At temperatures below freezing, water vapor changes to a solid to form ice crystals. Clouds are classified by form, as shown in **Figure 5,** and by altitude.

Cumulus Clouds

Puffy, white clouds that tend to have flat bottoms are called *cumulus clouds* (KYOO myoo luhs KLOWDZ). Cumulus clouds form when warm air rises. These clouds generally indicate fair weather. However, when these clouds get larger, they produce thunderstorms. Thunderstorms come from a kind of cumulus cloud called a *cumulonimbus cloud* (KYOO myoo loh NIM buhs KLOWD). Clouds that have names that include *-nimbus* or *nimbo-* are likely to produce precipitation.

Stratus Clouds

Clouds called *stratus clouds* (STRAYT uhs KLOWDZ) are clouds that form in layers. Stratus clouds cover large areas of the sky and often block out the sun. These clouds can be caused by a gentle lifting of a large body of air into the atmosphere. *Nimbostratus clouds* (NIM boh STRAYT uhs KLOWDZ) are dark stratus clouds that usually produce light to heavy, continuous rain. *Fog* is a stratus cloud that has formed near the ground.

Homework — BASIC

Cloud Models On a poster board, have students use cotton balls to make models of different types of clouds at different altitudes. Students should create labels to describe the clouds and the types of weather with which they are associated.

LS Visual/Intrapersonal

English Language Learners

MISCONCEPTION ALERT

Contrails What appears to be white smoke from an airplane's engine is not smoke at all. Condensation trails, or contrails, form as the combustion of the aircraft's fuel forms water vapor which condenses and freezes along the airplane's exhaust tail. A thick contrail that will not dissipate is a sign that a frontal system is approaching.

Cirrus Clouds

As you can see in **Figure 5,** *cirrus clouds* (SIR uhs KLOWDZ) are thin, feathery, white clouds found at high altitudes. Cirrus clouds form when the wind is strong. If they get thicker, cirrus clouds indicate that a change in the weather is coming.

Clouds and Altitude

Clouds are also classified by the altitude at which they form. **Figure 6** shows two altitude groups used to describe clouds and the altitudes at which they form in the middle latitudes. The prefix *cirro-* is used to describe clouds that form at high altitudes. For example, a cumulus cloud that forms high in the atmosphere is called a *cirrocumulus cloud.* The prefix *alto-* describes clouds that form at middle altitudes. Clouds that form at low altitudes do not have a specific prefix to describe them.

Reading Check At what altitude does an altostratus cloud form?

Figure 6 Cloud Types Based on Form and Altitude

High Clouds Because of the cold temperatures at high altitude, high clouds are made up of ice crystals. The prefix *cirro-* is used to describe high clouds.

8,000 m Cirrocumulus
Cirrus
Cirrostratus
6,000 m
Altostratus
Cumulonimbus

Middle Clouds Middle clouds can be made up of both water drops and ice crystals. The prefix *alto-* is used to describe middle clouds.

4,000 m
Altocumulus
Cumulus

2,000 m

Low Clouds Low clouds are made up of water drops. There is no specific prefix used to describe low clouds.

Stratocumulus
Nimbostratus
Stratus

Answer to Reading Check

Altostratus clouds form at middle altitudes.

CHAPTER RESOURCES

Technology

Transparencies
• Cloud Types Based on Form and Altitude

Concept Mapping Have students construct a concept map using section concepts and terms. Tell students that their map should explain the relative location of clouds in the atmosphere and should describe how they form. **LS** Visual

Quiz ———————— GENERAL

1. If an air mass is cooled and the amount of humidity in the air mass stays the same, does the relative humidity of the air mass increase or decrease? (It increases.)

2. What causes dew? (At night and in the early morning, the air cools and it can hold less moisture. Dew is water that condenses from the air in the early morning.)

3. How does hail form? (Hail forms when raindrops are carried to the tops of clouds by updrafts. The raindrops freeze and become hail. The hail grows larger as it is repeatedly covered with layers of freezing water.)

Alternative Assessment ———— ADVANCED

Story Have students write a short story that describes the travels of a water molecule from the moment it evaporates from the sea to the moment it returns to the sea. Students can also include illustrations with their stories. **LS** Verbal

Figure 7 *Snowflakes are six-sided ice crystals that can be several millimeters to several centimeters in size.*

precipitation any form of water that falls to the Earth's surface from the clouds

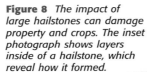

Precipitation

When water from the air returns to Earth's surface, it returns as precipitation. **Precipitation** is water, in solid or liquid form, that falls from the air to Earth. There are four major forms of precipitation—rain, snow, sleet, and hail.

Rain

The most common form of precipitation is *rain*. A cloud produces rain when the water drops in the cloud become large enough to fall. A water drop in a cloud begins as a droplet that is smaller than the period at the end of this sentence. Before such a water drop falls as rain, it must become about 100 times its original size.

Sleet and Snow

Sleet forms when rain falls through a layer of freezing air. The rain freezes in the air, which produces falling ice. *Snow* forms when temperatures are so cold that water vapor changes directly to a solid. Snow can fall as single ice crystals or can join to form snowflakes, as shown in **Figure 7.**

Hail

Balls or lumps of ice that fall from clouds are called *hail*. Hail forms in cumulonimbus clouds. When updrafts of air in the clouds carry raindrops high in the clouds, the raindrops freeze and hail forms. As hail falls, water drops coat it. Another updraft of air can send the hail up again. Here, the water drops collected on the hail freeze to form another layer of ice on the hail. This process can happen many times. Eventually, the hail becomes too heavy to be carried by the updrafts and so falls to Earth's surface, as shown in **Figure 8.**

Figure 8 *The impact of large hailstones can damage property and crops. The inset photograph shows layers inside of a hailstone, which reveal how it formed.*

Homework ———— ADVANCED

Weather Journal Two centuries ago, Emerson wrote that the sky is the "daily bread of our eyes." Careful observation of the sky remains an important skill. Encourage students to keep a daily journal of weather observations for at least a week. To help motivate students, have them consider writing their journal from the perspective of a 19th-century farmer. Each entry should describe the weather conditions at two times of the day and once at night. Based on their observations, students should predict the next day's weather. Students should note cloud types, wind direction, and temperature changes. Encourage students to go beyond the data they could find in a weather report and incorporate qualitative observations of the world around them. **LS** Visual/Intrapersonal

Summary

- Weather is the condition of the atmosphere at a certain time and place. Weather is affected by the amount of water vapor in the air.

- The water cycle describes the movement of water above, on, and below Earth's surface.

- Humidity describes the amount of water vapor in the air. Relative humidity is a way to express humidity.

- When the temperature of the air cools to its dew point, the air has reached saturation and condensation occurs.

- Clouds form as air cools to its dew point. Clouds are classified by form and by the altitude at which they form.

- Precipitation occurs when the water vapor that condenses in the atmosphere falls back to Earth in solid or liquid form.

Using Key Terms

1. In your own words, write a definition for each of the following terms: *relative humidity, condensation, cloud,* and *precipitation.*

Understanding Key Ideas

2. Which of the following clouds is most likely to produce light to heavy, continuous rain?
   a. cumulus cloud
   b. cumulonimbus cloud
   c. nimbostratus cloud
   d. cirrus cloud

3. How is relative humidity affected by the amount of water vapor in the air?

4. What does a relative humidity of 75% mean?

5. Describe the path of water through the water cycle.

6. What are four types of precipitation?

Critical Thinking

7. **Applying Concepts** Why are some clouds formed from water droplets, while others are made up of ice crystals?

8. **Applying Concepts** How can rain and hail fall from the same cumulonimbus cloud?

9. **Identifying Relationships** What happens to relative humidity as the air temperature drops below the dew point?

Interpreting Graphics

Use the image below to answer the questions that follow.

10. What type of cloud is shown in the image?

11. How is this type of cloud formed?

12. What type of weather can you expect when you see this type of cloud? Explain.

SCI LINKS
Developed and maintained by the National Science Teachers Association

For a variety of links related to this chapter, go to www.scilinks.org

Topic: The Water Cycle
SciLinks code: HSM1626

CONNECTION to
Physical Science — GENERAL

Water Molecules Explain that a water molecule has a positive end and a negative end. Opposite charges attract, so the positive end of one water molecule attracts the negative end of another. This attraction helps explain why small water droplets that collide are able to form relatively large raindrops.

Answers to Section Review

1. Sample answer: Relative humidity is the amount of water vapor the air contains compared with the maximum amount it can hold at a given temperature. Condensation is a process that occurs when air reaches its saturation point. A cloud is a mass of air that contains millions of condensed water droplets. Precipitation is solid or liquid water that falls from a cloud.

2. c

3. If the amount of water vapor in the air increases, the relative humidity also increases.

4. The air contains 75% of the maximum amount of water it can hold at a given temperature.

5. Sample answer: Water evaporates from the Earth's surface and rises into the atmosphere. The air cools as it rises. As the air cools, water condenses and falls as precipitation. The precipitation falls to the Earth.

6. rain, snow, sleet, and hail

7. Sample answer: Clouds that form at high altitudes are usually colder than clouds that form at lower altitudes. The cold, high-altitude clouds can be composed of ice crystals.

8. Sample answer: Cumulonimbus clouds can be very tall. Rain can form at the bottom of the cloud, and hail can form near the top of the cloud.

9. As the air temperature drops below the dew point, relative humidity increases to the saturation point, and condensation occurs.

10. a cumulus cloud

11. Cumulus clouds form when warm, moist air rises.

12. Sample answer: Cumulus clouds usually indicate fair weather. However, when cumulus clouds grow large, they can become cumulonimbus clouds, which often produce thunderstorms.

Focus

Overview

In this section, students learn about air masses and the ways that they affect weather in the United States. Students also learn about fronts—the boundaries between air masses.

🔔 Bellringer

Ask students to write down as many different qualities of air as possible. (Students might note that air can be humid or dry, can be hot or cold, or can have high pressure or low pressure.) Tell students that the air they are breathing now was hundreds of miles away yesterday. Ask them to think about what caused that air to move. Explain that air masses tend to flow from areas of high pressure to areas of low pressure, just as the air inside a balloon escapes when the balloon is punctured.

Motivate

Discussion ——— GENERAL

Air Masses and You Have students use **Figure 1** to determine which type of air mass is mainly responsible for the weather in your area. Have students describe the general temperatures and humidity typical of your area. Have students compare their results with information in this section. **LS** Visual

---

READING WARM-UP

Objectives

● Identify the four kinds of air masses that influence weather in the United States.
● Describe the four major types of fronts.
● Explain how fronts cause weather changes.
● Explain how cyclones and anticyclones affect the weather.

Terms to Learn

air mass   cyclone
front   anticyclone

READING STRATEGY

Reading Organizer As you read this section, make a table comparing cold, warm, occluded, and stationary fronts.

Air Masses and Fronts

Have you ever wondered how the weather can change so quickly? For example, the weather may be warm and sunny in the morning and cold and rainy by afternoon.

Changes in weather are caused by the movement and interaction of air masses. An **air mass** is a large body of air where temperature and moisture content are similar throughout. In this section, you will learn about air masses and their effect on weather.

Air Masses

Air masses are characterized by their moisture content and temperature. The moisture content and temperature of an air mass are determined by the area over which the air mass forms. These areas are called *source regions*. An example of a source region is the Gulf of Mexico. An air mass that forms over the Gulf of Mexico is warm and wet because this area is warm and has a lot of water that evaporates. There are many types of air masses, each of which is associated with a particular source region. The characteristics of these air masses are represented on maps by a two-letter symbol, as shown in **Figure 1.** The first letter indicates the moisture content that is characteristic of the air mass. The second letter represents the temperature that is characteristic of the air mass.

Figure 1 **Air Masses That Affect Weather in North America**

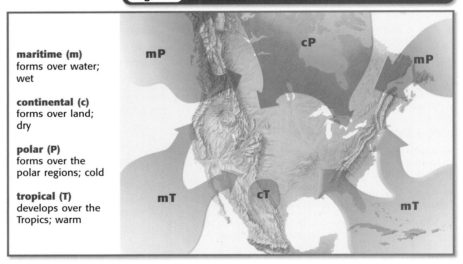

maritime (m)
forms over water; wet

continental (c)
forms over land; dry

polar (P)
forms over the polar regions; cold

tropical (T)
develops over the Tropics; warm

CHAPTER RESOURCES

Chapter Resource File

 • Lesson Plan
• Directed Reading A BASIC
• Directed Reading B SPECIAL NEEDS

Technology

 Transparencies
• Bellringer

Homework ——— GENERAL

Researching Weather Lore Have students research weather lore at the library or on the Internet to find out if the stories have a scientific basis. For example, students could research the saying, "Red sky at night, sailors delight; red sky at morning, sailors take warning." **LS** Intrapersonal/Logical

---

Figure 2 *Cold air masses that form over the North Atlantic Ocean can bring severe weather, such as blizzards, in the winter.*

Cold Air Masses

Most of the cold winter weather in the United States is influenced by three polar air masses. A continental polar (cP) air mass forms over northern Canada, which brings extremely cold winter weather to the United States. In the summer, a cP air mass generally brings cool, dry weather.

A maritime polar (mP) air mass that forms over the North Pacific Ocean is cool and very wet. This air mass brings rain and snow to the Pacific Coast in the winter and cool, foggy weather in the summer.

A maritime polar air mass that forms over the North Atlantic Ocean brings cool, cloudy weather and precipitation to New England in the winter, as shown in **Figure 2.** In the summer, the air mass brings cool weather and fog.

air mass a large body of air where temperature and moisture content are constant throughout

Warm Air Masses

Four warm air masses influence the weather in the United States. A maritime tropical (mT) air mass that develops over warm areas in the Pacific Ocean is milder than the maritime polar air mass that forms over the Pacific Ocean.

Other maritime tropical air masses develop over the warm waters of the Gulf of Mexico and the Atlantic Ocean. These air masses move north across the East Coast and into the Midwest. In the summer, they bring hot and humid weather, hurricanes, and thunderstorms, as shown in **Figure 3.** In the winter, they bring mild, often cloudy weather.

A continental tropical (cT) air mass forms over the deserts of northern Mexico and the southwestern United States. This air mass moves northward and brings clear, dry, and hot weather in the summer.

✓ **Reading Check** What type of air mass contributes to the hot and humid summer weather in the midwestern United States? (*See the Appendix for answers to Reading Checks.*)

Figure 3 *Warm air masses that develop over the Gulf of Mexico bring thunderstorms in the summer.*

Cultural Awareness GENERAL

Local Weather Local weather patterns are heavily influenced by air masses, which tend to bring predictable weather. All cultures have names for familiar weather patterns. For example, in Tunisia, Africa, weather forecasters often predict "hot and *chili*" conditions. This forecast may not make sense to people elsewhere, but to a Tunisian, *chili* refers to a hot wind blowing from the North African desert. Similarly, in parts of the eastern United States, people refer to the hot, dry, and relatively windless weeks of August as the "dog days" of summer. Have interested students research the names and characteristics of typical weather patterns in other countries. **LS** Interpersonal

Figure 4   **Fronts That Affect Weather in North America**

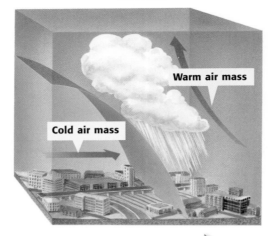

Cold Front

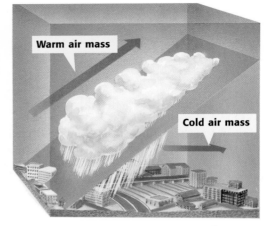

Warm Front

front the boundary between air masses of different densities and usually different temperatures

Fronts

Air masses that form from different areas often do not mix. The reason is that the air masses have different densities. For example, warm air is less dense than cold air. So, when two types of air masses meet, warm air generally rises. The area in which two types of air masses meet is called a **front.** The four kinds of fronts—cold fronts, warm fronts, occluded fronts, and stationary fronts—are shown in **Figure 4.** Fronts are associated with weather in the middle latitudes.

Cold Front

A cold front forms where cold air moves under warm air, which is less dense, and pushes the warm air up. Cold fronts can move quickly and bring thunderstorms, heavy rain, or snow. Cooler weather usually follows a cold front because the air mass behind the cold front is cooler and drier than the air mass that it is replacing.

Warm Front

A warm front forms where warm air moves over cold, denser air. In a warm front, the warm air gradually replaces the cold air. Warm fronts generally bring drizzly rain and are followed by clear and warm weather.

CONNECTION to History ——— GENERAL

WWI and Meteorology During World War I, European nations stopped broadcasting weather reports, fearing that they would be used by advancing enemy troops. This left nonaligned countries such as Norway to develop their own meteorology program. Norwegian meteorologists responded by forming the famous Bergen School, which greatly advanced the field of meteorology. They discovered that air masses formed from source regions and found that these masses traveled with the winds. Influenced by the war, the meteorologists described air masses using military terms. They imagined Europe as a battleground where different air masses fought like armies trying to advance on each other. The boundary between the air masses, where the "battle" occurs, was called the *front*.

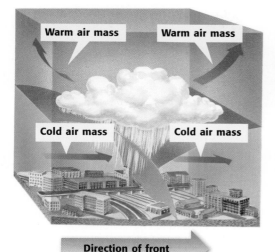

Occluded Front

Warm air mass   Warm air mass

Cold air mass   Cold air mass

Direction of front

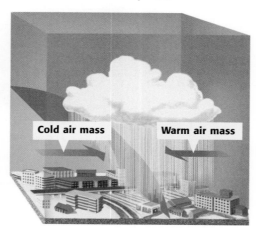

Stationary Front

Cold air mass   Warm air mass

Occluded Front

An occluded front forms when a warm air mass is caught between two colder air masses. The coldest air mass moves under and pushes up the warm air mass. The coldest air mass then moves forward until it meets a cold air mass that is warmer and less dense. The colder of these two air masses moves under and pushes up the warmer air mass. Sometimes, though, the two colder air masses mix. An occluded front has cool temperatures and large amounts of rain and snow.

✓ *Reading Check* **What type of weather would you expect an occluded front to produce?**

Stationary Front

A stationary front forms when a cold air mass meets a warm air mass. In this case, however, both air masses do not have enough force to lift the warm air mass over the cold air mass. So, the two air masses remain separated. This may happen because there is not enough wind to keep the air masses pushing against each other. A stationary front often brings many days of cloudy, wet weather.

Figure 5 This satellite image shows a cyclone system forming.

cyclone an area in the atmosphere that has lower pressure than the surrounding areas and has winds that spiral toward the center

anticyclone the rotation of air around a high-pressure center in the direction opposite to Earth's rotation

Air Pressure and Weather

You may have heard a weather reporter on TV or radio talking about areas of low pressure and high pressure. These areas of different pressure affect the weather.

Cyclones

Areas that have lower pressure than the surrounding areas do are called **cyclones.** Cyclones are areas where air masses come together, or converge, and rise. **Figure 5** shows a satellite image of the formation of a cyclone system.

Anticyclones

Areas that have high pressure are called **anticyclones.** Anticyclones are areas where air moves apart, or diverges, and sinks. The sinking air is denser than the surrounding air, and the pressure is higher. Cooler, denser air moves out of the center of these high-pressure areas toward areas of lower pressure. **Figure 6** shows how wind can spiral out of an anticyclone and into a cyclone.

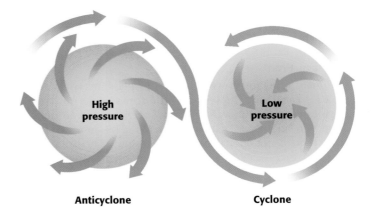

Figure 6 As the colder, denser air spirals out of the anticyclone, it moves towards areas of low pressure, which sometimes forms a cyclone.

High pressure

Low pressure

Anticyclone

Cyclone

CONNECTION to Life Science ——— GENERAL

Aching Joints and Air Pressure Why do people complain of aching joints before a thunderstorm? A study found that nearly 75% of arthritis sufferers felt more pain in their joints when air pressure was falling. Although this effect has been thoroughly documented, there is no definitive evidence of why it occurs.

Cyclones, Anticyclones, and Weather

You have learned what cyclones and anticyclones are. So, now you might be wondering how do cyclones and anticyclones affect the weather? As the air in the center of a cyclone rises, it cools and forms clouds and rain. The rising air in a cyclone causes stormy weather. In an anticyclone, the air sinks. As the air sinks, it gets warmer and absorbs moisture. The sinking air in an anticyclone brings dry, clear weather. By keeping track of cyclones and anticyclones, meteorologists can predict the weather.

Reading Check Describe the different types of weather that a cyclone and an anticyclone can produce.

CONNECTION TO Astronomy

Storms on Jupiter Cyclones and anticyclones occur on Jupiter, too! Generally, cyclones on Jupiter appear as dark ovals, and anticyclones appear as bright ovals. Jupiter's Great Red Spot is an anticyclone that has existed for centuries. Research the existence of cyclones and anticyclones on other bodies in our solar system.

SECTION Review

Summary

- Air masses are characterized by moisture content and temperature.
- A front occurs where two air masses meet.
- Four major types of fronts are cold, warm, occluded, and stationary fronts.
- Differences in air pressure cause cyclones, which bring stormy weather, and anticyclones, which bring dry, clear weather.

Using Key Terms

For each pair of terms, explain how the meanings of the terms differ.

1. *front* and *air mass*
2. *cyclone* and *anticyclone*

Understanding Key Ideas

3. What kind of front forms when a cold air mass displaces a warm air mass?
   a. a cold front
   b. a warm front
   c. an occluded front
   d. a stationary front
4. What are the major air masses that influence the weather in the United States?
5. What is one source region of a maritime polar air mass?
6. What are the characteristics of an air mass whose two-letter symbol is cP?
7. What are the four major types of fronts?
8. How do fronts cause weather changes?
9. How do cyclones and anticyclones affect the weather?

Math Skills

10. A cold front is moving toward the town of La Porte at 35 km/h. The front is 200 km away from La Porte. How long will it take the front to get to La Porte?

Critical Thinking

11. **Applying Concepts** How do air masses that form over the land and ocean affect weather in the United States?
12. **Identifying Relationships** Why does the Pacific Coast have cool, wet winters and warm, dry summers? Explain.
13. **Applying Concepts** Which air masses influence the weather where you live? Explain.

SCILINKS.

NSTA Developed and maintained by the National Science Teachers Association

For a variety of links related to this chapter, go to www.scilinks.org

Topic: Air Masses and Fronts
SciLinks code: HSM0032

Answer to Reading Check

An anticyclone can produce dry, clear weather.

CHAPTER RESOURCES

Chapter Resource File

- Section Quiz GENERAL
- Section Review GENERAL
- Vocabulary and Section Summary GENERAL

Answers to Section Review

1. Sample answer: An air mass is a large body of air that has a similar temperature and moisture level throughout. A front is a boundary between two air masses.
2. Sample answer: A cyclone is an area of low pressure with winds that spiral toward the center. An anticyclone is an area of high pressure with winds that flow outward.
3. a
4. continental polar, maritime polar, maritime tropical, and continental tropical
5. Sample answer: The North Pacific Ocean is one source region for maritime polar air masses.
6. A cP air mass is very cold and dry. It forms over areas near the poles, such as northern Canada.
7. The major types of fronts are cold fronts, warm fronts, stationary fronts, and occluded fronts.
8. Fronts are boundaries between air masses. When a front occurs, air masses of different temperature and humidity interact. The interactions of air masses cause weather changes.
9. The rising air of a cyclone often causes stormy weather. The sinking air of an anticyclone often causes dry, clear weather.
10. 200 km × 35 km/h = 5.7 h
11. Sample answer: Air masses that form over land have less moisture than those that form over the ocean. The amount of moisture carried in both types of air masses affects the amount of precipitation that the United States receives. Air masses that form over the ocean generally bring precipitation.
12. Sample answer: The Pacific Coast has cool, wet winters because it is affected by a maritime polar air mass during the winter. Summers on the Pacific Coast are warm and dry because the weather is influenced by a dry continental air mass.
13. Answers may vary.

Focus

Overview

In this section, students will learn about severe weather. The section explores thunderstorms, tornadoes, and hurricanes. Students learn about the causes of severe weather and about severe weather safety.

Bellringer

Have students write a one-paragraph description of a thunderstorm. Ask them to describe the weather conditions immediately before, during, and after a thunderstorm. Ask students to describe how the storm affects each of their senses.

Motivate

Demonstration — GENERAL

Modeling Thunder Inflate a balloon with air, and tie it closed. Explain that thunder occurs when lightning superheats air, which causes the gases to expand rapidly. The air in the balloon is under pressure, so it will also expand rapidly if the pressure is suddenly released. The rapid expansion of air causes vibrations that we hear as sound. Hold up a pin or needle, pause, and pop the balloon with a flourish.

LS Kinesthetic

READING WARM-UP

Objectives
- Describe how lightning forms.
- Describe the formation of thunderstorms, tornadoes, and hurricanes.
- Describe the characteristics of thunderstorms, tornadoes, and hurricanes.
- Explain how to stay safe during severe weather.

Terms to Learn
thunderstorm   tornado
lightning   hurricane
thunder

READING STRATEGY

Reading Organizer As you read this section, create an outline of the section. Use the headings from the section in your outline.

thunderstorm a usually brief, heavy storm that consists of rain, strong winds, lightning, and thunder

---

Severe Weather

CRAAAACK! BOOM! What made that noise? You didn't expect it, and it sure made you jump.

A big boom of thunder has probably surprised you at one time or another. And the thunder was probably followed by a thunderstorm. A thunderstorm is an example of severe weather. *Severe weather* is weather that can cause property damage and sometimes death.

Thunderstorms

Thunderstorms can be very loud and powerful. **Thunderstorms,** such as the one shown in **Figure 1,** are small, intense weather systems that produce strong winds, heavy rain, lightning, and thunder. Thunderstorms can occur along cold fronts. But thunderstorms can develop in other places, too. There are only two atmospheric conditions required to produce thunderstorms: warm and moist air near Earth's surface and an unstable atmosphere. The atmosphere is unstable when the surrounding air is colder than the rising air mass. The air mass will continue to rise as long as the surrounding air is colder than the air mass.

When the rising warm air reaches its dew point, the water vapor in the air condenses and forms cumulus clouds. If the atmosphere is extremely unstable, the warm air will continue to rise, which causes the cloud to grow into a dark, cumulonimbus cloud. Cumulonimbus clouds can reach heights of more than 15 km.

Figure 1 *A typical thunderstorm, such as this one over Dallas, Texas, generates an enormous amount of electrical energy.*

CHAPTER RESOURCES

Chapter Resource File
- Lesson Plan
- Directed Reading A BASIC
- Directed Reading B SPECIAL NEEDS

Technology
- Transparencies
  - Bellringer
  - *LINK TO PHYSICAL SCIENCE* How Lightning Forms

MISCONCEPTION ALERT

"The Same Place Twice" Inform students that the old saying, "Lightning never strikes twice in the same place," is not true. Lightning has struck the same place, and even the same person, more than once. Ray Sullivan, a retired national park ranger, has been hit seven times by lightning. Luckily, he has survived the strikes.

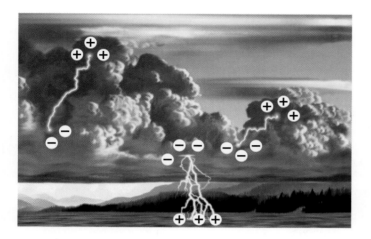

Figure 2 *The upper part of a cloud usually carries a positive electric charge, while the lower part of the cloud carries mainly negative charges.*

Lightning

Thunderstorms are very active electrically. **Lightning** is an electric discharge that occurs between a positively charged area and a negatively charged area, as shown in **Figure 2.** Lightning can happen between two clouds, between Earth and a cloud, or even between two parts of the same cloud. Have you ever touched someone after scuffing your feet on the carpet and received a mild shock? If so, you have experienced how lightning forms. While you walk around, friction between the floor and your shoes builds up an electric charge in your body. When you touch someone else, the charge is released.

When lightning strikes, energy is released. This energy is transferred to the air and causes the air to expand rapidly and send out sound waves. **Thunder** is the sound that results from the rapid expansion of air along the lightning strike.

lightning an electric discharge that takes place between two oppositely charged surfaces, such as between a cloud and the ground, between two clouds, or between two parts of the same cloud

thunder the sound caused by the rapid expansion of air along an electrical strike

Severe Thunderstorms

Severe thunderstorms can produce one or more of the following conditions: high winds, hail, flash floods, and tornadoes. Hailstorms damage crops, dent the metal on cars, and break windows. Flash flooding that results from heavy rains causes millions of dollars in property damage annually. And every year, flash flooding is a leading cause of weather-related deaths.

Lightning, as shown in **Figure 3,** happens during all thunderstorms and is very powerful. Lightning is responsible for starting thousands of forest fires each year and for killing or injuring hundreds of people a year in the United States.

Reading Check What is a severe thunderstorm? (*See the Appendix for answers to Reading Checks.*)

Figure 3 *Lightning often strikes the tallest object in an area, such as the Eiffel Tower in Paris, France.*

Is That a Fact!

The color of lightning can indicate atmospheric conditions. Blue lightning indicates hail, red lightning indicates rain, yellow or orange lightning indicates dust, and white lightning indicates low humidity.

Answer to Reading Check

A severe thunderstorm is a thunderstorm that produces high winds, hail, flash floods, or tornadoes.

Tornadoes

tornado a destructive, rotating column of air that has very high wind speeds, is visible as a funnel-shaped cloud, and touches the ground

Tornadoes happen in only 1% of all thunderstorms. A **tornado** is a small, spinning column of air that has high wind speeds and low central pressure and that touches the ground. A tornado starts out as a funnel cloud that pokes through the bottom of a cumulonimbus cloud and hangs in the air. The funnel cloud becomes a tornado when it makes contact with Earth's surface. **Figure 4** shows how a tornado forms.

Figure 4 How a Tornado Forms

❶ Wind moving in two directions causes a layer of air in the middle to begin to spin like a roll of toilet paper.

❷ The spinning column of air is turned to a vertical position by strong updrafts of air in the cumulonimbus cloud. The updrafts of air also begin to spin.

❸ The spinning column of air moves to the bottom of the cumulonimbus cloud and forms a funnel cloud.

❹ The funnel cloud becomes a tornado when it touches the ground.

BRAIN FOOD

Tornado Formation Most tornadoes develop from thunderstorms at the leading edge of a cold front. Ask students to think about why this is so. (The cool air wedges under the warm air, which may result in wind moving in opposite directions. This movement may cause a layer of air to spin. Rapidly rising warm air can turn the spinning layer into a vertical funnel.) **LS** Verbal

WEIRD SCIENCE

People have reported seeing "naked" chickens after tornadoes strike rural areas. A likely explanation is that tornadoes cause chickens to shed their feathers, or molt. Chickens often molt when attacked. As the chickens molt, the strong tornadic winds blow their feathers off.

Figure 5 *The tornado that hit Kissimmee, Florida, in 1998 had wind speeds of up to 416 km/h.*

Twists of Terror

About 75% of the world's tornadoes occur in the United States. Most of these tornadoes happen in the spring and early summer when cold, dry air from Canada meets warm, moist air from the Tropics. The size of a tornado's path of destruction is usually about 8 km long and 10 to 60 m wide. Although most tornadoes last only a few minutes, they can cause a lot of damage. Their ability to cause damage is due to their strong spinning winds. The average tornado has wind speeds between 120 and 180 km/h, but rarer, more violent tornadoes can have spinning winds of up to 500 km/h. The winds of tornadoes have been known to uproot trees and destroy buildings, as shown in **Figure 5.** Tornadoes are capable of picking up heavy objects, such as mobile homes and cars, and hurling them through the air.

hurricane a severe storm that develops over tropical oceans and whose strong winds of more than 120 km/h spiral in toward the intensely low-pressure storm center

Hurricanes

A large, rotating tropical weather system that has wind speeds of at least 120 km/h is called a **hurricane,** shown in **Figure 6.** Hurricanes are the most powerful storms on Earth. Hurricanes have different names in different parts of the world. In the western Pacific Ocean, hurricanes are called *typhoons*. Hurricanes that form over the Indian Ocean are called *cyclones*.

Most hurricanes form in the areas between 5° and 20° north latitude and between 5° and 20° south latitude over warm, tropical oceans. At higher latitudes, the water is too cold for hurricanes to form. Hurricanes vary in size from 160 to 1,500 km in diameter and can travel for thousands of kilometers.

✓ Reading Check What are some other names for hurricanes?

Figure 6 *This photograph of Hurricane Fran was taken from space.*

CONNECTION to History — GENERAL

Hurricanes and American History Hurricanes played a significant role in early American history. In 1609, a fleet of ships with settlers from England who were bound for Virginia was blown off course by a hurricane. Some of the ships landed in Bermuda instead, and the settlers started the first European colony there. Stories of the storm and the shipwrecks may have inspired William Shakespeare to write *The Tempest*.

Homework — ADVANCED

PORTFOLIO **Disaster Plan** Have students find out how to protect themselves during a thunderstorm, tornado, or hurricane. Using their findings, students should draw up a disaster plan for severe weather. The plan should include general information as well as things that might be specific to their family, such as what to do with the family pet(s), how to assist a person who uses a wheelchair or walker, and so on. Suggest that students review the plan with their family. **LS Intrapersonal**

Answer to Reading Check
Hurricanes are also called *typhoons* or *cyclones.*

Is That a Fact!

Before 1950, hurricanes were named or identified by their latitude and longitude. In the 1950s, meteorologists began assigning names to hurricanes. Today, the names are assigned in advance for 6-year cycles. The names are submitted by countries potentially in the paths of hurricanes and approved by the World Meteorological Organization.

Writing **Weather and Energy**
Tell students that creating severe weather takes a lot of energy. Have them research the relationship between energy and storm formation. For example, as a warm air mass rises, energy from water condensation helps fuel hurricanes. The energy released by a typical hurricane in 1 day is equal to detonating four hundred 20-megaton hydrogen bombs. Challenge students to research these concepts in books, magazines, and the Internet and to compile their findings into a short report. **LS** Intrapersonal

Group ACTIVITY — GENERAL

Hurricane Newscast Have students work in groups to learn about a hurricane of their choosing. Have students find out where the storm formed, what path it followed, what damage it did, and how people recovered from the damage. Ask students to focus on the people involved in the hurricane, from the meteorologists to relief workers. Have groups present the information they gathered as a series of simulated newscasts. **LS** Auditory/ Interpersonal **Co-op Learning**

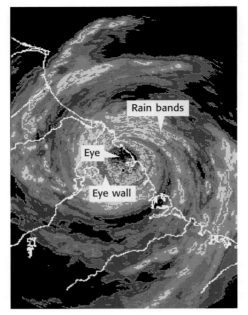

Figure 7 *The photo above gives you a bird's-eye view of a hurricane.*

Rain bands

Eye

Eye wall

How a Hurricane Forms

A hurricane begins as a group of thunderstorms moving over tropical ocean waters. Winds traveling in two different directions meet and cause the storm to spin. Because of the Coriolis effect, the storm turns counterclockwise in the Northern Hemisphere and clockwise in the Southern Hemisphere.

A hurricane gets its energy from the condensation of water vapor. Once formed, the hurricane is fueled through contact with the warm ocean water. Moisture is added to the warm air by evaporation from the ocean. As the warm, moist air rises, the water vapor condenses and releases large amounts of energy. The hurricane continues to grow as long as it is over its source of warm, moist air. When the hurricane moves into colder waters or over land, it begins to die because it has lost its source of energy. **Figure 7** and **Figure 8** show two views of a hurricane.

✓ Reading Check Where do hurricanes get their energy?

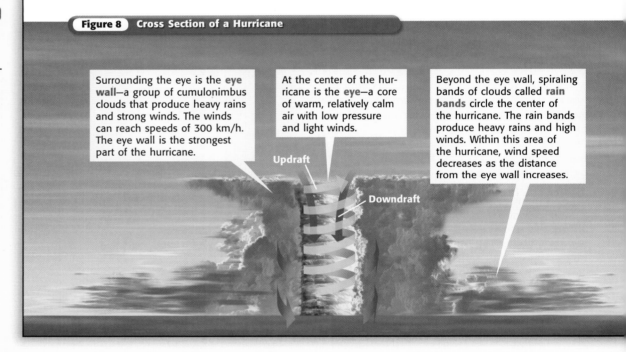

Figure 8 Cross Section of a Hurricane

Surrounding the eye is the **eye wall**—a group of cumulonimbus clouds that produce heavy rains and strong winds. The winds can reach speeds of 300 km/h. The eye wall is the strongest part of the hurricane.

At the center of the hurricane is the **eye**—a core of warm, relatively calm air with low pressure and light winds.

Beyond the eye wall, spiraling bands of clouds called **rain bands** circle the center of the hurricane. The rain bands produce heavy rains and high winds. Within this area of the hurricane, wind speed decreases as the distance from the eye wall increases.

Updraft

Downdraft

Answer to Reading Check
Hurricanes get their energy from the condensation of water vapor.

Damage Caused by Hurricanes

Hurricanes can cause a lot of damage when they move near or onto land. Wind speeds of most hurricanes range from 120 to 150 km/h. Some can reach speeds as high as 300 km/h. Hurricane winds can knock down trees and telephone poles and can damage and destroy buildings and homes.

While high winds cause a great deal of damage, most hurricane damage is caused by flooding associated with heavy rains and storm surges. A *storm surge* is a wall of water that builds up over the ocean because of the strong winds and low atmospheric pressure. The wall of water gets bigger as it nears the shore, and it reaches its greatest height when it crashes onto the shore. Depending on the hurricane's strength, a storm surge can be 1 to 8 m high and 65 to 160 km long. Flooding causes tremendous damage to property and lives when a storm surge moves onto shore, as shown in **Figure 9.**

Severe Weather Safety

Severe weather can be very dangerous, so it is important to keep yourself safe. One way to stay safe is to turn on the radio or TV during a storm. Your local radio and TV stations will let you know if a storm has gotten worse.

Thunderstorm Safety

Lightning is one of the most dangerous parts of a thunderstorm. Lightning is attracted to tall objects. If you are outside, stay away from trees, which can get struck down. If you are in the open, crouch down. Otherwise, you will be the tallest object in the area! Stay away from bodies of water. If lightning hits water while you are in it, you could be hurt or could even die.

Figure 9 *A hurricane's storm surge can cause severe damage to homes near the shoreline.*

Natural Disaster Plan

WRITING SKILL Every family should have a plan to deal with weather emergencies. With a parent, discuss what your family should do in the event of severe weather. Together, write up a plan for your family to follow in case of a natural disaster. Also, make a disaster supply kit that includes enough food and water to last several days.

Hurricane Tracking Meteorologists know where to look for hurricanes. Most hurricanes originate in an area called the *doldrums*, a narrow zone near the equator, and move in a curved path like a parabola. People have been tracking hurricanes for more than 50 years. New instruments, such as radar and geosynchronous weather satellites, allow meteorologists to track building pressure systems and make predictions about the path a tropical storm or a hurricane may take. U.S. military aircraft have even been used for informational reconnaissance, flying into hurricanes to measure wind velocities and direction, pressure, thermal structure, and the location of the eye. The ability to identify potential storm threats allows communities in the path of a hurricane time to prepare for the storm or to evacuate to safety. The National Hurricane Center monitors and stores information on hurricanes. Have students track a hurricane and write an autobiography of a hurricane from its birth to its death.
LS Verbal

MISCONCEPTION ALERT

Tropical Storm or Hurricane? Students may be confused by the terms *tropical storm* and *hurricane*. The difference between a hurricane and a tropical storm is wind speed. To qualify as a tropical storm, the wind speed must be at least 63 km/h but no greater than 119 km/h. If wind speed is greater than 119 km/h, the storm is considered to be a hurricane.

Figure 10 *During a tornado warning, it is best to protect yourself by crouching against a wall and covering the back of your head and neck with your hands or a book.*

Tornado Safety

Weather forecasters use watches and warnings to let people know about tornadoes. A *watch* is a weather alert that lets people know that a tornado may happen. A *warning* is a weather alert that lets people know that a tornado has been spotted.

If there is a tornado warning for your area, find shelter quickly. The best place to go is a basement or cellar. Or you can go to a windowless room in the center of the building, such as a bathroom, closet, or hallway, as **Figure 10** shows. If you are outside, lie down in a large, open field or a deep ditch.

Flood Safety

An area can get so much rain that it begins to flood. So, like tornadoes, floods have watches and warnings. However, little warning can usually be given. A flash flood is a flood that rises and falls very suddenly. The best thing to do during a flood is to find a high place to wait out the flood. You should always stay out of floodwaters. Even shallow water can be dangerous if it is moving fast.

Figure 11 *These store owners are boarding up their windows to protect the windows from strong winds during a hurricane.*

Hurricane Safety

If a hurricane is in your area, your local TV or radio station will keep you updated on its condition. People living on the shore may be asked to evacuate the area. If you live in an area where hurricanes strike, your family should have a disaster supply kit that includes enough water and food to last several days. To protect the windows in your home, you should cover them with plywood, as shown in **Figure 11.** Most important, you must stay indoors during the storm.

Science Bloopers

Native Meteorologists The Seminole Indians of Florida have used their own observations of nature to successfully predict severe weather. In one instance, their observations of plants and animals indicated that a hurricane was approaching. Although the weather bureau predicted the storm would miss the area, the Seminoles evacuated—and were spared the storm's destruction. In another instance, meteorologists were so sure of their predictions of a hurricane approaching that heavy equipment was moved away from the endangered area so that it would be available later to help relief efforts. The Seminoles thought otherwise and remained in the area. The hurricane never reached Florida.

Summary

- Thunderstorms are intense weather systems that produce strong winds, heavy rain, lightning, and thunder.
- Lightning is a large electric discharge that occurs between two oppositely charged surfaces. Lightning releases a great deal of energy and can be very dangerous.
- Tornadoes are small, rotating columns of air that touch the ground and can cause severe damage.

- A hurricane is a large, rotating tropical weather system. Hurricanes cause strong winds and can cause severe property damage.
- In the event of severe weather, it is important to stay safe. Listening to your local TV or radio station for updates and remaining indoors and away from windows are good rules to follow.

Using Key Terms

Complete each of the following sentences by choosing the correct term from the word bank.

| hurricane | storm surge |
| tornado | lightning |

1. Thunderstorms are very active electrically and often cause ___.

2. A ___ forms when a funnel cloud pokes through the bottom of a cumulonimbus cloud and makes contact with the ground.

Understanding Key Ideas

3. The safest thing to do if you are caught outdoors during a tornado is to
   a. stay near buildings and roads.
   b. head for an open area.
   c. seek shelter near a large tree.
   d. None of the above

4. Describe how tornadoes form.

5. At what latitudes do hurricanes usually form?

6. What is lightning? What happens when lightning strikes?

Critical Thinking

7. **Applying Concepts** What items do you think you would need in a disaster kit? Explain.

8. **Identifying Relationships** What happens to a hurricane as it moves over land? Explain.

Interpreting Graphics

Use the diagram below to answer the questions that follow.

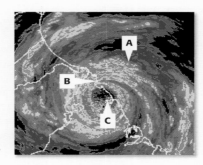

9. Describe what is happening at point C.
10. What is point B?
11. What kind of weather can you expect at point A?

Developed and maintained by the National Science Teachers Association

For a variety of links related to this chapter, go to www.scilinks.org

Topic: Severe Weather
SciLinks code: HSM1383

CHAPTER RESOURCES

Chapter Resource File

- Section Quiz GENERAL
- Section Review GENERAL
- Vocabulary and Section Summary GENERAL
- Reinforcement Worksheet BASIC
- SciLinks Activity GENERAL

SECTION
4

Focus

Overview

This section introduces instruments used to forecast and report the weather, such as thermometers, barometers, weather balloons, and radar. Students will also learn how meteorologists use weather maps to depict the data they gather.

Bellringer

Pose this question to students: "If you did not have the benefit of the weather forecast on the news, radio, or television, how would you forecast the weather?" (Answers will vary. Possible answers include observing the sky and noticing the direction and intensity of the winds.)

Motivate

Demonstration — GENERAL

Air Pressure and Barometers
Low pressure usually indicates stormy weather, and high pressure usually indicates clear weather. If possible, show students a barometer, and tell them that barometers are still widely used in weather forecasting. Show students how to read a barometer and how to use the movable pointer to track if air pressure is increasing or decreasing. **English Language Learners**
LS Visual

READING WARM-UP

Objectives
● Describe the different types of instruments used to take weather measurements.
● Explain how radar and weather satellites help meteorologists forecast the weather.
● Explain how to interpret a weather map.

Terms to Learn
thermometer
barometer
anemometer

READING STRATEGY

Reading Organizer As you read this section, make a table comparing the different instruments used to collect weather data.

Forecasting the Weather

You watch the weather forecast on the evening news. The news is good—there's no rain in sight. But how can the weather forecasters tell that it won't rain?

Weather affects how you dress and how you plan your day, so it is important to get accurate weather forecasts. But where do weather reporters get their information? And how do they predict the weather? A *weather forecast* is a prediction of weather conditions over the next 3 to 5 days. A *meteorologist* is a person who observes and collects data on atmospheric conditions to make weather predictions. In this section, you will learn how weather data are collected and shown.

Weather-Forecasting Technology

To accurately forecast the weather, meteorologists need to measure various atmospheric conditions, such as air pressure, humidity, precipitation, temperature, wind speed, and wind direction. Meteorologists use special instruments to collect data on weather conditions both near and far above Earth's surface.

High in the Sky

Weather balloons carry electronic equipment that can measure weather conditions as high as 30 km above Earth's surface. Weather balloons, such as the one in **Figure 1,** carry equipment that measures temperature, air pressure, and relative humidity. By tracking the balloons, meteorologists can also measure wind speed and direction.

✓ Reading Check How do meteorologists gather data on atmospheric conditions above Earth's surface? (*See the Appendix for answers to Reading Check.*)

Figure 1 *Weather balloons carry radio transmitters that send measurements to stations on the ground.*

CHAPTER RESOURCES

Chapter Resource File

📁 • **Lesson Plan**
   • **Directed Reading A** BASIC
   • **Directed Reading B** SPECIAL NEEDS

Technology

💾 **Transparencies**
   • Bellringer

Answer to Reading Check

Meteorologists use weather balloons to collect atmospheric data above Earth's surface.

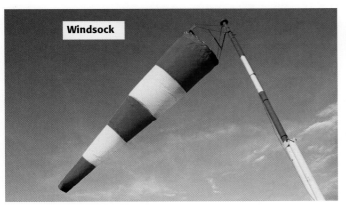

Windsock

Figure 2 *Meteorologists use these tools to collect atmospheric data.*

Thermometer

Anemometer

Measuring Air Temperature and Pressure

A tool used to measure air temperature is called a **thermometer.** Most thermometers use a liquid sealed in a narrow glass tube, as shown in **Figure 2.** When air temperature increases, the liquid expands and moves up the glass tube. As air temperature decreases, the liquid shrinks and moves down the tube.

A **barometer** is an instrument used to measure air pressure. A mercurial barometer consists of a glass tube that is sealed at one end and placed in a container full of mercury. As the air pressure pushes on the mercury inside the container, the mercury moves up the glass tube. The greater the air pressure is, the higher the mercury will rise.

Measuring Wind Direction

Wind direction can be measured by using a windsock or a wind vane. A windsock, shown in **Figure 2,** is a cone-shaped cloth bag open at both ends. The wind enters through the wide end and leaves through the narrow end. Therefore, the wide end points into the wind. A wind vane is shaped like an arrow with a large tail and is attached to a pole. As the wind pushes the tail of the wind vane, the wind vane spins on the pole until the arrow points into the wind.

Measuring Wind Speed

An instrument used to measure wind speed is called an **anemometer.** An anemometer, as shown in **Figure 2,** consists of three or four cups connected by spokes to a pole. The wind pushes on the hollow sides of the cups and causes the cups to rotate on the pole. The motion sends a weak electric current that is measured and displayed on a dial.

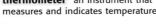

thermometer an instrument that measures and indicates temperature

barometer an instrument that measures atmospheric pressure

anemometer an instrument used to measure wind speed

Close

Reteaching — **BASIC**

Temperature Versus Pressure
Ask students what the difference is between a thermometer and a barometer. (A thermometer is sealed at both ends, so temperature is the only factor affecting the liquid. A barometer is open to the air at one end and subject to changes in air pressure.) Have students build models of each using two straws, colored water, clay for sealing the ends of the straws, and a paper cup. **LS** Kinesthetic

Quiz — **GENERAL**

1. What advantage do weather satellites have over ground-based weather stations? (Satellites can gather weather data at different altitudes and can track large systems better than land-based instruments can.)

2. Why are so many station models used to gather weather data in the United States? (The United States is very large, and Earth's atmosphere is constantly changing. Data from many stations help make forecasts more accurate.)

Alternative Assessment — **GENERAL**

Making a Weather Map Have students use the weather report from their local newspaper over a 1-week period to construct a picture of local weather conditions. Then, tell students to analyze their findings by applying what they have learned in this chapter. **LS** Visual

Figure 3 *Using Doppler radar, meteorologists can predict a tornado up to 20 minutes before it touches the ground.*

CONNECTION TO Biology

WRITING SKILL **Predicting the Weather** Throughout history, people have predicted approaching weather by interpreting natural signs. Animals and plants are usually more sensitive to changes in atmospheric conditions, such as air pressure, humidity, and temperature, than humans are. To find out more about natural signs, research this topic at the library or on the Internet. Write a short paper on your findings to share with the class.

Radar and Satellites

Radar is used to find the location, movement, and amount of precipitation. It can also detect what form of precipitation a weather system is carrying. You might have seen a kind of radar called *Doppler radar* used in a local TV weather report. **Figure 3** shows how Doppler radar is used to track precipitation. *Weather satellites* that orbit Earth provide the images of weather systems that you see on TV weather reports. Satellites can track storms and measure wind speeds, humidity, and temperatures at different altitudes.

Weather Maps

In the United States, the National Weather Service (NWS) and the National Oceanic and Atmospheric Administration (NOAA) collect and analyze weather data. The NWS produces weather maps based on information gathered from about 1,000 weather stations across the United States. On these maps, each station is represented by a station model. A *station model* is a small circle that shows the location of the weather station. As shown in **Figure 4,** surrounding the small circle is a set of symbols and numbers, which represent the weather data.

Figure 4 **A Station Model**

- Temperature (°F) — 38
- Amount of cloud cover
- Type of precipitation
- Dew point temperature (°F) — 27
- 196 Abbreviated version of barometric pressure in millibars
- Wind speed
- Wind direction

Is That a Fact!

Bats use the Doppler effect to locate prey and to navigate. Bats emit high-frequency sounds that bounce off objects. If the objects are moving, then the wave frequency changes. If the frequency does not change, then the bat knows the object is stationary.

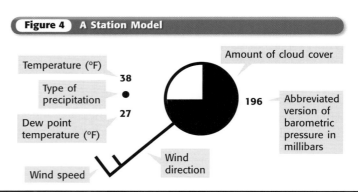

CONNECTION ACTIVITY
Math — **GENERAL**

Temperature Conversion Have students use the formulas below to convert 32°F, 72°F, and 5°F into degrees Celsius. Then, have students convert 100°C, 45°C, and 21°C into degrees Fahrenheit.

$°C = (°F − 32) × 5/9$

$°F = (°C × 9/5) + 32$

(0°C, 22.2°C, −15°C; 212°F, 113°F, 69.8°F)
LS Logical

Reading a Weather Map

Weather maps that you see on TV include lines called *isobars*. Isobars are lines that connect points of equal air pressure. Isobars that form closed circles represent areas of high or low pressure. These areas are usually marked on a map with a capital *H* or *L*. Fronts are also labeled on weather maps, as you can see on the weather map in **Figure 5**.

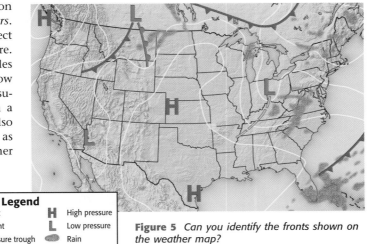

Legend

⌄⌄	Cold front	**H**	High pressure
⌒⌒	Warm front	**L**	Low pressure
═══	Low pressure trough	🌧	Rain
▨	Isobar		Fog

Figure 5 *Can you identify the fronts shown on the weather map?*

Using Key Terms

1. In your own words, write a definition for each of the following terms: *thermometer, barometer,* and *anemometer.*

Understanding Key Ideas

2. Which of the following instruments measures air pressure?
   a. thermometer
   b. barometer
   c. anemometer
   d. windsock

3. How does radar help meteorologists forecast the weather?

4. What does a station model represent?

Math Skills

5. If it is 75°F outside, what is the temperature in degrees Celsius? (Hint: $°F = (°C \times 9/5) + 32$)

Critical Thinking

6. **Applying Concepts** Why would a meteorologist compare a new weather map with one that is 24 h old?

7. **Making Inferences** In the United States, why is weather data gathered from a large number of station models?

8. **Making Inferences** How might several station models from different regions plotted on a map help a meteorologist?

For a variety of links related to this chapter, go to www.scilinks.org

Topic: Forecasting the Weather
SciLinks code: HSM0606

Answers to Section Review

1. Sample answer: A thermometer is a device used to measure temperature. A barometer is an instrument used to measure atmospheric pressure. An anemometer is an instrument used to measure wind speed.

2. b

3. Sample answer: Radar can detect the location, movement, and amount of precipitation.

4. A station model represents the location of a weather station and the weather data collected there.

5. $75 \ °F = (°C \times 9/5) + 32$
   $°C = (75 - 32) \div 9/5$
   $°C = 43 \div 1.8$
   $°C = 23.9°C$

6. Answers may vary. Sample answer: Meteorologists would compare a new weather map with one 24 h old to see how fast a front is moving.

7. Sample answer: Because the United States is very large, a large number of station models help give a more complete picture of weather and make weather forecasts more accurate.

8. Sample answer: Several station models plotted on a map would help a meteorologist get a better visual representation of what the weather is doing across the United States.

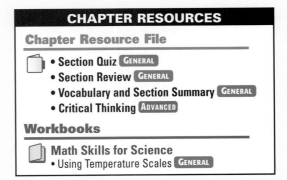

CHAPTER RESOURCES

Chapter Resource File

- Section Quiz **GENERAL**
- Section Review **GENERAL**
- Vocabulary and Section Summary **GENERAL**
- Critical Thinking **ADVANCED**

Workbooks

Math Skills for Science
- Using Temperature Scales **GENERAL**

Boiling Over!

Teacher's Notes

Time Required
One 45-minute class period

Lab Ratings

EASY —————————→ HARD

Teacher Prep 🜊
Student Set-Up 🜊🜊🜊
Concept Level 🜊🜊
Clean Up 🜊🜊

MATERIALS
The materials listed on the student page are enough for a group of 3–4 students.

Safety Caution
Remind students to review all safety cautions and icons before beginning this lab activity.

Preparation Notes
Begin the activity by leading a discussion of how thermometers work. Have students observe a regular thermometer. Ask students what parts make a thermometer work. (the bulb, a tube, and air in the tube)

Using Scientific Methods
Inquiry Lab

Boiling Over!

Safety Industries, Inc., would like to produce and sell thermometers that are safer than mercury thermometers. The company would like your team of inventors to design a thermometer that uses water instead of mercury. The company will offer a contract to the team that creates the best design of a water thermometer. Good luck!

OBJECTIVES

Construct a device that uses water to measure temperature.

Calibrate the new device by using a mercury thermometer.

MATERIALS

- bottle, plastic
- can, aluminum soda
- card, index, 3 in. × 5 in.
- clay, modeling (1 lb)
- container, yogurt, with lid
- cup, plastic-foam, large (2)
- film canister
- food coloring, red (1 bottle)
- funnel, plastic or paper cone
- gloves, heat-resistant
- hot plate
- ice, cube (5 or 6)
- pan, aluminum pie
- pitcher
- plastic tubing, 5 mm diameter, 30 cm long
- ruler, metric
- straw, plastic, inflexible, clear (1)
- tape, transparent (1 roll)
- thermometer, Celsius
- water, tap

SAFETY

Ask a Question

1. What causes the liquid in a thermometer to rise? How can I use this information to make a thermometer?

Form a Hypothesis

2. Brainstorm with a classmate to design a thermometer that uses only water to measure temperature. Sketch your design. Write a one-sentence hypothesis that describes how your thermometer will work.

Test the Hypothesis

3. Following your design, build a thermometer by using only materials from the materials list. Like a mercury thermometer, your thermometer needs a bulb and a tube. However, the liquid in your thermometer will be water.

4. To test your design, place the aluminum pie pan on a hot plate. Use the pitcher to carefully pour water into the pan until the pan is half full. Turn on the hot plate, and heat the water.

5. Put on your safety goggles and heat-resistant gloves, and carefully place the "bulb" of your thermometer in the hot water. Observe the water level in the tube. Does the water level rise?

6. If the water level does not rise, change your design as necessary and repeat steps 3–5. When the water level in your thermometer does rise, sketch the design of this thermometer as your final design.

7. After you decide on your final design, you must calibrate your thermometer by using a laboratory thermometer. Tape an index card to your thermometer's tube so that the part of the tube that sticks out from the "bulb" of your thermometer touches the card.

Daniel Bugenhagen
Yutan Jr.–Sr. High
Yutan, Nebraska

CHAPTER RESOURCES

Chapter Resource File
- **Datasheet for Chapter Lab**
- **Lab Notes and Answers**

Technology

 Classroom Videos
- Lab Video

LabBook

- Watching the Weather
- Let It Snow!
- Gone with the Wind

8 Place the plastic funnel or the cone-shaped paper funnel into a plastic-foam cup. Carefully pour hot water from the pie pan into the funnel. Be sure that no water splashes or spills.

9 Place your thermometer and a laboratory thermometer in the hot water. As your thermometer's water level rises, mark the level on the index card. At the same time, observe and record the temperature of the laboratory thermometer, and write this value beside your mark on the card.

10 Repeat steps 8–9 using warm tap water.

11 Repeat steps 8–9 using ice water.

12 Draw evenly spaced scale markings between your temperature markings on the index card. Write the temperatures that correspond to the scale marks on the index card.

Analyze the Results

1 **Analyzing Results** How well does your thermometer measure temperature?

Draw Conclusions

2 **Drawing Conclusions** Compare your thermometer design with other students' designs. How would you change your design to make your thermometer measure temperature better?

3 **Applying Conclusions** Take a class vote to see which design should be used by Safety Industries. Why was this thermometer design chosen? How did it differ from other designs in the class?

Lab Notes

A water thermometer has a receptacle containing water and air and a tube protruding from the receptacle. A trick to getting the water thermometer to work well is to allow a lot of air in the "bulb" because air expands more than water. As the air heats, it expands and pushes the water upward in the tube. One way to build such a thermometer is to put a straw in a soda can and seal the opening of the can with modeling clay so that water can escape only by moving upward, out of the straw. It is important that students' thermometers are tightly sealed. A sample design is shown below.

Analyze the Results
1. Answers may vary. Accept all reasonable responses.

Draw Conclusions
2. Answers may vary. Accept all reasonable responses.
3. Accept all reasonable responses.

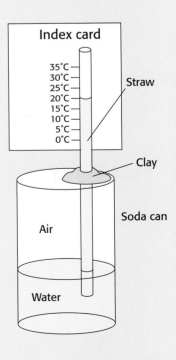

Chapter Review

Assignment Guide

SECTION	QUESTIONS
1	1, 2, 7–12, 17, 21, 29–32
2	3, 4, 13–14, 18, 19
3	5, 15, 20, 22–28
4	6, 16
2 and 3	24
2 and 4	33, 34

ANSWERS

Using Key Terms

1. Relative humidity is the amount of water vapor the air contains relative to the maximum amount it can hold at a given temperature. Dew point is the temperature to which air must cool to be saturated.

2. Condensation is the change of state from a gas to a liquid. Precipitation is water that falls from the atmosphere to the Earth.

3. An air mass is a large body of air that has the same moisture and temperature throughout. A front is the boundary between two different air masses.

4. Lightning is a large electric discharge that occurs between two oppositely charged surfaces. Thunder is the sound that results from the rapid expansion of air along a lightning strike.

USING KEY TERMS

For each pair of terms, explain how the meanings of the terms differ.

1. *relative humidity* and *dew point*

2. *condensation* and *precipitation*

3. *air mass* and *front*

4. *lightning* and *thunder*

5. *tornado* and *hurricane*

6. *barometer* and *anemometer*

UNDERSTANDING KEY IDEAS

Multiple Choice

7. The process in which water changes from a liquid to gas is called
   a. precipitation.
   b. condensation.
   c. evaporation.
   d. water vapor.

8. What is the relative humidity of air at its dew point?
   a. 0%   c. 75%
   b. 50%   d. 100%

9. Which of the following is NOT a type of condensation?
   a. fog   c. snow
   b. cloud   d. dew

10. High clouds made of ice crystals are called ___ clouds.
    a. stratus   c. nimbostratus
    b. cumulus   d. cirrus

11. Large thunderhead clouds that produce precipitation are called ___ clouds.
    a. nimbostratus   c. cumulus
    b. cumulonimbus   d. stratus

12. Strong updrafts within a thunderhead can produce
    a. snow.   c. sleet.
    b. rain.   d. hail.

13. A maritime tropical air mass contains
    a. warm, wet air.   c. warm, dry air.
    b. cold, moist air. d. cold, dry air.

14. A front that forms when a warm air mass is trapped between cold air masses and is forced to rise is a(n)
    a. stationary front. c. occluded front.
    b. warm front.   d. cold front.

15. A severe storm that forms as a rapidly rotating funnel cloud is called a
    a. hurricane.   c. typhoon.
    b. tornado.   d. thunderstorm.

16. The lines connecting points of equal air pressure on a weather map are called
    a. contour lines.   c. isobars.
    b. highs.   d. lows.

Short Answer

17. Explain the relationship between condensation and dew point.

5. A tornado is a small, rotating column of air with high wind speed that touches the ground. A hurricane is a large, rotating tropical weather system with wind speeds equal to or greater than 119 km/h.

6. A barometer is an instrument used to measure air pressure. An anemometer is an instrument used to measure wind speed.

Understanding Key Ideas

7. c	12. d
8. d	13. a
9. c	14. c
10. d	15. b
11. b	16. c

17. Air must cool to a temperature below its dew point before condensation can occur.

18. Stationary fronts generally bring many days of cloudy, wet weather.

19. An air mass that forms over the Gulf of Mexico is warm and wet.

18 Describe the conditions along a stationary front.

19 What are the characteristics of an air mass that forms over the Gulf of Mexico?

20 Explain how a hurricane develops.

21 Describe the water cycle, and explain how it affects weather.

22 List the major similarities and differences between hurricanes and tornadoes.

23 Explain how a tornado forms.

24 Describe an interaction between weather and ocean systems.

25 What is a station model? What types of information do station models provide?

26 What type of technology is used to locate and measure the amount of precipitation in an area?

27 List two ways to keep yourself informed during severe weather.

28 Explain why staying away from flood-water is important even when the water is shallow.

29 **Concept Mapping** Use the following terms to create a concept map: *evaporation*, *relative humidity*, *water vapor*, *dew*, *psychrometer*, *clouds*, and *fog*.

30 **Making Inferences** If both the air temperature and the amount of water vapor in the air change, is it possible for the relative humidity to stay the same? Explain.

31 **Applying Concepts** What can you assume about the amount of water vapor in the air if there is no difference between the wet- and dry-bulb readings of a psychrometer?

32 **Identifying Relationships** Explain why the concept of relative humidity is important to understanding weather.

INTERPRETING GRAPHICS

Use the weather map below to answer the questions that follow.

33 Where are thunderstorms most likely to occur? Explain your answer.

34 What are the weather conditions in Tulsa, Oklahoma? Explain your answer.

---

20. A hurricane begins as a group of thunderstorms moving over tropical ocean waters. Winds traveling in two different directions collide, which causes the storm to rotate over an area of low pressure. The hurricane is fueled by the condensation of water vapor.

21. The water cycle is the continuous movement of water from the Earth's surface, to the air, and back to the surface. Weather is affected by evaporation, condensation, and precipitation of water in the air.

CHAPTER RESOURCES

Chapter Resource File

- Chapter Review **GENERAL**
- Chapter Test A **GENERAL**
- Chapter Test B **ADVANCED**
- Chapter Test C **SPECIAL NEEDS**
- Vocabulary Activity **GENERAL**

Workbooks

Study Guide
- Assessment resources are also available in Spanish.

---

22. Sample answer: Both begin as a result of thunderstorms and are centered around low pressure. Hurricanes occur over water, and tornadoes generally occur over land.

23. Cold, dry air meets warm, moist air and starts to spin. Updrafts of air turn the spinning column vertical. The column moves to the bottom of the cloud and becomes a funnel cloud. A funnel cloud becomes a tornado when it touches the ground.

24. Sample answer: Evaporating ocean water fuels hurricanes in tropical regions.

25. Sample answer: A station model represents the location of a weather station and shows temperature, precipitation, wind direction, and other data.

26. Radar is used to find the location, movement, and amount of precipitation.

27. Sample answer: Turn the TV and radio to local stations for weather information.

28. Sample answer: Even shallow water can be dangerous if it is moving quickly.

Critical Thinking

29. An answer to this exercise can be found at the end of this book.

30. Sample answer: If air temperature rises, then the air can hold more water. If vapor content in the air also increases, then relative humidity could stay the same.

31. Sample answer: It can be assumed that the relative humidity is 100% because no water evaporated.

32. Sample answer: Precipitation can occur only when the air is saturated, which is when the relative humidity is 100%.

Interpreting Graphics

33. Thunderstorms are most likely to occur in Chicago because a cold front is approaching.

34. Tulsa is experiencing a stationary front and is probably receiving drizzly precipitation.

Standardized Test Preparation

Standardized Test Preparation

Teacher's Note

To provide practice under more realistic testing conditions, give students 20 minutes to answer all of the questions in this Standardized Test Preparation.

MISCONCEPTION ALERT

Answers to the standardized test preparation can help you identify student misconceptions and misunderstandings.

READING

Passage 1

1. B
2. H
3. D

✚ TEST DOCTOR

Question 3: Students may think that all the answer choices could be correct. It is true that violent tornadoes can destroy paved roads, damage crops, and damage homes. However, the question asks for a characteristic of violent storms. Answers A, B, and C list things a tornado can do, which are actions, not characteristics. The only answer that describes a characteristic of violent tornadoes is answer D.

READING

Read each of the passages below. Then, answer the questions that follow each passage.

Passage 1 In May 1997, a springtime tornado <u>wreaked</u> havoc on Jarrell, Texas. The Jarrell tornado was a powerful tornado, whose wind speeds were estimated at more than 410 km/h. The winds of the twister were so strong that they peeled the asphalt from paved roads, stripped fields of corn bare, and destroyed an entire neighborhood. Some tornadoes, such as the one that struck the town of Jarrell, are classified as violent tornadoes. Only 2% of the tornadoes that occur in the United States are categorized as violent tornadoes. Despite the fact that these types of tornadoes do not occur often, 70% of all tornado-related deaths are a result of violent tornadoes.

1. In the passage, what does the word *wreaked* mean?
   A smelled
   B caused
   C prevented
   D removed

2. Which of the following can be concluded from the passage?
   F Tornadoes often hit Jarrell, Texas.
   G Most tornadoes fall into the violent category.
   H The tornado that hit Jarrell was a rare type of tornado.
   I Tornadoes always happen during the spring.

3. Which of the following **best** describes a characteristic of violent tornadoes?
   A Violent tornadoes destroy paved roads.
   B Violent tornadoes damage crops.
   C Violent tornadoes damage homes.
   D Violent tornadoes have extremely strong winds.

Passage 2 Water evaporates into the air from Earth's surface. This water returns to Earth's surface as <u>precipitation</u>. Precipitation is water, in solid or liquid form, that falls from the air to Earth. The four major types of precipitation are rain, snow, sleet, and hail. The most common form of precipitation is rain.

A cloud produces rain when the cloud's water drops become large enough to fall. A raindrop begins as a water droplet that is smaller than the period at the end of this sentence. Before a water drop falls as rain, it must become about 100 times this beginning size. Water drops get larger by joining with other water drops. When the water drops become too heavy, they fall as precipitation.

1. In this passage, what does *precipitation* mean?
   A acceleration
   B haste
   C water that falls from the atmosphere to Earth
   D separating a substance from a solution as a solid

2. What is the main idea of the second paragraph?
   F Rain occurs when the water droplets in clouds become large enough to fall.
   G Raindrops are very small at first.
   H Water droplets join with other water droplets to become larger.
   I Rain is a form of precipitation.

3. According to the passage, which step happens last in the formation of precipitation?
   A Water droplets join.
   B Water droplets fall to the ground.
   C Water droplets become heavy.
   D Water evaporates into the air.

Passage 2

1. C
2. F
3. B

✚ TEST DOCTOR

Question 1: Both answers C and D are correct definitions for the word "precipitation." However, in this paragraph precipitation is defined as water returning to Earth's surface, so only answer C is correct.

Use each diagram below to answer the question that follows each diagram.

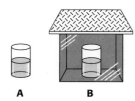

A   **B**

1. During an experiment, the setup shown in the diagram above is maintained for 72 h. Which of the following is the most likely outcome?

A Beaker A will hold less water than beaker B will.

B The amount of water in beaker A and beaker B will stay the same.

C The amount of water in beaker A and beaker B will change by about the same amount.

D Beaker B will hold less water than beaker A will.

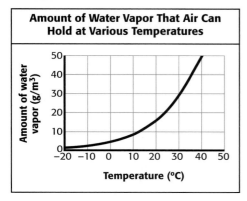

Amount of Water Vapor That Air Can Hold at Various Temperatures

2. Look at the line graph above. Which statement is consistent with the line graph?

F The ability of air to hold moisture increases as temperature increases.

G The ability of air to hold moisture decreases as temperature increases.

H The ability of air to hold moisture decreases and then increases as temperature increases.

I The ability of air to hold moisture stays the same regardless of temperature.

Read each question below, and choose the best answer.

1. The speed of light is 3.00×10^8 m/s. What is another way to express this measure?

A 3,000,000,000 m/s

B 300,000,000 m/s

C 3,000,000 m/s

D 300,000 m/s

2. A hurricane is moving 122 km/h. How long will it take to hit the coast, which is 549 km away?

F 4.2 h

G 4.5 h

H 4.8 h

I 5.2 h

3. A front is moving 15 km/h in an easterly direction. At that rate, how far will the front travel in 12 h?

A 0.8 km

B 1.25 km

C 27 km

D 180 km

4. On average, 2 out of every 100 tornadoes are classified as violent tornadoes. If there are 400 tornadoes in 1 year, which is the best prediction of the number of tornadoes that will be classified as violent tornadoes during that year?

F 2

G 4

H 8

I 16

5. The air temperature in the morning was 27°C. During the day, a front moved into the region and caused the temperature to drop to 18°C. By how many degrees did the temperature drop?

A 1°C

B 9°C

C 11°C

D 19°C

Standardized Test Preparation

TEST DOCTOR

Question 2: Some students may have difficulty interpreting graphs. To help students understand trends in graphs, have them choose two places on the curved line in the graph. It is best if students choose points that are easy to evaluate, such as points where grid lines cross. On this graph, students could choose the points where $x = 10$, $y = 10$ and $x = 30$, $y = 30$. Then, ask students to notice that when one number increased, the other also increased.

MATH

1. B
2. G
3. D
4. H
5. B

TEST DOCTOR

Question 4: This question asks students to evaluate a ratio. Students may have difficulty deciding which numbers should go together when comparing the ratio. Tell students to look for the words *out of* as a clue about which numbers are part of the same fraction in a ratio. In this case, "2 out of every 100 tornadoes" would indicate a fraction of 2/100. Then, the question can be interpreted as "How many tornadoes out of 400 are violent?" This interpretation produces a fraction of x/400.

CHAPTER RESOURCES

Chapter Resource File

 • Standardized Test Preparation **GENERAL**

State Resources

For specific resources for your state, visit **go.hrw.com** and type in the keyword **HSMSTR.**

Science Fiction

Background

Ray Bradbury is one of the world's most celebrated writers. He was born in the small town of Waukegan, Illinois, in 1920. He and his family moved several times and eventually ended up in Los Angeles. There he began a writing career that has spanned more than 60 years!

Bradbury has earned top honors in the field of literature, including the World Fantasy Award for lifetime work and the Grand Master Award from Science Fiction Writers of America. An unusual honor came when an astronaut named a crater on the moon Dandelion Crater after Ray Bradbury's novel *Dandelion Wine*.

Weird Science

CONNECTION ACTIVITY
History ——————— **BASIC**

Have students research a list of traditional weather signs. Once a class list is compiled, begin keeping a weather log. Students should record observations, make a prediction, and then check their predictions the following day.

Science in Action

Science Fiction

"All Summer in a Day" by Ray Bradbury

It is raining, just as it has been for seven long years. For the people who live on Venus, constant rain is a fact of life. But today is a special day—a day when the rain stops and the sun shines. This day comes once every seven years. At school, the students have been looking forward to this day for weeks. But Margot longs to see the sun even more than the others do. The reason for her longing makes the other kids jealous, and jealous kids can be cruel. What happens to Margot? Find out by reading Ray Bradbury's "All Summer in a Day" in the *Holt Anthology of Science Fiction*.

Language Arts ACTIVITY

WRITING SKILL What would living in a place where it rained all day and every day for seven years be like? Write a short story describing what your life would be like if you lived in such a place. In your story, describe what you and your friends would do for fun after school.

Weird Science

Can Animals Forecast the Weather?

Before ways of making sophisticated weather forecasts were developed, people observed animals and insects for evidence of changing weather. By observing the behavior of certain animals and insects, you, too, can detect changing weather! For example, did you know that birds fly higher when fair weather is coming? And a robin's song is high pitched in fair weather and low pitched as rain approaches. Ants travel in lines when rain is coming and scatter when the weather is clear. You can tell how hot the weather is by listening for the chirping of crickets—crickets chirp faster as the temperature rises!

Math ACTIVITY

To estimate the outdoor temperature in degrees Fahrenheit, count the number of times that a cricket chirps in 15 s and add 37. If you count 40 chirps in 15 s, what is the estimated temperature?

Answer to Language Arts Activity
Answers may vary. Accept any reasonable answer.

Answer to Math Activity
40 chirps + 37 = 77°F

Cristy Mitchell

Meteorologist Predicting floods, observing a tornado develop inside a storm, watching the growth of a hurricane, and issuing flood warnings are all in a day's work for Cristy Mitchell. As a meteorologist for the National Weather Service, Mitchell spends each working day observing the powerful forces of nature. When asked what made her job interesting, Mitchell replied, "There's nothing like the adrenaline rush you get when you see a tornado coming!"

Perhaps the most familiar field of meteorology is weather forecasting. However, meteorology is also used in air-pollution control, weather control, agricultural planning, and even criminal and civil investigations. Meteorologists also study trends in Earth's climate.

Meteorologists such as Mitchell use high-tech tools—computers and satellites—to collect data. By analyzing such data, Mitchell is able to forecast the weather.

Social Studies ACTIVITY

An almanac is a type of calendar that contains various information, including weather forecasts and astronomical data, for every day of the year. Many people used almanacs before meteorologists started to forecast the weather on TV. Use an almanac from the library to find out what the weather was on the day that you were born.

go.hrw.com

To learn more about these Science in Action topics, visit go.hrw.com and type in the keyword HZ5WEAF.

Current Science

Check out Current Science® articles related to this chapter by visiting go.hrw.com. Just type in the keyword HZ5CS16.

Climate
Chapter Planning Guide

Compression guide:
To shorten instruction
because of time limitations,
omit Section 2.

OBJECTIVES	LABS, DEMONSTRATIONS, AND ACTIVITIES	TECHNOLOGY RESOURCES
PACING • 90 min pp. 72–81 **Chapter Opener**	SE **Start-up Activity**, p. 73 GENERAL	OSP **Parent Letter** ■ GENERAL CD **Student Edition on CD-ROM** CD **Guided Reading Audio CD** ■ TR **Chapter Starter Transparency*** VID **Brain Food Video Quiz**
Section 1 What is Climate? • Explain the difference between weather and climate. • Identify five factors that determine climates. • Identify the three climate zones of the world.	TE **Connection Activity** Math, p. 75 GENERAL TE **Activity** Modeling the Earth and Sun, p. 76 ◆ BASIC SE **Quick Lab** A Cool Breeze, p. 77 GENERAL CRF **Datasheet for Quick Lab*** TE **Connection Activity** Geography, p. 77 ADVANCED SE **School-to-Home Activity** Using a Map, p. 78 GENERAL SE **Skills Practice Lab** Biome Business, p. 98 GENERAL CRF **Datasheet for Chapter Lab*** SE **Skills Practice Lab** For the Birds, p. 115 GENERAL CRF **Datasheet for LabBook*** LB **Whiz-Bang Demonstrations** How Humid Is It?* GENERAL	CRF **Lesson Plans*** TR **Bellringer Transparency*** TR The Seasons* TR The Circulation of Warm and Cold Air* TR The Earth's Land Biomes* VID **Lab Videos for Earth Science** CD **Science Tutor**
PACING • 45 min pp. 82–85 **Section 2 The Tropics** • Locate and describe the tropical zone. • Describe the biomes found in the tropical zone.	TE **Activity** Country Profile, p. 82 GENERAL TE **Connection Activity** Life Science, p. 83 GENERAL SE **Science in Action** Math, Social Studies, and Language Arts Activities, pp. 104–105 GENERAL	CRF **Lesson Plans*** TR **Bellringer Transparency*** TR *LINK TO LIFE SCIENCE* Gas Exchange in Leaves* CRF **SciLinks Activity*** GENERAL CD **Science Tutor**
PACING • 45 min pp. 86–91 **Section 3 Temperate and Polar Zones** • Locate and describe the temperate zone and the polar zone. • Describe the different biomes found in the temperate zone and the polar zone. • Explain what a microclimate is.	TE **Activity** Camp Climate, p. 86 GENERAL TE **Demonstration** Mock Permafrost, p. 89 ◆ GENERAL SE **School-to-Home Activity** Your Biome, p. 90 GENERAL LB **Calculator-Based Labs** What Causes the Seasons?* ◆ ADVANCED SE **Connection to Physics** Hot Roofs!, p. 91 ◆ GENERAL	CRF **Lesson Plans*** TR **Bellringer Transparency*** CD **Science Tutor**
PACING • 45 min pp. 92–97 **Section 4 Changes in Climate** • Describe how the Earth's climate has changed over time. • Summarize four different theories that attempt to explain why the Earth's climate has changed. • Explain the greenhouse effect and its role in global warming.	TE **Demonstration** The Greenhouse Effect, p. 92 ◆ GENERAL TE **Activity** Ancient Climates, p. 93 ADVANCED TE **Activity** Volcanic Eruptions, p. 94 GENERAL TE **Connection Activity** Real World, p. 95 ADVANCED SE **School-to-Home Activity** Reducing Pollution, p. 97 GENERAL LB **Long-Term Projects & Research Ideas** Sun-Starved in Fairbanks* ADVANCED	SE **Internet Activity**, p. 93 GENERAL CRF **Lesson Plans*** TR **Bellringer Transparency*** TR The Milankovitch Theory* CD **Science Tutor**

PACING • 90 min

CHAPTER REVIEW, ASSESSMENT, AND STANDARDIZED TEST PREPARATION

CRF **Vocabulary Activity*** ■ GENERAL
SE **Chapter Review**, pp. 100–101 GENERAL
CRF **Chapter Review*** ■ GENERAL
CRF **Chapter Tests A*** ■ GENERAL, **B*** ADVANCED, **C*** SPECIAL NEEDS
SE **Standardized Test Preparation**, pp. 102–103 GENERAL
CRF **Standardized Test Preparation*** GENERAL
CRF **Performance-Based Assessment*** GENERAL
OSP **Test Generator** GENERAL
CRF **Test Item Listing*** GENERAL

Online and Technology Resources

Visit **go.hrw.com** for a
variety of free resources
related to this textbook.
Enter the keyword
HZ5CLM.

Holt Online Learning

Students can access interactive
problem-solving help and active
visual concept development
with the *Holt Science and
Technology* Online Edition
available at **www.hrw.com**.

Guided Reading Audio CD
Also in Spanish

A direct reading of each chapter for
auditory learners, reluctant readers,
and Spanish-speaking students.

**Science Tutor
CD-ROM**
Excellent for remediation
and test practice.

SKILLS DEVELOPMENT RESOURCES	SECTION REVIEW AND ASSESSMENT	STANDARDS CORRELATIONS
SE Pre-Reading Activity, p. 72 `GENERAL` **OSP** Science Puzzlers, Twisters & Teasers `GENERAL`		National Science Education Standards SAI 1
CRF Directed Reading A* ■ `BASIC`, B* `SPECIAL NEEDS` **CRF** Vocabulary and Section Summary* ■ `GENERAL` **SE** Reading Strategy Discussion, p. 74 `GENERAL` **TE** Inclusion Strategies, p. 78 ◆	**SE** Reading Checks, pp. 74, 76, 78, 79, 80 `GENERAL` **TE** Homework, p. 79 **TE** Reteaching, p. 80 `BASIC` **TE** Quiz, p. 80 `GENERAL` **TE** Alternative Assessment, p. 80 `GENERAL` **SE** Section Review,* p. 81 ■ `GENERAL` **CRF** Section Quiz* ■ `GENERAL`	SAI 1; SPSP 1, 3; ES 1f, 1j, 3d; *Chapter Lab:* SAI 1; SPSP 2 *LabBook:* UCP 2, 3; SAI 1; ST 1
CRF Directed Reading A* ■ `BASIC`, B* `SPECIAL NEEDS` **CRF** Vocabulary and Section Summary* ■ `GENERAL` **SE** Reading Strategy Reading Organizer, p. 82 `GENERAL` **SE** Connection to Social Studies Living in the Tropics, p. 83 `GENERAL` **SE** Connection to Biology Animal and Plant Adaptations, p. 84 `GENERAL` **MS** Math Skills for Science Rain-Forest Math* `GENERAL` **SS** Science Skills Finding Useful Sources* `GENERAL`	**SE** Reading Checks, pp. 82, 85 `GENERAL` **TE** Reteaching, p. 84 `BASIC` **TE** Quiz, p. 84 `GENERAL` **TE** Alternative Assessment, p. 84 `GENERAL` **SE** Section Review,* p. 85 ■ `GENERAL` **CRF** Section Quiz* ■ `GENERAL`	UCP 2, 3; SAI 1, 2; ST 1; SPSP 2; HNS 1, 3
CRF Directed Reading A* ■ `BASIC`, B* `SPECIAL NEEDS` **CRF** Vocabulary and Section Summary* ■ `GENERAL` **SE** Reading Strategy Reading Organizer, p. 86 `GENERAL` **TE** Inclusion Strategies, p. 88 **CRF** Reinforcement Worksheet A Tale of Three Climates* `BASIC`	**SE** Reading Checks, pp. 86, 88, 91 `GENERAL` **TE** Homework, p. 89 `ADVANCED` **TE** Reteaching, p. 90 `BASIC` **TE** Quiz, p. 90 `GENERAL` **TE** Alternative Assessment, p. 90 `GENERAL` **SE** Section Review,* p. 91 ■ `GENERAL` **CRF** Section Quiz* ■ `GENERAL`	SAI 1, 2; SPSP 2; HNS 1, 3
CRF Directed Reading A* ■ `BASIC`, B* `SPECIAL NEEDS` **CRF** Vocabulary and Section Summary* ■ `GENERAL` **SE** Reading Strategy Paired Summarizing, p. 92 `GENERAL` **SE** Connection to Astronomy Sunspots, p. 95 `GENERAL` **SE** Math Practice The Ride to School, p. 96 `GENERAL` **CRF** Critical Thinking Cyberspace Heats Up* `ADVANCED` **SS** Science Skills Understanding Bias* `GENERAL`	**SE** Reading Checks, pp. 93, 94, 97 `GENERAL` **TE** Reteaching, p. 96 `BASIC` **TE** Quiz, p. 96 `GENERAL` **TE** Alternative Assessment, p. 96 `GENERAL` **SE** Section Review,* p. 97 ■ `GENERAL` **CRF** Section Quiz* ■ `GENERAL`	UCP 2, 3; SAI 1, 2; ST 2; SPSP 3, 4, 5; HNS 1; ES 1k, 2a

One-Stop Planner® CD-ROM

This convenient CD-ROM includes:
- Lab Materials QuickList Software
- Holt Calendar Planner
- Customizable Lesson Plans
- Printable Worksheets
- ExamView® Test Generator

CNN student News™

cnnstudentnews.com

Find the latest news, lesson plans, and activities related to important scientific events.

SCLINKS. NSTA

www.scilinks.org

Maintained by the **National Science Teachers Association.** See Chapter Enrichment pages for a complete list of topics.

Current Science®

Check out *Current Science* articles and activities by visiting the HRW Web site at **go.hrw.com.** Just type in the keyword **HZ5CS17T.**

Classroom Videos

- **Lab Videos** demonstrate the chapter lab.
- **Brain Food Video Quizzes** help students review the chapter material.
- **CNN Videos** bring science into your students' daily life.

Visual Resources

CHAPTER STARTER TRANSPARENCY

What If . . . ?

The brochure boasts of the most adventurous summer camp in the world. You can't wait to lace up your hiking boots and head for the outdoors. But before you fly halfway around the world, you check the recommended supply list: light summer clothes, sunscreen, rain gear, heavy down-filled jacket, ski mask, and thick gloves. Wait a minute! You are traveling to only one destination, so why are you required to bring such a wide variety of clothes? On further investigation, you learn that your outdoor adventure advertises the opportunity to "climb the climates of the world in just three days." Your destination is Africa's tallest mountain, Kilimanjaro.

You spend the first day hiking through a hot, sweltering rain forest. Day two

finds you treading through a grassy meadow that slopes up the side of the first peak, called Mawensi.

On the third day, you start to get cold. The frozen ground crunches under your feet. Within 2 hours your feet feel like blocks of ice, and breathing is difficult. You finally reach the summit just as the clouds part, revealing steam rising off the rain forest 3,000 m below. Maybe the trip was worth the effort after all.

Climate changes as elevation increases, just as it changes from the equator to the poles. In this chapter you will learn what factors affect climate, how climate is influenced by human and natural activity, and what type of environment is found in which climate.

BELLRINGER TRANSPARENCIES

Section: What Is Climate?
Pretend you are entering a contest for a free trip to a place with perfect climate. To win, write a description of your idea of the perfect climate in 25 words or less. Do you know of any real place where your dream climate really exists?

Record your response in your **science journal.**

Section: The Tropics
Imagine you are a zoologist hired to design a camel and a deer exhibit for your community's new zoo. Describe the differences between a deer and a camel. Where and in what kind of climate are you most likely to find these animals? What would you have to provide for each of these animals so they would continue to flourish?

Write your exhibit proposal in your **science journal.**

TEACHING TRANSPARENCIES

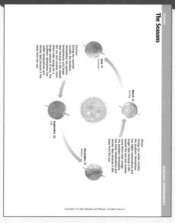

The Seasons

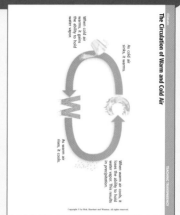

The Circulation of Warm and Cold Air

TEACHING TRANSPARENCIES

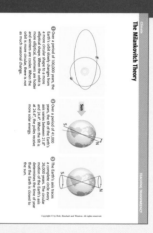

The Milankovitch Theory

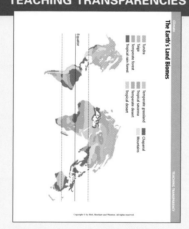

The Earth's Land Biomes

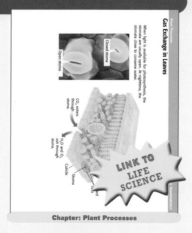

Gas Exchange in Leaves

Chapter: Plant Processes

CONCEPT MAPPING TRANSPARENCY

Use the following terms to complete the concept map below:
ocean currents, seasons, latitude, climate, prevailing winds, curved, mountains, large bodies of water

Planning Resources

LESSON PLANS

Lesson Plan   SAMPLE

Section: Waves

Pacing
Regular Schedule: with lab(s):2 days   without lab(s):2 days
Block Schedule: with lab(s):1 1/2 days   without lab(s):1 day

Objectives
1. Relate the seven properties of life to a living organism.
2. Describe seven themes that can help you to organize what you learn about science.
3. Identify the tiny structures that make up all living organisms.
4. Differentiate between reproduction and heredity and between metabolism and homeostasis.

National Science Education Standards Covered
LSInter6:Cells have particular structures that underlie their functions.
LSMat1:Most cell functions involve chemical reactions.
LSBeh1:Cells store and use information to guide their functions.
UCP1:Cell functions are regulated.
SI1: Cells can differentiate and form complete multicellular organisms.
PS1: Species evolve over time.
ESS1: The great diversity of organisms is the result of more than 3.5 billion years of evolution.
ESS2: Natural selection and its evolutionary consequences provide a scientific explanation for the fossil record of ancient life forms as well as for the striking molecular similarities observed among the diverse species of living organisms.
ST1: The millions of different species of plants, animals, and microorganisms that live on Earth today are related by descent from common ancestors.
ST2: The energy for life primarily comes from the sun.
SPSP1: The complexity and organization of organisms accommodates the need for obtaining, transforming, transporting, releasing, and eliminating the matter and energy used to sustain the organism.
SPSP6: As matter and energy flows through different levels of organization of living systems—cells, organs, communities—and between living systems and the physical environment, chemical elements are recombined in different ways.
HNS1: Organisms have behavioral responses to internal changes and to external stimuli.

PARENT LETTER

SAMPLE

Dear Parent,

Your son's or daughter's science class will soon begin exploring the chapter entitled "The World of Physical Science." In this chapter, students will learn about how the scientific method applies to the world of physical science and the role of physical science in the world. By the end of the chapter, students should demonstrate a clear understanding of the chapter's main ideas and be able to discuss the following topics:

1. physical science as the study of energy and matter (Section 1)
2. the role of physical science in the world around them (Section 1)
3. careers that rely on physical science (Section 1)
4. steps used in the scientific method (Section 2)
5. examples of technology (Section 2)
6. how the scientific method is used to answer questions and solve problems (Section 2)
7. how our knowledge of science changes over time (Section 2)
8. how models represent real objects or systems (Section 3)
9. examples of different ways models are used in science (Section 3)
10. the importance of the International System of Units (Section 4)
11. the appropriate units to use for particular measurements (Section 4)
12. how area and density are derived quantities (Section 4)

Questions to Ask Along the Way

You can help your son or daughter learn about these topics by asking interesting questions such as the following:

• What are some surprising careers that use physical science?
• What is a characteristic of a good hypothesis?
• Where is it a good idea to use a model?
• Why do Americans measure things in terms of inches and yards and meters?

ALSO IN SPANISH

TEST ITEM LISTING

TEST ITEM LISTING
The World of Earth Science   SAMPLE

MULTIPLE CHOICE

1. A limitation of models is that
   a. they are large enough to see.   c. they model unfamiliar things.
   b. they do not act exactly like the things they model.
   c. they are smaller than the things that they model.
   d. they model unfamiliar things.
   Answer: B   Difficulty: 1   Section: 3   Objective: 2

2. The length 10 m is equal to
   a. 100 cm.   c. 1,000 mm.
   b. 1,000 cm.   d. Both (b) and (c)
   Answer: B   Difficulty: 1   Section: 3   Objective: 2

3. To be valid, a hypothesis must be
   a. testable.   c. made into a law.
   b. supported by evidence.   d. Both (a) and (b)
   Answer: B   Difficulty: 1   Section: 2   Objective: 2 1

4. The statement "Sheila has a stain on her shirt" is an example of a(n)
   a. law.   c. observation.
   b. hypothesis.   d. prediction.
   Answer: B   Difficulty: 1   Section: 2   Objective: 2

5. A hypothesis is often developed out of
   a. observations.   c. laws.
   b. experiments.   d. Both (a) and (b)
   Answer: B   Difficulty: 1   Section: 2   Objective: 2

6. How many milliliters are in 3.5 kL?
   a. 3,500 mL.   c. 3,500,000 mL.
   b. 0.0035 mL.   d. 35,000 mL.
   Answer: B   Difficulty: 1   Section: 3   Objective: 2

7. A map of Seattle is an example of a
   a. law.   c. model.
   b. theory.   d. unit.
   Answer: B   Difficulty: 1   Section: 3   Objective: 2

8. A lab has the safety icons shown below. These icons mean that you should wear
   a. only safety goggles.   c. safety goggles and a lab apron.
   b. only a lab apron.   d. safety goggles, a lab apron, and gloves.
   Answer: B   Difficulty: 1   Section: 1   Objective: 2

9. The law of conservation of mass says the total mass before a chemical change is
   a. less than the total mass after the change.
   b. less than the total mass after the change.
   c. the same as the total mass after the change.
   d. not the same as the total mass after the change.
   Answer: B   Difficulty: 1   Section: 3   Objective: 2

10. In which of the following areas might you find a geochemist at work?
    a. studying the chemistry of rocks   c. studying fishes
    b. studying forestry   d. studying the atmosphere
    Answer: B   Difficulty: 1   Section: 3   Objective: 2

One-Stop Planner® CD-ROM

This CD-ROM includes all of the resources shown here and the following time-saving tools:

• *Lab Materials QuickList Software*
• *Customizable lesson plans*
• *Holt Calendar Planner*
• *The powerful ExamView® Test Generator*

Meeting Individual Needs

DIRECTED READING A
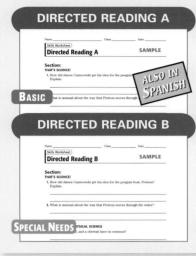
Directed Reading A — SAMPLE

Section: THAT'S SCIENCE!

1. How did James Czarnowski get his idea for the penguin... Explain.

ALSO IN SPANISH

BASIC

DIRECTED READING B
Directed Reading B — SAMPLE

Section: THAT'S SCIENCE!

1. How did James Czarnowski get his idea for the penguin boat, Proteus? Explain.

2. What is unusual about the way that Proteus moves through the water?

SPECIAL NEEDS

VOCABULARY ACTIVITY
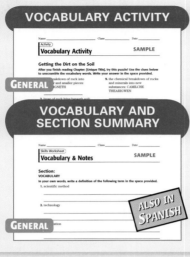
Vocabulary Activity — SAMPLE

Getting the Dirt on the Soil

After you finish reading Chapter: [Unique Title], try this puzzle! Use the clues below to unscramble the vocabulary words. Write your answer in the space provided.

GENERAL

VOCABULARY AND SECTION SUMMARY
Vocabulary & Notes — SAMPLE

Section: VOCABULARY

In your own words, write a definition of the following term in the space provided.

1. scientific method

2. technology

ALSO IN SPANISH

GENERAL

REINFORCEMENT
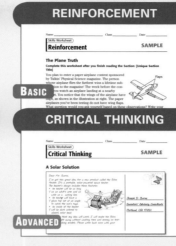
Reinforcement — SAMPLE

The Plane Truth

Complete this worksheet after you finish reading the Section: [Unique Section Title]

You plan to enter a paper airplane contest sponsored by Talkin' Physical Science magazine...

BASIC

CRITICAL THINKING
Critical Thinking — SAMPLE

A Solar Solution

ADVANCED

SCILINKS ACTIVITY
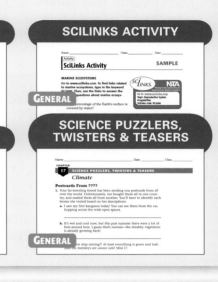
SciLinks Activity — SAMPLE

MARINE ECOSYSTEMS

GENERAL

SCIENCE PUZZLERS, TWISTERS & TEASERS
SCIENCE PUZZLERS, TWISTERS & TEASERS
Climate

Postcards From ????

1. Your far-traveling friend has been sending you postcards from all over the world...

GENERAL

Labs and Activities

LONG-TERM PROJECTS & RESEARCH IDEAS

PROJECT 45 — STUDENT WORKSHEET — DESIGN YOUR OWN

Sun-Starved in Fairbanks

It's New Year's Day in Fairbanks, Alaska. The stars shine brightly in the dark morning sky. It's 9 A.M., but the sun won't rise for at least another 2 hours!...

INTERNET KEYWORDS: Season Affective Disorder (SAD)

The Winter Blues

INTERNET KEYWORDS: Iditarod, dog sled mushers

Research Ideas

ADVANCED

WHIZ-BANG DEMONSTRATIONS
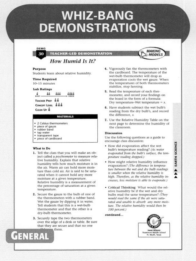
DEMO 30 — TEACHER-LED DEMONSTRATION — MAKING MODELS

How Humid Is It?

Purpose
Students learn about relative humidity.

Time Required
10–15 minutes

Lab Ratings

Materials
- 2 Celsius thermometers
- piece of gauze
- rubber band
- tap water
- transparent tape
- piece of cardboard

What to Do

Discussion

GENERAL

CALCULATOR-BASED LABS
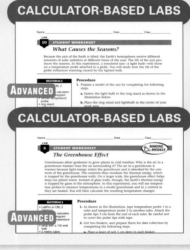
LAB 10 — STUDENT WORKSHEET

What Causes the Seasons?

ADVANCED

MATERIALS

Procedure

CALCULATOR-BASED LABS
LAB 6 — STUDENT WORKSHEET — MAKING MODELS

The Greenhouse Effect

MATERIALS

Procedure

ADVANCED

DATASHEETS FOR QUICKLABS
TEACHER RESOURCE PAGE
Quick Lab — DATASHEET FOR QUICK LAB
Reaction to Stress — SAMPLE

Background

DATASHEETS FOR CHAPTER LABS
TEACHER RESOURCE PAGE
Skills Practice Lab — DATASHEET FOR CHAPTER LAB
Using Scientific Methods — SAMPLE

Teacher's Notes
TIME REQUIRED
One 45-minute class period.

DATASHEETS FOR LABBOOK
TEACHER RESOURCE PAGE
Skills Practice Lab — DATASHEET FOR LABBOOK LAB
Does It All Add Up? — SAMPLE

Teacher's Notes
TIME REQUIRED
One 45-minute class period.

Review and Assessments

SECTION QUIZ

Section Quiz — SAMPLE

Section:

In the space provided, write the letter of the description that best matches the term or phrase.

ALSO IN SPANISH

GENERAL

SECTION REVIEW
Section Review — SAMPLE

Section: KEY TERMS

1. What do paleontologists study?

2. How does a trace fossil differ from petrified wood?

ALSO IN SPANISH

GENERAL

CHAPTER REVIEW
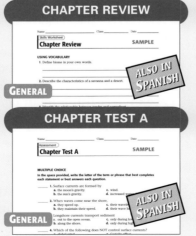
Chapter Review — SAMPLE

USING VOCABULARY

1. Define biome in your own words.

2. Describe the characteristics of a savanna and a desert.

ALSO IN SPANISH

GENERAL

CHAPTER TEST A
Chapter Test A — SAMPLE

MULTIPLE CHOICE
In the space provided, write the letter of the term or phrase that best completes each statement or best answers each question.

1. Surface currents are formed by
   a. the moon's gravity.   c. wind.
   b. the sun's gravity.   d. increased water density.

2. When waves come near the shore,
   a. they speed up.   c. their wavelength increases.
   b. they maintain their speed.   d. their wave height increases.

ALSO IN SPANISH

GENERAL

CHAPTER TEST B

Chapter Test B — SAMPLE

MULTIPLE CHOICE
In the space provided, write the letter of the term or phrase that best completes each statement or best answers each question.

1. Surface currents are formed by
   a. the moon's gravity.   c. wind.
   b. the sun's gravity.   d. increased water density.

2. When waves come near the shore,
   a. they speed up.   c. their wavelength increases.
   b. they maintain their speed.   d. their wave height increases.

ADVANCED

CHAPTER TEST C
Chapter Test C — SAMPLE

MULTIPLE CHOICE
In the space provided, write the letter of the term or phrase that best completes each statement or best answers each question.

1. Surface currents are formed by
   a. the moon's gravity.   c. wind.
   b. the sun's gravity.   d. increased water density.

2. When waves come near the shore,
   a. they speed up.   c. their wavelength increases.
   b. they maintain their speed.   d. their wave height increases.

SPECIAL NEEDS

STANDARDIZED TEST PREPARATION
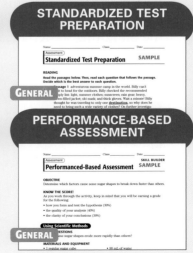
Standardized Test Preparation — SAMPLE

READING
Read the passages below. Then, read each question that follows the passage. Decide which is the best answer to each question.

GENERAL

PERFORMANCE-BASED ASSESSMENT
Performance-Based Assessment — SKILL BUILDER SAMPLE

OBJECTIVE
Determine which factors cause some sugar shapes to break down faster than others.

KNOW THE SCORE!

Using Scientific Methods

MATERIALS AND EQUIPMENT

GENERAL

This Chapter Enrichment provides relevant and interesting information to expand and enhance your presentation of the chapter material.

Section 1

What Is Climate?

Climatology

● The study of climate can be traced back to Greek scientists of the sixth century BCE. In fact, the word *climate* comes from the Greek word *klíma,* meaning "an inclination" of the sun's rays. Climatology can be divided into three branches—global climatology, regional climatology, and physical climatology. Global climatology investigates the general circulation of wind and water currents around the Earth. Regional climatology studies the characteristic weather patterns and related phenomena of a particular region. Physical climatology analyzes statistics concerning climatic factors such as temperature, moisture, wind, and air pressure.

Global Winds

● Global winds are patterns of air circulation that travel across the Earth. These winds include the trade winds, the prevailing westerlies, and the polar easterlies.

● In both hemispheres, the trade winds blow from 30° latitude to the equator. The Coriolis effect makes the trade winds curve to the right in the Northern Hemisphere, moving northeast to southwest. In the Southern Hemisphere, the trade winds curve to the left and move from southeast to northwest.

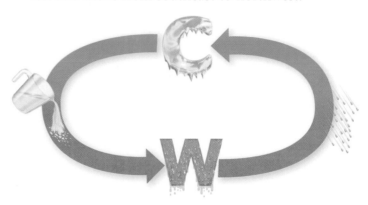

● The prevailing westerlies are found in both the Northern and Southern Hemispheres between 30° and 60° latitude. In the Northern Hemisphere, the westerlies blow from the southwest to the northeast. In the Southern Hemisphere, they blow from the northwest to the southeast.

● The polar easterlies extend from the poles to 60° latitude in both hemispheres. The polar easterlies blow from the northeast to the southwest in the Northern Hemisphere. In the Southern Hemisphere, these winds blow from the southeast to the northwest.

Section 2

The Tropics

Climate Classification

● Because climate is a complicated and somewhat abstract concept, more than 100 classification models have been devised, which vary according to the data on which the classifications are based. For instance, there have been attempts to classify climates according to factors such as soil formation, rock weathering, and even effects on human comfort!

● In 1966, Werner Terjung, an American geographer, developed a physiological climate classification. This system categorized climates according to their effects on people's comfort levels. The system focused on four factors that might affect human comfort— temperature, relative humidity, wind speed, and solar radiation.

Section 3

Temperate and Polar Zones

The Köppen System

● The most widely used climate classification system is the Köppen system. This system, named for Wladimir Köppen, the German botanist and climatologist who developed it, uses vegetation regions and average weather statistics to classify local climates. Each vegetation region is characterized by the natural vegetation that is predominant there. Critics have found fault with the Köppen system because it considers only average monthly temperatures and precipitation, ignoring other factors, such as winds, cloud cover, and daily temperature extremes.

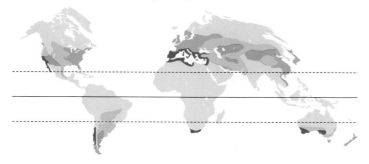

Section 4

Changes in Climate

Pangaea

● In 1620, the British philosopher Francis Bacon noted that Africa and South America looked as if they could fit together like puzzle pieces. But it was not until the early 20th century that the German meteorologist Alfred Wegener proposed a theory that all the continents were once one landmass. Wegener's hypothesis was supported by the existence of similar plant and animal fossils on different continents. Although his theory was initially ridiculed, Wegener was vindicated after World War II when sea-floor spreading and a mechanism for continental drift were discovered.

Pangaea

Is That a Fact!

◆ *Pangaea*, the name Wegener gave to the supercontinent, is Greek for "all Earth."

The Greenhouse Effect

● Gases such as water vapor, carbon dioxide and methane are known as greenhouse gases because they absorb and reradiate thermal energy in Earth's atmosphere. Greenhouse gases are necessary for life on Earth because they keep Earth's average temperature at 15°C. Without them, Earth would be frozen; the average temperature would be about –18°C.

Is That a Fact!

◆ Burning 1 gal of gasoline can produce 9 kg of carbon dioxide.

SciLinks is maintained by the National Science Teachers Association to provide you and your students with interesting, up-to-date links that will enrich your classroom presentation of the chapter.

Visit www.scilinks.org and enter the SciLinks code for more information about the topic listed.

Topic: What Is Climate?
SciLinks code: HSM1659

Topic: Climates of the World
SciLinks code: HSM0302

Topic: Modeling Earth's Climate
SciLinks code: HSM0976

Topic: Changes in Climate
SciLinks code: HSM0252

Overview

Tell students that this chapter describes different climates around the world and the factors that influence climate. This chapter also explains how climate can change over time.

Assessing Prior Knowledge

Students should be familiar with the following topics:

- weather patterns
- latitudes of the Earth

Identifying Misconceptions

Students may think that the Earth is farther away from the sun during winter and closer to the sun in the summer. Point out that the seasons are caused by the Earth's tilt, not by the distance between the Earth and the sun. Students may also think that the only factor that influences climate is a location's distance from the equator. Explain that this chapter will introduce many factors that influence climate.

Climate

About the PHOTO

Would you like to hang out on this ice with the penguins? You probably would not. You would be shivering, and your teeth would be chattering. However, these penguins feel comfortable. They have thick feathers and lots of body fat to keep them warm. Like other animals, penguins have adapted to their climate, which allows them to live comfortably in that climate. So, you will never see one of these penguins living comfortably on a hot, sunny beach in Florida!

PRE-READING ACTIVITY

FOLDNOTES **Pyramid** Before you read the chapter, create the FoldNote entitled "Pyramid" described in the **Study Skills** section of the Appendix. Label the sides of the pyramid with "Tropical climate," "Temperate climate," and "Polar climate." As you read the chapter, define each climate zone, and write characteristics of each climate zone on the appropriate pyramid side.

Standards Correlations

National Science Education Standards

The following codes indicate the National Science Education Standards that correlate to this chapter. The full text of the standards is at the front of the book.

Chapter Opener
SAI 1

Section 1 What Is Climate?
SAI 1; SPSP 1, 3; ES 1j, 3d

Section 2 The Tropics
SAI 2; HNS 1, 3; SPSP 2; LabBook: UCP 2, 3; SAI 1; ST 1

Section 3 Temperate and Polar Zones
SAI 1, 2; HNS 1, 3; SPSP 2

Section 4 Changes in Climate
UCP 2, 3; SAI 1, 2; ST 2; SPSP 3, 4, 5; HNS 1; ES 1k, 2a; LabBook: UCP 2, 3; SAI 1

Chapter Lab
SAI 1, UCP 2

Chapter Review
UCP 2; SAI 1; ES 1d, 1f, 1j, 3d

Science in Action
SPSP 5; HNS 1, 2

START-UP ACTIVITY

MATERIALS

FOR EACH GROUP
- adhesive putty
- globe
- lamp
- thermometers (2)

Safety Caution: Remind students to review all safety cautions and icons before beginning this lab activity. Students should not touch the lamp's bulb while it is on or immediately after it has been turned off.

Teacher's Notes: If you have time, encourage students to repeat the experiment, positioning one thermometer at the equator and one at the South Pole. Have students compare their results.

Answers

1. yes; The final temperature at the globe's North Pole was cooler than the final temperature at the globe's equator.

2. The temperature readings at the North Pole and the equator are different because the globe's equator received more direct energy from the lamp than the globe's North Pole received.

START-UP ACTIVITY

What's Your Angle?

Try this activity to see how the angle of the sun's solar rays influences temperatures on Earth.

Procedure

1. Place a **lamp** 30 cm from a **globe**.

2. Point the lamp so that the light shines directly on the globe's equator.

3. Using **adhesive putty**, attach a **thermometer** to the globe's equator in a vertical position. Attach **another thermometer** to the globe's North Pole so that the tip points toward the lamp.

4. Record the temperature reading of each thermometer.

5. Turn on the lamp, and let the light shine on the globe for 3 minutes.

6. After 3 minutes, turn off the lamp and record the temperature reading of each thermometer again.

Analysis

1. Was there a difference between the final temperature at the globe's North Pole and the final temperature at the globe's equator? If so, what was it?

2. Explain why the temperature readings at the North Pole and the equator may be different.

What If . . . ?

The brochure boasts of the most adventurous summer camp in the world. You can't wait to lace up your hiking boots and head for the outdoors. But before you fly halfway around the world, you check the recommended supply list: light summer clothes, sunscreen, rain gear, heavy down-filled jacket, ski mask, and thick gloves. Wait a minute! You are traveling to only one destination, so why are you required to bring such a wide variety of clothes? On further investigation, you learn that your outdoor adventure advertises the opportunity to "climb the climates of the world in just three days." Your destination is Africa's tallest mountain, Kilimanjaro.

You spend the first day hiking through a hot, sweltering rain forest. Day two finds you treading through a grassy meadow that slopes up the side of the first peak, called Mawensii.

On the third day, you start to get cold. The frozen ground crunches under your feet. Within 2 hours your feet feel like blocks of ice, and breathing is difficult. You finally reach the summit just as the clouds part, revealing steam rising off the rain forest 3,000 m below. Maybe the trip was worth the effort after all!

Climate changes as elevation increases, just as it changes from the equator to the poles. In this chapter you will learn what factors affect climate, how climate is influenced by human and natural activity, and what type of environment is found in which climate.

Chapter Starter Transparency
Use this transparency to help students begin thinking about the relationship between elevation and climate.

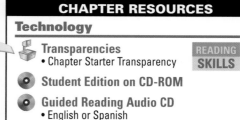

CHAPTER RESOURCES

Technology

Transparencies
- Chapter Starter Transparency

READING SKILLS

Student Edition on CD-ROM

Guided Reading Audio CD
- English or Spanish

Classroom Videos
- Brain Food Video Quiz

Workbooks

Science Puzzlers, Twisters & Teasers
- Climate **GENERAL**

Focus

Overview

In this section, students will learn the difference between weather and climate. They will examine how latitude, prevailing winds, geography, and ocean currents affect an area's climate. Finally, students will learn about the three major climate zones of the world.

 Bellringer

Have students imagine that they have entered a contest for a free trip to a place that has a perfect climate. To win, they must describe their idea of a perfect climate in 25 words or less.

Motivate

Discussion ——— GENERAL

Latitude and Climate Ask students to find locations on a United States or world map where they would like to visit. Write the locations and their latitudinal positions on the board. Review with students that latitude is the distance north or south from the equator, expressed in degrees. Ask students to help you list some observations about the climate in each location. Make sure students notice the relationship between latitude and climate. **L$** **Verbal**

What Is Climate?

Suppose you receive a call from a friend who is coming to visit you tomorrow. To decide what clothing to bring, he asks about the current weather in your area.

You step outside to see if rain clouds are in the sky and to check the temperature. But what would you do if your friend asked you about the climate in your area? What is the difference between weather and climate?

Climate Vs. Weather

The main difference between weather and climate is the length of time over which both are measured. **Weather** is the condition of the atmosphere at a particular time. Weather conditions vary from day to day and include temperature, humidity, precipitation, wind, and visibility. **Climate,** on the other hand, is the average weather condition in an area over a long period of time. Climate is mostly determined by two factors—temperature and precipitation. Different parts of the world can have different climates, as shown in **Figure 1.** But why are climates so different? The answer is complicated. It includes factors in addition to temperature and precipitation, such as latitude, wind patterns, mountains, large bodies of water, and ocean currents.

✓ **Reading Check** How is climate different from weather? (*See the Appendix for answers to Reading Checks.*)

Figure 1 *How does the climate in northern Africa differ from the climate where you live?*

Objectives

- Explain the difference between weather and climate.
- Identify five factors that determine climates.
- Identify the three climate zones of the world.

Terms to Learn

weather	elevation
climate	surface current
latitude	biome
prevailing winds	

READING STRATEGY

Discussion Read this section silently. Write down questions that you have about this section. Discuss your questions in a small group.

CHAPTER RESOURCES

Chapter Resource File

- **Lesson Plan**
- **Directed Reading A** BASIC
- **Directed Reading B** SPECIAL NEEDS

Technology

Transparencies
- Bellringer

Answer to Reading Check

Climate is the average weather condition in an area over a long period of time. Weather is the condition of the atmosphere at a particular time.

Latitude

Think of the last time you looked at a globe. Do you recall the thin, horizontal lines that circle the globe? Those lines are called lines of latitude. **Latitude** is the distance north or south, measured in degrees, from the equator. In general, the temperature of an area depends on its latitude. The higher the latitude is, the colder the climate tends to be. One of the coldest places on Earth, the North Pole, is 90° north of the equator. However, the equator, at latitude 0°, is usually hot.

As shown in **Figure 2,** if you were to take a trip to different latitudes in the United States, you would experience different climates. For example, the climate in Washington, D.C., which is at a higher latitude, is different from the climate in Texas.

Solar Energy and Latitude

Solar energy, which is energy from the sun, heats the Earth. The amount of direct solar energy a particular area receives is determined by latitude. **Figure 3** shows how the curve of the Earth affects the amount of direct solar energy at different latitudes. Notice that the sun's rays hit the equator directly, at almost a 90° angle. At this angle, a small area of the Earth's surface receives more direct solar energy than at a lesser angle. As a result, that area has high temperatures. However, the sun's rays strike the poles at a lesser angle than they do the equator. At this angle, the same amount of direct solar energy that hits the area at the equator is spread over a larger area at the poles. The result is lower temperatures at the poles.

Figure 2 *Winter in south Texas (top) is different from winter in Washington D.C. (bottom).*

weather the short-term state of the atmosphere, including temperature, humidity, precipitation, wind, and visibility

climate the average weather condition in an area over a long period of time

latitude the distance north or south from the equator; expressed in degrees

Figure 3 The sun's rays strike the Earth's surface at different angles because the surface is curved.

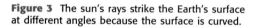

Equator

Sun's rays

Modeling the Earth and Sun

Ask two volunteers to act as the Earth and the sun. Give the "sun" a flashlight and the "Earth" a globe with a half-meridian mounting. Turn off the lights, and have the volunteers sit on the floor. Ask the "sun" to shine the flashlight on the globe, and ask the "Earth" to slowly spin the globe counterclockwise. Have the class notice which parts of the globe are most exposed to the light. Next, have the "Earth" slowly make a complete revolution around the "sun" while rotating the globe at the same time. Make sure that the volunteer always keeps the axis of the globe oriented in the same direction. Stop the "Earth" at each season so that students can observe the flashlight's rays on the two hemispheres. If necessary, repeat this activity with other volunteers.

LS Kinesthetic/Visual **Co-op Learning**

Seasons and Latitude

In most places in the United States, the year consists of four seasons. But there are places in the world that do not have such seasonal changes. For example, areas near the equator have approximately the same temperatures and same amount of daylight year-round. Seasons happen because the Earth is tilted on its axis at a 23.5° angle. This tilt affects how much solar energy an area receives as Earth moves around the sun. **Figure 4** shows how latitude and the tilt of the Earth determine the seasons and the length of the day in a particular area.

✓ **Reading Check** Why is there less seasonal change near the equator?

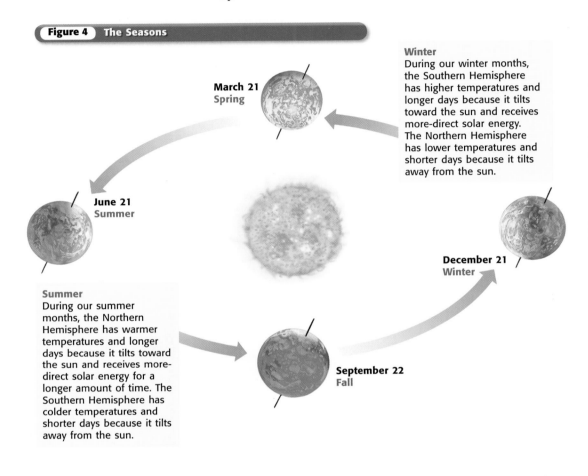

Figure 4   The Seasons

March 21
Spring

Winter
During our winter months, the Southern Hemisphere has higher temperatures and longer days because it tilts toward the sun and receives more-direct solar energy. The Northern Hemisphere has lower temperatures and shorter days because it tilts away from the sun.

June 21
Summer

December 21
Winter

Summer
During our summer months, the Northern Hemisphere has warmer temperatures and longer days because it tilts toward the sun and receives more-direct solar energy for a longer amount of time. The Southern Hemisphere has colder temperatures and shorter days because it tilts away from the sun.

September 22
Fall

Answer to Reading Check

Locations near the equator have less seasonal variation because the tilt of the Earth does not change the amount of energy these locations receive from the sun.

Figure 5 The Circulation of Warm Air and Cold Air

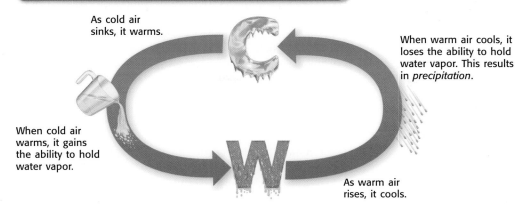

As cold air sinks, it warms.

When warm air cools, it loses the ability to hold water vapor. This results in *precipitation*.

When cold air warms, it gains the ability to hold water vapor.

As warm air rises, it cools.

Prevailing Winds

Winds that blow mainly from one direction are **prevailing winds**. Before you learn how the prevailing winds affect climate, take a look at **Figure 5** to learn about some of the basic properties of air.

Prevailing winds affect the amount of precipitation that a region receives. If the prevailing winds form from warm air, they may carry moisture. If the prevailing winds form from cold air, they will probably be dry.

The amount of moisture in prevailing winds is also affected by whether the winds blow across land or across a large body of water. Winds that travel across large bodies of water absorb moisture. Winds that travel across land tend to be dry. Even if a region borders the ocean, the area might be dry. **Figure 6** shows an example of how dry prevailing winds can cause the land to be dry though the land is near an ocean.

prevailing winds winds that blow mainly from one direction during a given period

Sahara

Prevailing winds

Africa

Figure 6 *The Sahara Desert, in northern Africa, is extremely dry because of the dry prevailing winds that blow across the continent.*

QUICK LAB

A Cool Breeze

1. Hold a **thermometer** next to the top edge of a **cup** of **water** containing two **ice cubes.** Record the temperature next to the cup.

2. Have your lab partner fan the surface of the cup with a **paper fan.** Record the temperature again. Has the temperature changed? Why or why not?

CONNECTION ACTIVITY
Geography — ADVANCED

Writing **Monsoons** Monsoons are recurrent global weather patterns that dramatically affect the populations, economies, and environments of South Asia. The wet summer monsoon usually begins mid-June, when temperatures rise sharply in Asia's interior and cause the air above the land to warm and rise. This movement creates a low pressure area that draws warm, moist air inland from the Indian and Pacific Oceans. This moisture-laden air cools as it moves across the continent, causing heavy rains, thunderstorms, and flooding to occur. The heaviest rains occur where this air mass meets the foothills of the Himalayas. During the winter, the interior of Asia cools rapidly. This cool, dense air creates an immense high-pressure center, which forces cool, dry air to flow outward toward the oceans. As the air mass travels, it warms and becomes even drier. Warm, dry winters result. Encourage students to write a report about the effect of monsoons on South Asia. **LS Intrapersonal**

Answer to School-to-Home Activity

Mountain ranges in the United States are the Sierra Nevada, the Rocky Mountains, and the Appalachian Mountains; yes; Climate varies from one side of the mountain range to the other, so one side is densely vegetated and the other side is much drier and less vegetated. The prevailing winds blow from the side with the most vegetation.

Using the Figure—BASIC

Wet Winds Remind students that winds traveling across large bodies of water, such as the ocean, absorb moisture. Have students study **Figure 7.** The inset photographs were taken in California's Sierra Nevada mountain range. Ask students to examine the photographs closely and describe as many details as possible. Then ask students to consider which side of the mountain is likely to be closer to a large body of water. (the left side)

LS Visual   English Language Learners

Answer to Reading Check

The atmosphere becomes less dense and loses its ability to absorb and hold thermal energy at higher elevations.

 **SCHOOL to HOME**

Using a Map

With your parent, use a physical map to locate the mountain ranges in the United States. Does climate vary from one side of a mountain range to the other? If so, what does this tell you about the climatic conditions on either side of the mountain? From what direction are the prevailing winds blowing?

 ACTiViTY

Mountains

Mountains can influence an area's climate by affecting both temperature and precipitation. Kilimanjaro is the tallest mountain in Africa. It has snow-covered peaks year-round, even though it is only about 3° (320 km) south of the equator. Temperatures on Kilimanjaro and in other mountainous areas are affected by elevation. **Elevation** is the height of surface landforms above sea level. As the elevation increases, the ability of air to transfer energy from the ground to the atmosphere decreases. Therefore, as elevation increases, temperature decreases.

Mountains also affect the climate of nearby areas by influencing the distribution of precipitation. **Figure 7** shows how the climates on two sides of a mountain can be very different.

✓ Reading Check Why does the atmosphere become cooler at higher elevations?

Figure 7 *Mountains block the prevailing winds and affect the climate on the other side.*

The Wet Side
Mountains force air to rise. The air cools as it rises, releasing moisture as snow or rain. The land on the windward side of the mountain is usually green and lush because the wind releases its moisture.

The Dry Side
After dry air crosses the mountain, the air begins to sink. As the air sinks, it is warmed and absorbs moisture. The dry conditions created by the sinking, warm air usually produce a desert. This side of the mountain is in a *rain shadow.*

 INCLUSION Strategies

- **Developmentally Delayed**   • **Hearing Impaired**
- **Learning Disabled**

Organize students into small groups. Give each group a clear plastic rectangular pan, a paper cup, hot water, and cold water. Have students poke 10 holes into the sides of the paper cup and tape the cup to the corner of the pan. Fill the pan two-thirds full with cold water. Have students put three drops of food coloring into the hot water and pour it into the paper cup. Have students record and explain their observations. (Students will observe the colored water diffuse through the holes in the cup. The hot water will not mix very much with the cold water. Most of the hot water will "float" on top. Explain that hot and cold air move in similar ways as hot and cold water do.) **LS** Kinesthetic   English Language Learners

Large Bodies of Water

Large bodies of water can influence an area's climate. Water absorbs and releases heat slower than land does. Because of this quality, water helps to moderate the temperatures of the land around it. So, sudden or extreme temperature changes rarely take place on land near large bodies of water. For example, the state of Michigan, which is surrounded by the Great Lakes, has more-moderate temperatures than other places at the same latitude. The lakes also increase the moisture content of the air, which leads to heavy snowfall in the winter. This "lake effect" can cause 350 inches of snow to drop in one year!

Ocean Currents

The circulation of ocean surface currents has a large effect on an area's climate. **Surface currents** are streamlike movements of water that occur at or near the surface of the ocean. **Figure 8** shows the pattern of the major ocean surface currents.

As surface currents move, they carry warm or cool water to different locations. The surface temperature of the water affects the temperature of the air above it. Warm currents heat the surrounding air and cause warmer temperatures. Cool currents cool the surrounding air and cause cooler temperatures. The Gulf Stream current carries warm water northward off the east coast of North America and past Iceland. Iceland is an island country located just below the Arctic Circle. The warm water from the Gulf Stream heats the surrounding air and creates warmer temperatures in southern Iceland. Iceland experiences milder temperatures than Greenland, its neighboring island. Greenland's climate is cooler because Greenland is not influenced by the Gulf Stream.

✓ **Reading Check** Why does Iceland experience milder temperatures than Greenland?

elevation the height of an object above sea level

surface current a horizontal movement of ocean water that is caused by wind and that occurs at or near the ocean's surface

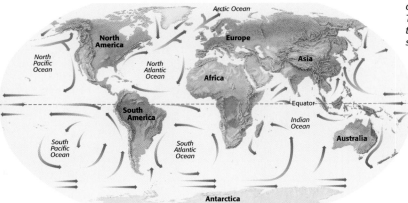

Figure 8 *The red arrows represent the movement of warm surface currents. The blue arrows represent the movement of cold surface currents.*

Homework — ADVANCED

Using Maps Have students look at a map and find cities that are at about the same latitude in a single continent. For example, Guadalajara and Tampico, in Mexico, are at about the same latitude, as are San Francisco, California, and Wichita, Kansas. Students should research the annual rainfall and temperature for each city. They can create a bar graph showing the differences in rainfall for each city, and students should attempt to explain the patterns they notice by identifying physical features on the map. If their data contradict what they have learned in this section, ask them to suggest explanations. **LS Visual**

Answer to Reading Check

The Gulf Stream current carries warm water past Iceland, which heats the air and causes milder temperatures.

SCIENCE HUMOR

Western and eastern Oregon have very different climates because the Cascades divide the state. Oregonians living east of the Cascades complain, "It's so dry, the jackrabbits carry canteens." West of the Cascades, people say, "It's so wet, folks don't tan, they rust!"

Is That a Fact!

Large lakes, such as the Great Lakes, in the United States and Canada, and Lake Victoria, in Africa, affect local climates. This phenomenon, called the *lake effect*, helps keep the surrounding land cooler in the summer and warmer in the winter.

Reteaching ── BASIC

Climate Factors Ask volunteers to list on the board the factors that influence climate. (temperature, precipitation, latitude, wind patterns, mountains, large bodies of water, and ocean currents) Ask students to describe how these factors influence climate. Have volunteers take turns writing these descriptions under each heading. **LS** Verbal

Quiz ── GENERAL

1. Why are the poles colder than the equator? (The sun's rays strike the Earth's surface at a less direct angle at the poles than at the equator, so solar energy is spread over a larger area.)

2. Is precipitation more likely when the prevailing winds are formed from warm air or from cold air? (warm air)

Alternative Assessment ── GENERAL

Climate Game Organize students into teams to play a climate game show. Have each team write 10 questions about material in the section. Have one team ask questions to the other teams. Have the other teams "buzz in" to answer the questions. **LS** Verbal/Interpersonal

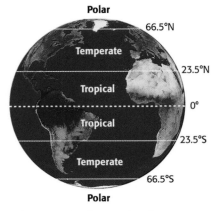

Figure 9 *The three major climate zones are determined by latitude.*

biome a large region characterized by a specific type of climate and certain types of plant and animal communities

Climates of the World

Have you seen any polar bears in your neighborhood lately? You probably have not. That's because polar bears live only in very cold arctic regions. Why are the animals in one part of the world so different from the animals in other parts? One of the differences has to do with climate. Plants and animals that have adapted to one climate may not be able to live in another climate. For example, frogs would not be able to survive at the North Pole.

Climate Zones

The Earth's three major climate zones—tropical, temperate, and polar—are shown in **Figure 9.** Each zone has a temperature range that relates to its latitude. However, in each of these zones, there are several types of climates because of differences in the geography and the amount of precipitation. Because of the various climates in each zone, there are different biomes in each zone. A **biome** is a large region characterized by a specific type of climate and certain types of plant and animal communities. **Figure 10** shows the distribution of the Earth's land biomes. In which biome do you live?

✔ Reading Check What factors distinguish one biome from another biome?

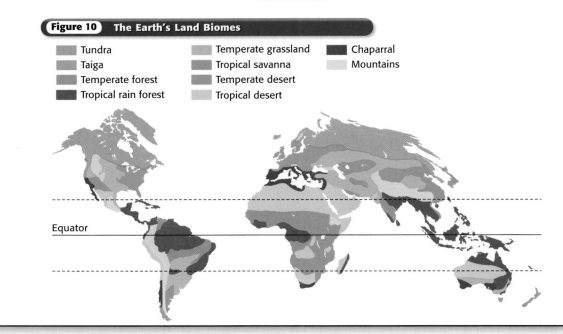

Figure 10	The Earth's Land Biomes

- Tundra
- Taiga
- Temperate forest
- Tropical rain forest
- Temperate grassland
- Tropical savanna
- Temperate desert
- Tropical desert
- Chaparral
- Mountains

Equator

Answer to Reading Check
Each biome has a different climate and different plant and animal communities.

SECTION Review

Summary

- Weather is the condition of the atmosphere at a particular time. This condition includes temperature, humidity, precipitation, wind, and visibility.
- Climate is the average weather condition in an area over a long period of time.
- The higher the latitude, the cooler the climate.
- Prevailing winds affect the climate of an area by the amount of moisture they carry.

- Mountains influence an area's climate by affecting both temperature and precipitation.
- Large bodies of water and ocean currents influence the climate of an area by affecting the temperature of the air over the water.
- The three climate zones of the world are the tropical zone, the temperate zone, and the polar zone.

Using Key Terms

1. In your own words, write a definition for each of the following terms: *weather, climate, latitude, prevailing winds, elevation, surface currents,* and *biome.*

Understanding Key Ideas

2. Which of the following affects climate by causing the air to rise?
   a. mountains
   b. ocean currents
   c. large bodies of water
   d. latitude

3. What is the difference between weather and climate?

4. List five factors that determine climates.

5. Explain why there is a difference in climate between areas at 0° latitude and areas at 45° latitude.

6. List the three climate zones of the world.

Critical Thinking

7. **Analyzing Relationships** How would seasons be different if the Earth did not tilt on its axis?

8. **Applying Concepts** During what months does Australia have summer? Explain.

Interpreting Graphics

Use the map below to answer the questions that follow.

9. Would you expect the area that the arrow points to to be moist or dry? Explain your answer.

10. Describe how the climate of the same area would change if the prevailing winds traveled from the opposite direction. Explain how you came to this conclusion.

SCI LINKS
NSTA
Developed and maintained by the National Science Teachers Association

For a variety of links related to this chapter, go to www.scilinks.org

Topic: What Is Climate?
SciLinks code: HSM1659

CHAPTER RESOURCES

Chapter Resource File

- Section Quiz GENERAL
- Section Review GENERAL
- Vocabulary and Section Summary GENERAL
- Datasheet for Quick Lab

Technology

Transparencies
- The Earth's Land Biomes

Answers to Section Review

1. Sample answer: Weather is the condition of the atmosphere at a certain time. Climate is the average weather in an area over a long period of time. Latitude is the distance in degrees north or south of the equator. Prevailing winds are winds that blow mainly in one direction. Elevation is the height of surface landforms above sea level. Surface currents are streamlike movements of water that occur at or near the surface of the ocean. A biome is a large region characterized by a specific type of climate and certain types of plants and animals.

2. a

3. Weather is the condition of the atmosphere at a particular time. Climate is the average weather of a given area.

4. latitude, prevailing winds, mountains, large bodies of water, and ocean currents

5. Areas at different latitudes receive different amounts of solar energy because the Earth's surface is curved, and because the Earth is tilted on its axis.

6. tropical zone, temperate zone, and polar zone

7. If the Earth were not tilted on its axis, there would be no seasons.

8. Australia has summer during December, January, February, and March. This is because Australia is in the Earth's Southern Hemisphere, and the Southern Hemisphere is tilted away from the sun during these months.

9. dry

10. Accept all reasonable answers. If the prevailing winds blew from the Atlantic ocean, the area would have a wet climate with plenty of precipitation.

Focus

Overview

In this section, students learn the location and the characteristics of the tropical climate zone and the different biomes that are found in this climate.

 Bellringer

Ask students to describe the differences between a deer and a camel. Where would they find these animals? Ask students to think about how climate influences the animals that live in certain areas.

Motivate

ACTiViTY ——————— GENERAL

Writing **Country Profile** Have each student choose a country in the tropics to focus on for this section. Students should record the area's latitude and geographic characteristics. Tell students to find pictures from magazines or the Internet of the people, plants, and animals that live in the country. Then have students use the pictures to create a poster of the country they chose. Students should include information on average monthly rainfall and temperature. **LS** Visual

---

The Tropics

Where in the world do you think you could find a flying dragon gliding above you from one treetop to the next?

Don't worry. This flying dragon, or tree lizard, is only about 20 cm long, and it eats only insects. With winglike skin flaps, the flying dragon can glide from one treetop to the next. But, you won't find this kind of animal in the United States. These flying dragons live in Southeast Asia, which is in the tropical zone.

READING WARM-UP

Objectives
- Locate and describe the tropical zone.
- Describe the biomes found in the tropical zone.

Terms to Learn
tropical zone

READING STRATEGY

Reading Organizer As you read this section, make a table comparing *tropical rain forests, tropical savannas,* and *tropical deserts.*

The Tropical Zone

The region that surrounds the equator and that extends from about 23.5° north latitude to 23.5° south latitude is called the **tropical zone.** The tropical zone is also known as the Tropics. Latitudes in the tropical zone receive the most solar radiation. Temperatures are therefore usually hot, except at high elevations.

Within the tropical zone, there are three major types of biomes—tropical rain forest, tropical desert, and tropical savanna. These three biomes have high temperatures. But they differ in the amount of precipitation, soil characteristics, vegetation, and kinds of animals. **Figure 1** shows the distribution of these biomes.

✓ *Reading Check* **At what latitudes would you find the tropical zone?** (*See the Appendix for answers to Reading Checks.*)

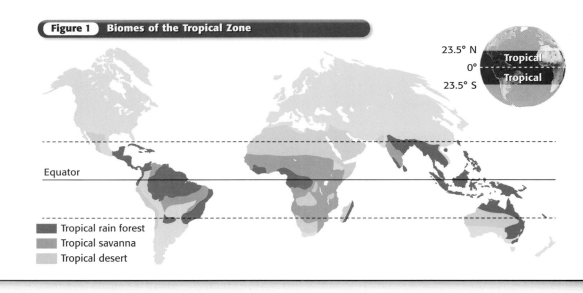

Figure 1   Biomes of the Tropical Zone

23.5° N
0°
23.5° S
Tropical
Tropical

Equator

- ■ Tropical rain forest
- ■ Tropical savanna
- ■ Tropical desert

CHAPTER RESOURCES

Chapter Resource File

- **Lesson Plan**
- **Directed Reading A** BASIC
- **Directed Reading B** SPECIAL NEEDS

Technology

Transparencies
- Bellringer
- **LINK TO LIFE SCIENCE** Gas Exchange in Leaves

Workbooks

Math Skills for Science
- Rainforest Math GENERAL

Answer to Reading Check

You would find the tropical zone from 23.5° north latitude to 23.5° south latitude.

Tropical Rain Forest

- Average Temperature Range
  25°C to 28°C (77°F to 82°F)
- Average Yearly Precipitation
  200 cm or more
- Soil Characteristics
  thin and nutrient poor

Figure 2 *In tropical rain forests, many of the trees form above-ground roots that provide extra support for the trees in the thin, nutrient-poor soil.*

Tropical Rain Forests

Tropical rain forests are always warm and wet. Because they are located near the equator, they receive strong sunlight year-round. So, there is little difference between seasons in tropical rain forests.

Tropical rain forests contain the greatest number of animal and plant species of any biome. Animals found in tropical rain forests include monkeys, parrots, tree frogs, tigers, and leopards. Plants found in tropical rain forests include mahogany, vines, ferns, and bamboo. But in spite of the lush vegetation, shown in **Figure 2,** the soil in rain forests is poor. The rapid decay of plants and animals returns nutrients to the soil. But these nutrients are quickly absorbed and used by the plants. The nutrients that are not immediately used by the plants are washed away by the heavy rains. The soil is left thin and nutrient poor.

tropical zone the region that surrounds the equator and that extends from about 23.5° north latitude to 23.5° south latitude

CONNECTION TO Social Studies

WRITING SKILL **Living in the Tropics** The tropical climate is very hot and humid. People who live in the Tropics have had to adapt to feel comfortable in that climate. For example, in the country of Samoa, some people live in homes that have no walls, which are called *fales*. Fales have only a roof, which provides shade. The openness of the home allows cool breezes to flow through the home. Research other countries in the Tropics. See how the climate influences the way the people live in those countries. Then, in your **science journal,** describe how the people's lifestyle helps them adapt to the climate.

WEIRD SCIENCE

In addition to having land biomes, Earth has marine biomes. However, marine biomes are less influenced by latitude than they are by water depth. Some of the animals that inhabit the deeper biomes have very interesting adaptations. For example, the anglerfish, which lives in total darkness uses a luminescent "lure" that trails from the fish's jaw and attracts prey within reach of its enormous, sharp teeth.

Close

Reteaching — BASIC

Concept Mapping Have students create a concept map that shows how each of the three biomes in the tropical zone is influenced by precipitation and temperature. **LS** Visual

Quiz — GENERAL

1. What are three biomes in the tropical zone? (tropical rain forest, tropical savannas, and tropical deserts)

2. What do all tropical biomes have in common? (They are all between 23.5° north latitude and 23.5° south latitude.)

Alternative Assessment — GENERAL

Building a Biome
PORTFOLIO Tell students that they are going to create an imaginary biome. Tell them to write the characteristics of their biome on a sheet of paper. Students should include the biome's annual precipitation, average temperature, topography, and latitude. When students have finished creating their imaginary biomes, ask them to write down the types of organisms that they think would inhabit their biomes. If students want, they can make drawings of some of the imaginary organisms. Invite students to share their work with the class. **LS** Intrapersonal

Tropical Savanna
- Average Temperature Range 27°C to 32°C (80°F to 90°F)
- Average Yearly Precipitation 100 cm
- Soil Characteristics generally nutrient poor

Figure 3 *The grass of a tropical savanna can be as tall as 5 m.*

Tropical Savannas

Tropical savannas, or grasslands, are composed of tall grasses and a few scattered trees. The climate is usually very warm. Tropical savannas have a dry season that lasts four to eight months and that is followed by short periods of rain. Savanna soils are generally nutrient poor. However, grass fires, which are common during the dry season, leave the soils nutrient enriched. An African savanna is shown in **Figure 3.**

Many plants have adapted to fire and use it to promote development. For example, some species need fire to break open their seeds' outer skin. Only after this skin is broken can each seed grow. For other species, heat from the fire triggers the plants to drop their seeds into the newly enriched soil.

Animals that live in tropical savannas include giraffes, lions, crocodiles, and elephants. Plants include tall grasses, trees, and thorny shrubs.

CONNECTION TO Biology

WRITING SKILL **Animal and Plant Adaptations** Animals and plants adapt to the climate in which they live. These adaptations cause certain animals and plants to be unique to particular biomes. For example, the camel, which is unique to the desert, has adapted to going for long periods of time without water. Research other animals or plants that live in the Tropics. Then, in your **science journal,** describe the characteristics that help them survive in the Tropics.

Is That a Fact!

The world's largest desert, the Sahara, covers more than 9 million square kilometers—about the size of the United States. In contrast, the largest desert in the United States is the Mojave Desert. It covers 38,900 km², which is nearly twice the size of New Jersey.

CONNECTION to Real World — GENERAL

Desertification Deserts are expanding at an accelerating rate. In the last 100 years, the estimated area of land occupied by deserts rose from 9.4% to 23.3%. Many factors have contributed to this phenomenon, including climatic shifts, overgrazing, and overuse of the land through inefficient agricultural practices. As a class, find out what is being done to stop desertification in western Africa and other areas of the world.

Tropical Deserts

A desert is an area that receives less than 25 cm of rainfall per year. Because of this low yearly rainfall, deserts are the driest places on Earth. Desert plants, such as those shown in **Figure 4**, are adapted to survive in places that have little water. Animals such as rats, lizards, snakes, and scorpions have also adapted to survive in these deserts.

There are two kinds of deserts—hot deserts and cold deserts. Hot deserts are caused by cool, sinking air masses. Many hot deserts, such as the Sahara, in Africa, are tropical deserts. Daily temperatures in tropical deserts often vary from very hot daytime temperatures (50°C) to cool nighttime temperatures (20°C). Because of the dryness of deserts, the soil is poor in organic matter, which is needed for plants to grow.

✓ **Reading Check** What animals would you find in a tropical desert?

Tropical Desert

- **Average Temperature Range** 16°C to 50°C (61°F to 120°F)
- **Average Yearly Precipitation** 0–25 cm
- **Soil Characteristics** poor in organic matter

Figure 4 *Plants such as succulents have fleshy stems and leaves to store water.*

SECTION Review

Summary

- The tropical zone is located around the equator, between 23.5° north and 23.5° south latitude.
- Temperatures are usually hot in the tropical zone.
- Tropical rain forests are warm and wet. They have the greatest number of plant and animal species of any biome.
- Tropical savannas are grasslands that have a dry season.
- Tropical deserts are hot and receive little rain.

Using Key Terms

1. In your own words, write a definition for the term *tropical zone.*

Understanding Key Ideas

2. Which of the following tropical biomes has less than 50 cm of precipitation a year?
   a. rain forest   c. grassland
   b. desert   d. savanna

3. What are the soil characteristics of a tropical rain forest?

4. In what ways have savanna vegetation adapted to fire?

Math Skills

5. Suppose that in a tropical savanna, the temperature was recorded every hour for 4 h. The recorded temperatures were 27°C, 28°C, 29°C, and 29°C. Calculate the average temperature for this 4 h period.

Critical Thinking

6. **Analyzing Relationships** How do the tropical biomes differ?

7. **Making Inferences** How would you expect the adaptations of a plant in a tropical rain forest to differ from the adaptations of a tropical desert plant? Explain.

8. **Analyzing Data** An area has a temperature range of 30°C to 40°C and received 10 cm of rain this year. What biome is this area in?

SCI**LINKS**
Developed and maintained by the National Science Teachers Association

For a variety of links related to this chapter, go to www.scilinks.org

Topic: Climates of the World
SciLinks code: HSM0302

CHAPTER RESOURCES

Chapter Resource File

- Section Quiz **GENERAL**
- Section Review **GENERAL**
- Vocabulary and Section Summary **GENERAL**
- Reinforcement Worksheet **BASIC**
- SciLinks Activity **GENERAL**

Focus

Overview

In this section, students will learn the location and the characteristics of the temperate climate zone and the polar climate zone. They will also learn about microclimates and about different biomes that are found in these climate zones.

🎵 Bellringer

Tell students that they are taking a trip to the North Pole. In order to pack, they need to know what the climate is like. Have students write a description of what they would expect the climate to be like at the North Pole.

Motivate

Group ACTiViTY — GENERAL

Camp Climate Have groups write a brochure for a summer camp in a temperate biome of their choice. Suggest that they include information about the environment that will entice people to come and helpful tips about how to prepare for the area's climate.

LS Visual Co-op Learning

READING WARM-UP

Objectives

● Locate and describe the temperate zone and the polar zone.

● Describe the different biomes found in the temperate zone and the polar zone.

● Explain what a microclimate is.

Terms to Learn

temperate zone
polar zone
microclimate

READING STRATEGY

Reading Organizer As you read this section, create an outline of the section. Use the headings from the section in your outline.

Temperate and Polar Zones

Which season is your favorite? Do you like the change of colors in the fall, the flowers in the spring, or do you prefer the hot days of summer?

If you live in the continental United States, chances are you live in a biome that experiences seasonal change. Seasonal change is one characteristic of the temperate zone. Most of the continental United States is in the temperate zone, which is the climate zone between the Tropics and the polar zone.

The Temperate Zone

The climate zone between the Tropics and the polar zone is the **temperate zone.** Latitudes in the temperate zone receive less solar energy than latitudes in the Tropics do. Because of this, temperatures in the temperate zone tend to be lower than in the Tropics. Some biomes in the temperate zone have a mild change of seasons. Other biomes in the country can experience freezing temperatures in the winter and very hot temperatures in the summer. The temperate zone consists of the following four biomes—temperate forest, temperate grassland, chaparral, and temperate desert. Although these biomes have four distinct seasons, the biomes differ in temperature and precipitation and have different plants and animals. **Figure 1** shows the distribution of the biomes found in the temperate zone.

✓ Reading Check Where is the temperate zone? (*See the Appendix for answers to Reading Checks.*)

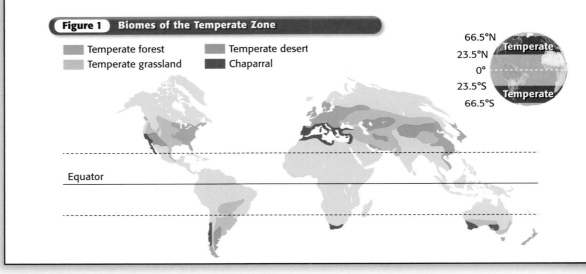

Figure 1 **Biomes of the Temperate Zone**

  Temperate forest
  Temperate grassland
  Temperate desert
  Chaparral

66.5°N
23.5°N
0°
23.5°S
66.5°S
Temperate
Temperate

Equator

CHAPTER RESOURCES

Chapter Resource File

📁 • **Lesson Plan**
     • **Directed Reading A** BASIC
     • **Directed Reading B** SPECIAL NEEDS

Technology

💾 **Transparencies**
     • Bellringer

Answer to Reading Check

The temperate zone is located between the Tropics and the polar zone.

Temperate Forest

- Average Temperature Range
  0°C to 28°C (32°F to 82°F)
- Average Yearly Precipitation
  76 to 250 cm
- Soil Characteristics
  very fertile, organically rich

Temperate Forests

The temperate forest biomes tend to have high amounts of rainfall and seasonal temperature differences. Summers are often warm, and winters are often cold. Animals such as deer, bears, and foxes live in temperate forests. **Figure 2** shows deciduous trees in a temperate forest. *Deciduous* describes trees that lose their leaves at the end of the growing season. The soils in deciduous forests are usually fertile because of the high organic content from decaying leaves that drop every winter. Another type of tree found in the temperate forest is the evergreen. *Evergreens* are trees that keep their leaves year-round.

Temperate Grasslands

Temperate grasslands, such as those shown in **Figure 3,** are regions that receive too little rainfall for trees to grow. This biome has warm summers and cold winters. Examples of animals that are found in temperate grasslands include bison in North America and kangaroo in Australia. Grasses are the most common kind of plant found in this biome. Because grasslands have the most-fertile soils of all biomes, much of the grassland has been plowed to make room for croplands.

Figure 3 *At one time, the world's grasslands covered about 42% of Earth's total land surface. Today, they occupy only about 12% of the Earth's total land surface.*

Figure 2 *Deciduous trees have leaves that change color and drop when temperatures become cold.*

temperate zone the climate zone between the Tropics and the polar zone

Temperate Grassland

- Average Temperature Range
  −6°C to 26°C (21°F to 78°F)
- Average Yearly Precipitation
  38 to 76 cm
- Soil Characteristics
  most-fertile soils of all biomes

Teach

CONNECTION ACTIVITY
Life Science ——— **GENERAL**

Writing **Fragmentation** The settlement of humans in temperate forests around the world has greatly fragmented these areas. Much of the temperate forest has been converted to agricultural land or has been logged. Fragmentation has a negative impact on many plants and animals that have certain habitat requirements. In fact, fragmentation has led to the extinction of many species. The temperate forest is also vulnerable to air pollution resulting from industrial activity. Acid precipitation has damaged forests, either killing the trees or making them more susceptible to disease. Have students write a persuasive essay explaining the importance of conserving Earth's temperate forests. **LS** Intrapersonal

MISCONCEPTION
///ALERT

Temperate Rain Forest You don't need to travel to the Tropics to find a rain forest. Western Washington State is home to the largest temperate rain forest in the world. Moss-covered trees more than 500 years old stand 60 m tall and are 5 m in diameter. The ground is covered by ferns, moss, salmon-berries, and the thorny Hercules'-club. The growth is not as diverse as in the tropical forests, but it is every bit as lush. The forest receives 380 cm of rain each year! Have students find out more about this remarkable ecosystem and the efforts to preserve it.

Harvesting Fog Chile's arid northern desert land is one of the driest places on Earth. It receives so little rainfall that the yearly average is listed as "immeasurable." Surprisingly, people live there. They get drinking water by harvesting the fog. The village of Chungungo has built 75 fog-catching nets that supply 11,000 L of clean water per day. The nets, which look like giant volleyball nets, are positioned in the hills above the town. As the mountain fog passes through the nets, beads of water collect and are channeled to a pipeline that supplies the village with water. Scientists believe that this technology could be used in 30 other countries to supply safe and inexpensive water for drinking and agriculture.

Answer to Reading Check

Temperate deserts are cold at night because low humidity and cloudless skies allow energy to escape.

Chaparral

- **Average Temperature Range** 11°C to 26°C (51°F to 78°F)
- **Average Yearly Precipitation** 48 to 56 cm
- **Soil Characteristics** rocky, nutrient-poor soils

Figure 4 *Some plant species found in chaparral require fire to reproduce.*

Figure 5 *The Great Basin Desert is in the rain shadow of the Sierra Nevada.*

Chaparrals

Chaparral regions, as shown in **Figure 4,** have cool, wet winters and hot, dry summers. Animals, such as coyotes and mountain lions live in chaparrals. The vegetation is mainly evergreen shrubs. These shrubs are short, woody plants with thick, waxy leaves. The waxy leaves are adaptations that help prevent water loss in dry conditions. These shrubs grow in rocky, nutrient-poor soil. Like tropical-savanna vegetation, chaparral vegetation has adapted to fire. In fact, some plants, such as chamise, can grow back from their roots after a fire.

Temperate Deserts

The temperate desert biomes, like the one shown in **Figure 5,** tend to be cold deserts. Like all deserts, cold deserts receive less than 25 cm of precipitation yearly. Examples of animals that live in temperate deserts are lizards, snakes, bats, and toads. And the types of plants found in temperate deserts include cacti, shrubs, and thorny trees.

Temperate deserts can be very hot in the daytime. But, unlike hot deserts, they are often very cold at night. This large change in temperature between day and night is caused by low humidity and cloudless skies. These conditions allow for a large amount of energy to heat the Earth's surface during the day. However, these same characteristics allow the energy to escape at night. This causes temperatures to drop. You probably rarely think of snow and deserts together. But temperate deserts often receive light snow during the winter.

✓ **Reading Check** Why are temperate deserts cold at night?

Temperate Desert

- **Average Temperature Range** 1°C to 50°C (34°F to 120°F)
- **Average Yearly Precipitation** 0 to 25 cm
- **Soil Characteristics** poor in organic matter

 INCLUSION *Strategies*

- *Behavior Control Issues*   • *Visually Impaired*
- *Gifted and Talented*

Organize students into small groups. Assign each group two biomes to categorize. Groups will need their textbook, additional resource books such as an encyclopedia, two large sheets of paper, various magazines to cut pictures from, and glue. For each biome, ask each group to record on paper the definition, a description with a picture, typical plants or animals that live in the biome, one or two locations of the biome, and something unique about this biome. For extra credit, ask students to hypothesize how geography may affect the climate of the locations they chose. Have groups share with the rest of the class what they documented. **LS** Visual/Kinesthetic

Figure 6 Biomes of the Polar Zone

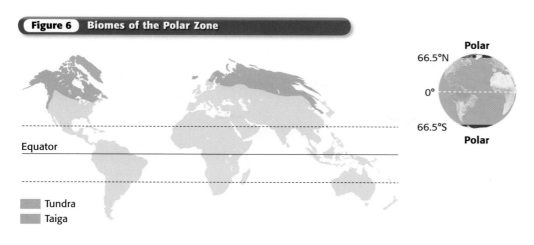

Tundra
Taiga

The Polar Zone

The climate zone located at the North or South Pole and its surrounding area is called the **polar zone.** Polar climates have the coldest average temperatures of all the climate zones. Temperatures in the winter stay below freezing. The temperatures during the summer remain cool. **Figure 6** shows the distribution of the biomes found in the polar zone.

polar zone the North or South Pole and its surrounding area

Tundra

The tundra biome, as shown in **Figure 7,** has long, cold winters with almost 24 hours of night. It also has short, cool summers with almost 24 hours of daylight. In the summer, only the top meter of soil thaws. Underneath the thawed soil lies a permanently frozen layer of soil, called *permafrost.* This frozen layer prevents the water in the thawed soil from draining. Because of the poor drainage, the upper soil layer is muddy. This muddy layer of soil makes a great breeding ground for insects, such as mosquitoes. Many birds migrate to the tundra during the summer to feed on the insects. Other animals that live in the tundra are caribou, reindeer, and polar bears. Plants in this biome include mosses and lichens.

Tundra

- **Average Temperature Range** −27°C to 5°C (−17°F to 41°F)
- **Average Yearly Precipitation** 0 to 25 cm
- **Soil Characteristics** frozen

Figure 7 *In the tundra, mosses and lichens cover rocks.*

WEIRD SCIENCE

Lichens are organisms that thrive in the polar zone. Some lichens in the Arctic have been determined to be 4,500 years old. To protect themselves from the cold, some lichens live 2 cm inside rocks! Despite their ability to survive in extremely harsh arctic conditions, most lichens have an extremely low tolerance for sulfur dioxide in air pollution. As a result, they are usually not found in industrialized areas.

Taiga

- Average Temperature Range −10°C to 15°C (14°F to 59°F)
- Average Yearly Precipitation 40 to 61 cm
- Soil Characteristics acidic

Figure 8 *The taiga, such as this one in Washington, have mostly evergreens for trees.*

microclimate the climate of a small area

SCHOOL to HOME

WRITING SKILL **Your Biome** With your parents, explore the biome in the area where you live. What kinds of animals and plants live in your area? Write a one-page paper that describes the biome and why the biome of your area has its particular climate.

ACTIVITY

Taiga (Northern Coniferous Forest)

Just south of the tundra lies the taiga biome. The taiga, as shown in **Figure 8,** has long, cold winters and short, warm summers. Animals commonly found here are moose, bears, and rabbits. The majority of the trees are evergreen needle-leaved trees called *conifers,* such as pine, spruce, and fir trees. The needles and flexible branches allow these trees to shed heavy snow before they can be damaged. Conifer needles are made of acidic substances. When the needles die and fall to the soil, they make the soil acidic. Most plants cannot grow in acidic soil. Because of the acidic soil, the forest floor is bare except for some mosses and lichens.

Microclimates

The climate and the biome of a particular place can also be influenced by local conditions. **Microclimate** is the climate of a small area. The alpine biome is a cold biome found on mountains all around the world. The alpine biome can even be found on mountains in the Tropics! How is this possible? The high elevation affects the area's climate and therefore its biome. As the elevation increases, the air's ability to transfer heat from the ground to the atmosphere by conduction decreases, which causes temperatures to decrease. In winter, the temperatures are below freezing. In summer, average temperatures range from 10°C to 15°C. Plants and animals have had to develop special adaptations to live in this severe climate.

Cities

Cities are also microclimates. In a city, temperatures can be 1°C to 2°C warmer than the surrounding rural areas. Have you ever walked barefoot on a black asphalt street on a hot summer day? Doing so burns your feet because buildings and pavement made of dark materials absorb solar radiation instead of reflecting it. There is also less vegetation in a city to take in the sun's rays. This absorption and re-radiation of heat by buildings and pavement heats the surrounding air. In turn, the temperatures rise.

Reading Check Why do cities have higher temperatures than the surrounding rural areas?

CONNECTION TO Physics

Hot Roofs! Scientists studied roofs on a sunny day when the air temperature was 13°C. They recorded roof temperatures ranging from 18°C to 61°C depending on color and material of the roof. Place thermometers on outside objects that are made of different types of materials and that are different colors. Please stay off the roof! Is there a difference in temperatures? **ACTIVITY**

SECTION Review

Summary

- The temperate zone is located between the Tropics and the polar zone. It has moderate temperatures.
- Temperate forests, temperate grasslands, and temperate deserts are biomes in the temperate zone.
- The polar zone includes the North or South Pole and its surrounding area. The polar zone has the coldest temperatures.
- The tundra and the taiga are biomes within the polar zone.

Using Key Terms

1. In your own words, write a definition for the term *microclimate*.

Complete each of the following sentences by choosing the correct term from the word bank.

> temperate zone   polar zone
> microclimate

2. The coldest temperatures are found in the ___.

3. The ___ has moderate temperatures.

Understanding Key Ideas

4. Which of the following biomes has the driest climate?
   a. temperate forests
   b. temperate grasslands
   c. chaparrals
   d. temperate deserts

5. Explain why the temperate zone has lower temperatures than the Tropics.

6. Describe how the latitude of the polar zone affects the climate in that area.

7. Explain why the tundra can sometimes experience 24 hours of daylight or 24 hours of night.

8. How do conifers make the soil they grow in too acidic for other plants to grow?

Math Skills

9. Texas has an area of about 700,000 square kilometers. Grasslands compose about 20% of this area. About how many square kilometers of grassland are there in Texas?

Critical Thinking

10. **Identifying Relationships** Which biome would be more suitable for growing crops, temperate forest or taiga? Explain.

11. **Making Inferences** Describe the types of animals and vegetation you might find in the Alpine biome.

SCILINKS **NSTA**
Developed and maintained by the National Science Teachers Association

For a variety of links related to this chapter, go to www.scilinks.org

Topic: Modeling Earth's Climate
SciLinks code: HSM0976

Answer to Reading Check

Cities have higher temperatures than the surrounding rural areas because buildings and pavement absorb solar radiation instead of reflecting it.

CHAPTER RESOURCES

Chapter Resource File

- **Section Quiz** GENERAL
- **Section Review** GENERAL
- **Vocabulary and Section Summary** GENERAL
- **Reinforcement Worksheet** BASIC

Workbooks

Science Skills
- Finding Useful Sources GENERAL

Answers to Section Review

1. Sample answer: A microclimate is the climate of a small area.
2. polar zone
3. temperate zone
4. d
5. The temperate zone has lower temperatures than the Tropics because it is located at a higher latitude.
6. Because the polar zone is at a higher latitude than the other climate zones, it receives less direct solar energy and therefore has lower temperatures.
7. The Earth is tilted so that during the summer, high latitudes are pointed toward the sun. Therefore, polar regions receive 24 hours of daylight each day. In the winter, the Earth is tilted so that high latitudes are pointed away from the sun. Therefore, polar regions experience 24 hours of night each day.
8. The needles of conifers are acidic. When the needles fall to the ground, they make the soil acidic, which makes it difficult for many other plants to grow.
9. $700,000 \text{ km}^2 \times 0.20 = 140,000 \text{ km}^2$
10. Sample answer: A temperate forest would be better for growing crops than the taiga because the soil in the forest is very fertile and organically rich. The taiga would be a difficult place to grow crops because the soil is acidic from the conifer needles.
11. Students should choose plants and animals that are adapted to very cold climates in the mountains. Sample answer: mountain goat, snow leopard, moss

Focus

Overview

In this section, students will learn how the Earth's climate has changed in the past. Students will learn about different causes of climate change. Students will also learn about the greenhouse effect and its role in global warming.

🔊 Bellringer

Have students imagine that the climate of the area where they live has changed, so it is now warmer than it used to be. Have students write down five different ways they think the area would be affected by warmer temperatures.

Motivate

Demonstration — GENERAL

The Greenhouse Effect Tell students that the glass windows in a greenhouse are similar to the Earth's atmosphere. The glass allows radiant energy to enter but prevents thermal energy from escaping. Have students place a thermometer in a plastic bag on a sunny window-sill. Place another thermometer next to the plastic bag. After 30 minutes, have a student read the two thermometers and compare the difference in temperature.

English Language Learners

LS Kinesthetic

READING WARM-UP

Objectives
- Describe how the Earth's climate has changed over time.
- Summarize four different theories that attempt to explain why the Earth's climate has changed.
- Explain the greenhouse effect and its role in global warming.

Terms to Learn
ice age
global warming
greenhouse effect

READING STRATEGY

Paired Summarizing Read this section silently. In pairs, take turns summarizing the material. Stop to discuss ideas that seem confusing.

ice age a long period of climate cooling during which ice sheets cover large areas of Earth's surface; also known as a glacial period

---

Changes in Climate

As you have probably noticed, the weather changes from day to day. Sometimes, the weather can change several times in one day! But have you ever noticed the climate change?

On Saturday, your morning baseball game was canceled because of rain, but by that afternoon the sun was shining. Now, think about the climate where you live. You probably haven't noticed a change in climate, because climates change slowly. What causes climatic change? Studies indicate that human activity may cause climatic change. However, natural factors also can influence changes in the climate.

Ice Ages

The geologic record indicates that the Earth's climate has been much colder than it is today. In fact, much of the Earth was covered by sheets of ice during certain periods. An **ice age** is a period during which ice collects in high latitudes and moves toward lower latitudes. Scientists have found evidence of many major ice ages throughout the Earth's geologic history. The most recent ice age began about 2 million years ago.

Glacial Periods

During an ice age, there are periods of cold and periods of warmth. These periods are called glacial and interglacial periods. During *glacial periods,* the enormous sheets of ice advance. As they advance, they get bigger and cover a larger area, as shown in **Figure 1.** Because a large amount of water is frozen during glacial periods, the sea level drops.

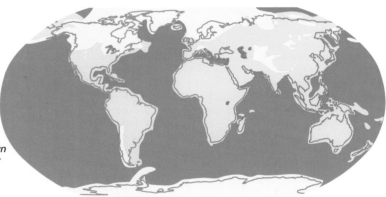

Figure 1 *During glacial periods, ice sheets (as shown in light blue), cover a larger portion of the Earth.*

CHAPTER RESOURCES

Chapter Resource File

- **Lesson Plan**
- **Directed Reading A** BASIC
- **Directed Reading B** SPECIAL NEEDS

Technology

Transparencies
- Bellringer
- The Milankovitch Theory

Interglacial Periods

Warmer times that happen between glacial periods are called *interglacial periods*. During an interglacial period, the ice begins to melt and the sea level rises again. The last interglacial period began 10,000 years ago and is still happening. Why do these periods occur? Will the Earth have another glacial period in the future? These questions have been debated by scientists for the past 200 years.

Motions of the Earth

There are many theories about the causes of ice ages. Each theory tries to explain the gradual cooling that begins an ice age. This cooling leads to the development of large ice sheets that periodically cover large areas of the Earth's surface.

The *Milankovitch theory* explains why an ice age isn't just one long cold spell. Instead, the ice age alternates between cold and warm periods. Milutin Milankovitch, a Yugoslavian scientist, proposed that changes in the Earth's orbit and in the tilt of the Earth's axis cause ice ages. His theory is shown in **Figure 2.** In a 100,000 year period, the Earth's orbit changes from elliptical to circular. This changes the Earth's distance from the sun. In turn, it changes the temperature on Earth. Changes in the tilt of the Earth also influence the climate. The more the Earth is tilted, the closer the poles are to the sun.

✓ **Reading Check** **What are the two things Milankovitch says causes ice ages?** (*See the Appendix for answers to Reading Checks.*)

INTERNET ACTIVITY

For another activity related to this chapter, go to **go.hrw.com** and type in the keyword **HZ5CLMW.**

Teach

ACTiViTY ——— **ADVANCED**

Ancient Climates Have students find out why scientists study the dust concentrations and gas composition of glacial ice in places such as Antarctica and Greenland. In an oral or written presentation, have students explain why these and other data provide evidence about the last glacial period and other ice ages.
LS Verbal/Intrapersonal

Answer to Reading Check

Changes in the Earth's orbit and the tilt of the Earth's axis are the two things that Milankovitch says cause ice ages.

Figure 2 **The Milankovitch Theory**

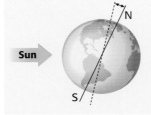
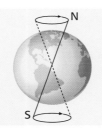

❶ Over a period of 100,000 years, the Earth's orbit slowly changes from a more circular shape to a more elliptical shape and back again. When Earth's orbit is elliptical, Earth receives more energy from the sun. When its orbit is more circular, Earth receives less energy from the sun.

❷ Over a period of 41,000 years, the tilt of the Earth's axis varies between 22.2° and 24.5°. When the tilt is at 24.5°, the poles receive more solar energy.

❸ The Earth's axis traces a complete circle every 26,000 years. The circular motion of the Earth's axis determines the time of year that the Earth is closest to the sun.

MISCONCEPTION ALERT

Ice Ages and Glacial Periods Students may be confused about the difference between an ice age and a glacial period. An ice age is the gradual cooling of the planet over thousands of years. During this time, glaciers repeatedly spread outward from the Earth's poles toward the equator. Ice ages are characterized by glacial periods (when glaciers spread) and interglacial periods (when glaciers retreat). Glacial periods can happen rather quickly—often in less than 30 years. Ice cores indicate that sudden glaciation periods could be caused by changes in major ocean currents or by volcanic eruptions. Currently, we are in an interglacial period of an ice age.

ACTiViTY ——— GENERAL

writing **Volcanic Eruptions**
Have students research
and write a short report
on a large volcanic eruption.
Reports should include where
the volcano is located, what
damage the eruption caused,
and what the eruption's long-
term effects were. **LS** Intrapersonal

CONNECTION to
Geology ——— GENERAL

**Climate Change Due to Plate
Tectonics** Tectonic activity
will continue to rearrange the
Earth's continents in the future.
Europe and North America will
continue to spread apart, allow-
ing greater circulation between
the Arctic and Atlantic Oceans.
At the same time, Antarctica
will move away from the South
Pole. Ask students to imagine
that they have been transported
50 million years into the future.
How is the Earth different in
terms of the events just described?
Have students create a story or
comic about the Earth of the
distant future. (Sample answer:
Earth will be much warmer. The
sea level will be higher because
ocean currents will reach both polar
regions, warming them. Antarctica
will no longer be an icebound continent. Additionally, the continents
will be rearranged, and some of
today's prominent geographic features, such as the Rocky Mountains,
will be significantly eroded.)
LS Intrapersonal/Visual

Figure 3 *Much of Pangaea—the part
that is now Africa, South America, India,
Antarctica, Australia, and Saudi Arabia—
was covered by continental ice sheets.*

Plate Tectonics

The Earth's climate is further influenced by plate
tectonics and continental drift. One theory pro-
poses that ice ages happen when the continents
are positioned closer to the polar regions. About
250 million years ago, all the continents were connected near the South Pole in one giant landmass
called *Pangaea,* as shown in **Figure 3.** During this
time, ice covered a large area of the Earth's surface. As Pangaea broke apart, the continents moved
toward the equator, and the ice age ended. During the last ice age, many large landmasses were
positioned in the polar zones. Antarctica, northern
North America, Europe, and Asia were covered by
large sheets of ice.

Volcanic Eruptions

Many natural factors can affect global climate. Catastrophic
events, such as volcanic eruptions, can influence climate. Volcanic eruptions send large amounts of dust, ash, and smoke
into the atmosphere. Once in the atmosphere, the dust, smoke,
and ash particles act as a shield. This shield blocks the sun's
rays, which causes the Earth to cool. **Figure 4** shows how dust
particles from a volcanic eruption block the sun.

✓ Reading Check How can volcanoes change the climate?

Figure 4 Volcanic Dust in the Atmosphere

Volcanic eruptions, such as the 1980
eruption of Mount St. Helens, as
shown at right, produce dust that
reflects sunlight.

Sun's rays
Mount St. Helens
Dust layer
Atmosphere

Answer to Reading Check
Dust, ash, and smoke from volcanic
eruptions block the sun's rays, which
causes the Earth to cool.

Figure 5 Some scientists believe that a 10 km chunk of rock smashed into the Earth 65 million years ago, which caused the climatic change that resulted in the extinction of dinosaurs.

Asteroid Impact

Imagine a rock the size of a car flying in from outer space and crashing in your neighborhood. This rock, like the one shown in **Figure 5,** is called an asteroid. An *asteroid* is a small, rocky object that orbits the sun. Sometimes, asteroids enter our atmosphere and crash into the Earth. What would happen if an asteroid 1 km wide, which is more than half a mile long, hit the Earth? Scientists believe that if an asteroid this big hit the Earth, it could change the climate of the entire world.

When a large piece of rock slams into the Earth, it causes debris to shoot into the atmosphere. *Debris* is dust and smaller rocks. This debris can block some of the sunlight and thermal energy. This would lower average temperatures, which would change the climate. Plants wouldn't get the sunlight they needed to grow, and animals would find surviving difficult. Scientists believe such an event is what caused dinosaurs to become extinct 65 million years ago when a 10 km asteroid slammed into the Earth and changed the Earth's climate.

The Sun's Cycle

Some changes in the climate can be linked to changes in the sun. You might think that the sun always stays the same. However, the sun follows an 11-year cycle. During this cycle, the sun changes from a solar maximum to a solar minimum. During a solar minimum, the sun produces a low percentage of high-energy radiation. But when the sun is at its solar maximum, it produces a large percentage of high-energy radiation. This increase in high-energy radiation warms the winds in the atmosphere. This change in turn affects climate patterns around the world.

CONNECTION TO Astronomy

Sunspots Sunspots are dark areas on the sun's surface. The number of sunspots changes with the sun's cycle. When the cycle is at a solar maximum, there are many sunspots. When the cycle is at a solar minimum, there are fewer sunspots. If the number of sunspots was low in 1997, in what year will the next low point in the cycle happen?

Reteaching ——— BASIC

Changing Climate Ask students to describe the climate in their area. Then review the factors that might affect the climate. Have students describe how each factor would affect the climate in their area.

 Intrapersonal

Quiz ——— GENERAL

1. Why does the sea level fall during glacial periods? (because much of Earth's water is frozen during a glacial period)

2. How might a major volcanic eruption have brought about an ice age? (Dust, smoke, and ash from a volcanic eruption entered the atmosphere and acted as a shield, blocking out many of the sun's rays and causing the Earth to cool.)

3. How might global warming affect coastal areas? (The warmer temperatures could cause polar icecaps to melt, which would raise the sea level and cause flooding in coastal areas.)

Alternative Assessment ——— GENERAL

Climate Collage Have students make a collage about global cooling or warming. They can include images of how they think the Earth would appear and descriptions of the likely causes of climate change. English Language Learners

Visual

The Ride to School

1. The round-trip distance from your home to school is 20 km.

2. You traveled from home to school and from school to home 23 times in a month.

3. The vehicle in which you took your trips travels 30 km/gal.

4. If burning 1 gal of gasoline produces 9 kg of carbon dioxide, how much carbon dioxide did the vehicle release during the month?

global warming a gradual increase in the average global temperature

greenhouse effect the warming of the surface and lower atmosphere of Earth that occurs when carbon dioxide, water vapor, and other gases in the air absorb and trap thermal energy

Global Warming

A gradual increase in the average global temperature that is due to a higher concentration of gases, such as carbon dioxide in the atmosphere, is called **global warming.** To understand how global warming works, you must first learn about the greenhouse effect.

Greenhouse Effect

The Earth's natural heating process, in which gases in the atmosphere trap thermal energy, is called the **greenhouse effect.** The car in **Figure 6** shows how the greenhouse effect works. The car's windows stop most of the thermal energy from escaping, and the inside of the car gets hot. On Earth, instead of glass stopping the thermal energy, atmospheric gases absorb the thermal energy. When this happens, the thermal energy stays in the atmosphere and keeps the Earth warm. Many scientists believe that the rise in global temperatures is due to an increase of carbon dioxide, an atmospheric gas. Most evidence shows that the increase in carbon dioxide is caused by the burning of fossil fuels.

Another factor that may add to global warming is the clearing of forests. In many countries, forests are being burned to clear land for farming. Burning of the forests releases more carbon dioxide. Because plants use carbon dioxide to make food, destroying the trees decreases a natural way of removing carbon dioxide from the atmosphere.

Figure 6 *Sunlight streams into the car through the clear, glass windows. The seats absorb the radiant energy and change it into thermal energy. The energy is then trapped in the car.*

Answer to Math Practice

10 km × 2 = 20 km/day
20 km/day × 23 trips = 460 km/mo
460 km ÷ 30 km/gal = 15.3 kg CO_2

Answer to School-to-Home Activity

Sample answer: The city could pass legislation that requires all vehicle emissions to be below a certain standard. The city could provide incentives for car pooling. The city could also improve the public transportation system and create more public transportation routes.

Consequences of Global Warming

Many scientists think that if the global temperature continues to rise, the ice caps will melt and cause flooding. Melted ice-caps would raise the sea level and flood low-lying areas, such as the coasts.

Areas that receive little rainfall, such as deserts, might receive even less because of increased evaporation. Desert animals and plants would find surviving harder. Warmer and drier climates could harm crops in the Midwest of the United States. But farther north, such as in Canada, weather conditions for farming could improve.

✓ Reading Check How would warmer temperatures affect deserts?

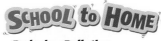

SCHOOL to HOME

Reducing Pollution
Your city just received a warning from the Environmental Protection Agency for exceeding the automobile fuel emissions standards. Discuss with your parent ways that the city can reduce the amount of automobile emissions.

ACTIVITY

SECTION Review

Summary

● The Earth's climate experiences glacial and interglacial periods.

● The Milankovitch theory states that the Earth's climate changes as its orbit and the tilt of its axis change.

● Climate changes can be caused by volcanic eruptions, asteroid impact, the sun's cycle, and by global warming.

● Excess carbon dioxide is believed to contribute to global warming.

Using Key Terms

1. Use the following term in a sentence: *ice age*.

2. In your own words, write a definition for each of the following terms: *global warming* and *greenhouse effect*.

Understanding Key Ideas

3. Describe the possible causes of an ice age.

4. Which of the following can cause a change in the climate due to dust particles?
   a. volcanic eruptions
   b. plate tectonics
   c. solar cycles
   d. ice ages

5. How has the Earth's climate changed over time?

6. What might have caused the Earth's climate to change?

7. Which period of an ice age are we in currently? Explain.

8. Explain how the greenhouse effect warms the Earth.

Math Skills

9. After a volcanic eruption, the average temperature in a region dropped from 30° to 18°C. By how many degrees Celsius did the temperature drop?

Critical Thinking

10. **Analyzing Relationships** How will the warming of the Earth affect agriculture in different parts of the world? Explain.

11. **Predicting Consequences** How would deforestation (the cutting of trees) affect global warming?

SCI LINKS®

NSTA
Developed and maintained by the
National Science Teachers Association

For a variety of links related to this chapter, go to www.scilinks.org

Topic: Changes in Climate
SciLinks code: HSM0252

Answer to Reading Check

The deserts would receive even less rainfall, making it harder for plants and animals in the desert to survive.

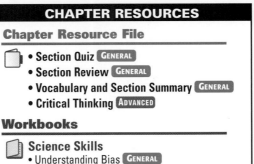

CHAPTER RESOURCES

Chapter Resource File
- Section Quiz **GENERAL**
- Section Review **GENERAL**
- Vocabulary and Section Summary **GENERAL**
- Critical Thinking **ADVANCED**

Workbooks

Science Skills
- Understanding Bias **GENERAL**

Answers to Section Review

1. Sample answer: Milankovitch theorized that ice ages were caused by changes in the Earth's orbit and changes in the tilt of the Earth's axis.

2. Sample answer: Global warming is the gradual increase in the average global temperature due to a higher concentration of greenhouse gases in the atmosphere. The greenhouse effect is the warming of the surface and lower atmosphere of the Earth that occurs when carbon dioxide, water vapor, and other gases in the air absorb and trap thermal energy.

3. Ice ages could be caused by changes in the Earth's orbit, in the tilt of the Earth's axis, by plate tectonics, volcanic eruptions, or asteroid impacts.

4. a

5. The Earth has experienced periods of cold and warm temperatures called glacial and interglacial periods.

6. The Earth's climate may have changed because of the change in the Earth's orbit, a change in the tilt of the Earth's axis, plate tectonics, volcanic eruptions, impact from a large asteroid, the sun's cycle, and global warming.

7. We are in an interglacial period. Ice sheets are melting instead of advancing.

8. The greenhouse effect occurs when gases in the atmosphere trap thermal energy and warm the Earth.

9. $30°C - 18°C = 12°C$

10. Sample answer: Global warming might improve farming at higher latitudes. Closer to the equator, an increase in evaporation and less rainfall might make growing crops difficult.

11. Answers may vary. Sample answer: Trees store carbon, so deforestation could cause carbon dioxide levels in the air to increase, which might increase global warming.

Biome Business

Teacher's Notes

Time Required

One 45-minute class period

Lab Ratings

EASY —————————→ HARD

Teacher Prep 🧪
Student Set-Up 🧪
Concept Level 🧪🧪
Clean Up 🧪

MATERIALS

Note that student groups will need a general map to identify their biome location.

Preparation Notes

Remind students not to use seasonal terms such as *spring* and *fall* because some of the biomes in the Southern Hemisphere may experience seasons that are opposite from the seasons of the Northern Hemisphere.

Skills Practice Lab

Biome Business

OBJECTIVES

Interpret data in a climatograph.

Identify the biome for each climatograph.

You have just been hired as an assistant to a world-famous botanist. You have been provided with climatographs for three biomes. A *climatograph* is a graph that shows the monthly temperature and precipitation of an area in a year.

You can use the information provided in the three graphs to determine what type of climate each biome has. Next to the climatograph for each biome is an unlabeled map of the biome. Using the maps and the information provided in the graphs, you must figure out what the environment is like in each biome. You can find the exact location of each biome by tracing the map of the biome and matching it to the map at the bottom of the page.

- Tundra
- Taiga
- Temperate forest
- Tropical rain forest
- Temperate grassland
- Tropical savanna
- Temperate desert
- Tropical desert
- Chaparral
- Mountains

Procedure

1. Look at each climatograph. The shaded areas show the average precipitation for the biome. The red line shows the average temperature.

2. Use the climatographs to determine the climate patterns for each biome. Compare the map of each biome with the map below to find the exact location of each biome.

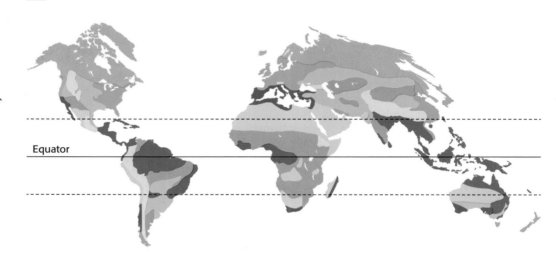

Equator

David Sparks
Redwater Jr. High
Redwater, Texas

CHAPTER RESOURCES

Chapter Resource File
- • Datasheet for Chapter Lab
- • Lab Notes and Answers

Technology
- 🎞 **Classroom Videos**
  - • Lab Video

LabBook

- • Global Impact
- • For the Birds

Analyze Results

1 **Analyzing Data** Describe the precipitation patterns of each biome by answering the following questions:

 a. In which month does the biome receive the most precipitation?

 b. Do you think that the biome is dry, or do you think that it is wet from frequent rains?

2 **Analyzing Data** Describe the temperature patterns of each biome by answering the following questions:

 a. In the biome, which months are warmest?

 b. Does the biome seem to have temperature cycles, like seasons, or is the temperature almost always the same?

 c. Do you think that the biome is warm or cold? Explain.

Draw Conclusions

3 **Drawing Conclusions** Name each biome.

4 **Applying Conclusions** Where is each biome located?

Biome B

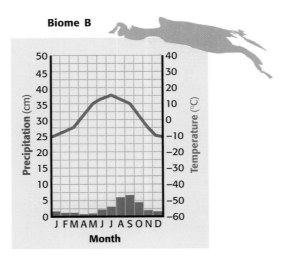

Biome A

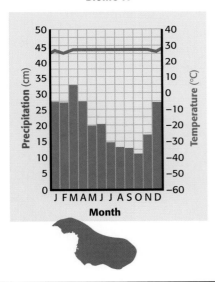

Biome C

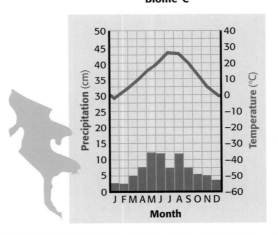

Analyze the Results

1.a. In Biome A, the rain is heaviest in March. In Biome B, the rain is heaviest in September. In Biome C, the rain is heaviest in May.

 b. Biome A is very wet. Biomes B and C are relatively dry, but some months are rainier than others.

2.a. Biome A has a relatively constant temperature throughout the year. Biomes B and C experience their warmest months from June to August.

 b. Biome A has a constant temperature throughout the year. Biomes B and C experience temperature cycles.

 c. Biome A is warm, and the temperature is high year-round. Biome B has a cooler climate, and the climatograph shows cooler temperatures year-round. Biome C has a moderate climate in the early and late months of the year, but the temperature is quite hot in the middle months of the year.

Draw Conclusions

3. Biome A is a tropical rain forest. Biome B is a taiga. Biome C is a temperate grassland.

4. Biome A is located on the western coast of Africa, near the equator. Biome B is located in northern Asia. Biome C is located in the midwestern United States.

Assignment Guide

Section	Questions
1	1, 6, 9, 12, 13, 18–20, 24–26
2	7
3	2, 8, 14, 15, 23
4	10, 16, 21,
1 and 2	3
1 and 4	4, 5, 17
2 and 3	11, 22

ANSWERS

Using Key Terms

1. Sample answer: A biome is one large region characterized by a specific type of climate, and the tropical zone is an even larger region, consisting of several biomes.

2. Sample answer: Weather is the condition of the atmosphere at a particular time, and climate is the average weather condition of an area.

3. Sample answer: The temperate zone is between the Tropics and the polar zone. The polar zone includes the North and South Poles and their surrounding areas.

4. global warming

5. microclimate

Understanding Key Ideas

6. d	9. c
7. a	10. c
8. b	11. b

USING KEY TERMS

For each pair of terms, explain how the meanings of the terms differ.

1 *biome* and *tropical zone*

2 *weather* and *climate*

3 *temperate zone* and *polar zone*

Complete each of the following sentences by choosing the correct term from the word bank.

biome	microclimate
ice age	global warming

4 One factor that could add to ___ is an increase in pollution.

5 A city is an example of a(n) ___.

UNDERSTANDING KEY IDEAS

Multiple Choice

6 Which of the following is a factor that affects climate?
  a. prevailing winds
  b. latitude
  c. ocean currents
  d. All of the above

7 The biome that has a temperature range of 28°C to 32°C and an average yearly precipitation of 100 cm is the
  a. tropical savanna.
  b. tropical desert.
  c. tropical rain forest.
  d. None of the above

8 Which of the following biomes is NOT found in the temperate zone?
  a. temperate forest
  b. taiga
  c. chaparral
  d. temperate grassland

9 In which of the following is the tilt of the Earth's axis considered to have an effect on climate?
  a. global warming
  b. the sun's cycle
  c. the Milankovitch theory
  d. asteroid impact

10 Which of the following substances contributes to the greenhouse effect?
  a. smoke
  b. smog
  c. carbon dioxide
  d. All of the above

11 In which of the following climate zones is the soil most fertile?
  a. the tropical climate zone
  b. the temperate climate zone
  c. the polar climate zone
  d. None of the above

---

12. Higher latitudes receive less solar radiation because the sun's rays strike the Earth's surface at a less direct angle. This spreads the same amount of solar energy over a larger area, resulting in lower temperatures.

13. The amount of precipitation an area receives can depend on whether the region's prevailing winds form from a warm air mass or from a cold air mass. If the winds form from a warm air mass, they will probably carry moisture. If the winds form from a cold air mass, they will probably be dry. Precipitation is more likely to occur when the prevailing winds are warm and moist.

14. Answers may vary. Sample answer: Alpine biomes on tropical mountains are examples of a microclimate. Less dense air at higher elevations retains less thermal energy and less precipitation than air at lower elevations.

15. The tundras and deserts receive very little precipitation.

16. Carbon dioxide is a greenhouse gas. Deforestation decreases the amount of trees, which naturally recycle carbon dioxide in the atmosphere. If the trees are burned, carbon dioxide will be released into the atmosphere, and global warming will increase.

Short Answer

12 Why do higher latitudes receive less solar radiation than lower latitudes do?

13 How does wind influence precipitation patterns?

14 Give an example of a microclimate. What causes the unique temperature and precipitation characteristics of this area?

15 How are tundras and deserts similar?

16 How does deforestation influence global warming?

CRITICAL THINKING

17 **Concept Mapping** Use the following terms to create a concept map: *global warming, deforestation, changes in climate, greenhouse effect, ice ages,* and *the Milankovitch theory.*

18 **Analyzing Processes** Explain how ocean surface currents cause milder climates.

19 **Identifying Relationships** Describe how the tilt of the Earth's axis affects seasonal changes in different latitudes.

20 **Evaluating Conclusions** Explain why the climate on the eastern side of the Rocky Mountains differs drastically from the climate on the western side.

21 **Applying Concepts** What are some steps you and your family can take to reduce the amount of carbon dioxide that is released into the atmosphere?

22 **Applying Concepts** If you wanted to live in a warm, dry area, which biome would you choose to live in?

23 **Evaluating Data** Explain why the vegetation in areas that have a tundra climate is sparse even though these areas receive precipitation that is adequate to support life.

INTERPRETING GRAPHICS

Use the diagram below to answer the questions that follow.

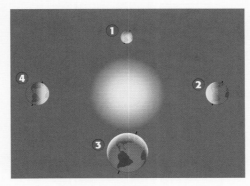

24 At what position—1, 2, 3, or 4—is it spring in the Southern Hemisphere?

25 At what position does the South Pole receive almost 24 hours of daylight?

26 Explain what is happening in each climate zone in both the Northern and Southern Hemispheres at position 4.

---

19. Sample answer: Due to the Earth's tilt, higher latitudes in the Northern Hemisphere receive more solar energy in June, July, and August, causing summer during that period. Because the Southern Hemisphere is tilted away from the sun during these months, higher latitudes in that hemisphere receive less direct solar energy, which causes winter.

20. Sample answer: The climate differs on each side of the Rocky Mountains because the mountains affect the distribution of precipitation. The western side receives more precipitation because, as the warm air is forced to rise, it releases precipitation. As the dry air crosses the mountain, it sinks, warming and absorbing moisture. Therefore, the eastern side is much warmer and drier.

21. Sample answer: conserve electricity, use public transportation, and plant trees

22. tropical savanna or tropical desert

23. Tundra soil is frozen for most of the year. In the summer, only the top meter thaws. The frozen soil underneath prevents the water from properly draining, which makes it difficult for some vegetation to grow.

Interpreting Graphics

24. 3

25. 2

26. In the tropical zone, temperatures are warm. The temperate zone in the Northern Hemisphere is experiencing summer. The temperate zone in the Southern Hemisphere is experiencing winter. The polar zone in the Northern Hemisphere is experiencing almost 24 hours of daylight. The polar zone in the Southern Hemisphere is experiencing almost 24 hours of night.

Critical Thinking

17.  An answer to this exercise can be found at the end of this book.

18. Sample answer: Warm surface currents heat the surrounding air. A warm surface current might bring warmer temperatures to an area of land at a higher latitude that might normally be colder.

CHAPTER RESOURCES

Chapter Resource File

- Chapter Review GENERAL
- Chapter Test A GENERAL
- Chapter Test B ADVANCED
- Chapter Test C SPECIAL NEEDS
- Vocabulary Activity GENERAL

Workbooks

Study Guide
- Assessment resources are also available in Spanish.

Standardized Test Preparation

Standardized Test Preparation

Teacher's Note

To provide practice under more realistic testing conditions, give students 20 minutes to answer all of the questions in this Standardized Test Preparation.

MISCONCEPTION ALERT

Answers to the standardized test preparation can help you identify student misconceptions and misunderstandings.

READING

Passage 1

1. C
2. G
3. C

+ TEST DOCTOR

Question 1: Some students may think the word *decipher* means "to question" or to "calculate" because students may relate these words to how scientists use computers to determine why climate changes, which is discussed in the passage.

Question 3: This fact is mentioned in the sentence: "For example, 6,000 years ago today's desert in North Africa was grassland and shallow lakes." If students chose A, they may not have realized that the climate of North Africa has changed.

READING

Read each of the passages below. Then, answer the questions that follow each passage.

Passage 1 Earth's climate has gone through many changes. For example, 6,000 years ago today's desert in North Africa was grassland and shallow lakes. Hippopotamuses, crocodiles, and early Stone Age people shared the shallow lakes that covered the area. For many years, scientists have known that Earth's climate has changed. What they didn't know was why it changed. Today, scientists can use supercomputers and complex computer programs to help them find the answer. Now, scientists may be able to <u>decipher</u> why North Africa's lakes and grasslands became a desert. And that information may be useful for predicting future heat waves and ice ages.

1. In this passage, what does *decipher* mean?
   - **A** to question
   - **B** to cover up
   - **C** to explain
   - **D** to calculate

2. According to the passage, which of the following statements is true?
   - **F** Scientists did not know that Earth's climate has changed.
   - **G** Scientists have known that Earth's climate has changed.
   - **H** Scientists have known why Earth's climate has changed.
   - **I** Scientists know that North Africa was always desert.

3. Which of the following is a fact in the passage?
   - **A** North African desert areas never had lakes.
   - **B** North American desert areas never had lakes.
   - **C** North African desert areas had shallow lakes.
   - **D** North Africa is covered with shallow lakes.

Passage 2 El Niño, which is Spanish for "the child," is the name of a weather event that occurs in the Pacific Ocean. Every 2 to 12 years, the inter-action between the ocean surface and atmospheric winds creates El Niño. This event influences weather patterns in many regions of the world. For example, in Indonesia and Malaysia, El Niño meant <u>drought</u> and forest fires in 1998. Thousands of people in these countries suffered respiratory ailments caused by breathing the smoke from these fires. Heavy rains in San Francisco created extremely high mold-spore counts. These spores caused problems for people who have allergies. In San Francisco, the spore count in February is usually between 0 and 100. In 1998, the count was often higher than 8,000.

1. In this passage, what does *drought* mean?
   - **A** windy weather
   - **B** stormy weather
   - **C** long period of dry weather
   - **D** rainy weather

2. What can you infer about mold spores from reading the passage?
   - **F** Some people in San Francisco are allergic to mold spores.
   - **G** Mold spores are only in San Francisco.
   - **H** A higher mold-spore count helps people with allergies.
   - **I** The mold-spore count was low in 1998.

3. According to the passage, which of the following statements is true?
   - **A** El Niño causes droughts in Indonesia and Malaysia.
   - **B** El Niño occurs every year.
   - **C** El Niño causes fires in San Francisco.
   - **D** El Niño last occurred in 1998.

Passage 2

1. C
2. F
3. A

+ TEST DOCTOR

Question 1: If students chose B, they may think that *drought* means "stormy weather" because heavy rains were mentioned in the passage. However, droughts are long periods of dry weather.

The chart below shows types of organisms in an unknown biome. Use the chart below to answer the questions that follow.

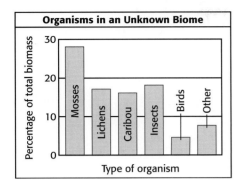

Organisms in an Unknown Biome

1. *Biomass* is a term that means "the total mass of all living things in a certain area." The graph above shows the relative percentages of the total biomass for different plants and animals in a given area. What type of biome does the graph represent?

   A rain forest
   B chaparral
   C tundra
   D taiga

2. Approximately what percentage of biomass is made up of caribou?

   F 28%
   G 25%
   H 16%
   I 5%

3. Approximately what percentage of biomass is made up of lichens and mosses?

   A 45%
   B 35%
   C 25%
   D 16%

MATH

Read each question below, and choose the best answer.

1. In a certain area of the savanna that is 12 km long and 5 km wide, there are 180 giraffes. How many giraffes are there per square kilometer in this area?

   A 12
   B 6
   C 4
   D 3

2. If the air temperature near the shore of a lake measures 24°C and the temperature increases by 0.055°C every 10 m traveled away from the lake, what would the air temperature 1 km from the lake be?

   F 5°C
   G 25°C
   H 29.5°C
   I 35°C

3. In a temperate desert, the temperature dropped from 50°C at noon to 37°C by nightfall. By how many degrees Celsius did the noon temperature drop?

   A 13°C
   B 20°C
   C 26°C
   D 50°C

4. Earth is tilted on its axis at a 23.5° angle. What is the measure of the angle that is complementary to a 23.5° angle?

   F 66.5°
   G 67.5°
   H 156.5°
   I 336.5°

5. After a volcanic eruption, the average temperature in a region dropped from 30°C to 18°C. By what percentage did the temperature drop?

   A 30%
   B 25%
   C 40%
   D 15%

Standardized Test Preparation

CHAPTER RESOURCES

Chapter Resource File

• Standardized Test Preparation GENERAL

State Resources

 For specific resources for your state, visit **go.hrw.com** and type in the keyword **HSMSTR.**

Scientific Debate

Debate —————— GENERAL

Organize the class into two teams. Have each team research global warming. After their research is complete, have each team prepare a position paper which states and supports their stance on the issues central to global warming. Using their position papers, have the teams engage in a debate about global warming. **LS** Interpersonal

Science, Technology, and Society

ACTIVITY —————— GENERAL

Have students design a model of an ice core. Have students fill a plastic foam cup one-third full with water. Place the cup of water in the freezer overnight. Add about 2 cm of water to the cup of frozen water. Then sprinkle ashes into the water to simulate the debris released from a volcanic eruption. Have the students put the cup in the freezer overnight again. Students may continue to add layers to their ice core to simulate conditions such as acid rain. Make sure students record each layer and mark the layer on the plastic foam cup. When the cup is filled, have students carefully remove the ice from the cup and analyze their findings. **LS** Kinesthetic

Science in Action

Scientific Debate

Global Warming

Many scientists believe that pollution from burning fossil fuels is causing temperatures on Earth to rise. Higher average temperatures can cause significant changes in climate. These changes may make survival difficult for animals and plants that have adapted to a biome.

However, other scientists believe that there isn't enough evidence to prove that global warming exists. They argue that any increase in temperatures around the world can be caused by a number of factors other than pollution, such as the sun's cycle.

Language Arts ACTIVITY

WRITING SKILL Read articles that present a variety of viewpoints on global warming. Then, write your own article supporting your viewpoint on global warming.

Science, Technology, and Society

Ice Cores

How do scientists know what Earth's climate was like thousands of years ago? Scientists learn about Earth's past climates by studying ice cores. An ice core is collected by drilling a tube of ice from glaciers and polar ice sheets. Layers in the ice core contain substances that landed in the snow during a particular year or season, such as dust from desert storms, ash from volcanic eruptions, and carbon dioxide from pollution. By studying the layers of the ice cores, scientists can learn what factors influenced the past climates.

Math ACTIVITY

An area has an average yearly rainfall of 20 cm. In 1,000 years, if the average yearly rainfall decreases by 6%, what would the new average yearly rainfall be?

Answer to Language Arts Activity
Students should supply articles with a variety of viewpoints on global warming.

Answer to Math Activity
20 cm × 0.06 = 1.2 cm
20 cm − 1.2 cm = 18.8 cm

Mercedes Pascual

Climate Change and Disease Mercedes Pascual is a theoretical ecologist at the University of Michigan. Pascual has been able to help the people of Bangladesh save lives by using information about climate changes to predict outbreaks of the disease cholera. Cholera can be a deadly disease that people usually contract by drinking contaminated water. Pascual knew that in Bangladesh, outbreaks of cholera peak every 3.7 years. She noticed that this period matches the frequency of the El Niño Southern Oscillations, which is a weather event that occurs in the Pacific Ocean. El Niño affects weather patterns in many regions of the world, including Bangladesh. El Niño increases the temperatures of the sea off the coast of Bangladesh. Pascual found that increased sea temperatures lead to higher numbers of the bacteria that cause cholera. In turn, more people contract cholera. But because of the research conducted by Pascual and other scientists, the people of Bangladesh can better predict and prepare for outbreaks of cholera.

Social Studies ACTIVITY

WRITING SKILL Research the effects of El Niño. Write a report describing El Niño and its affect on a country other than Bangladesh.

go.hrw.com
To learn more about these Science in Action topics, visit go.hrw.com and type in the keyword HZ5CLMF.

Current Science
Check out Current Science® articles related to this chapter by visiting go.hrw.com. Just type in the keyword HZ5CS17.

Go Fly a Bike!

Teacher's Notes

Time Required

One 45-minute class period

Lab Ratings

EASY ——————————————— HARD

Teacher Prep 🜖

Student Set-Up 🜖🜖🜖

Concept Level 🜖🜖

Clean Up 🜖🜖

MATERIALS

The materials listed on the student page are enough for a group of 3 to 4 students.

Safety Caution

Remind students to review all safety cautions and icons before beginning this lab activity.

Preparation Notes

Conduct this activity on a day when the wind is blowing but not when the wind speed is greater than 50 km/h. Use straight, plastic straws. Before the activity, explain that an *anemometer* is a device that measures wind speed. It works because the wind pushes the cups at the same speed that the wind is moving.

Go Fly a Bike!

Your friend Daniel just invented a bicycle that can fly! Trouble is, the bike can fly only when the wind speed is between 3 m/s and 10 m/s. If the wind is not blowing hard enough, the bike won't get enough lift to rise into the air, and if the wind is blowing too hard, the bike is difficult to control. Daniel needs to know if he can fly his bike today. Can you build a device that can estimate how fast the wind is blowing?

MATERIALS

- clay, modeling
- cups, paper, small (5)
- hole punch
- marker, colored
- pencil, sharp, with an eraser
- ruler, metric
- scissors
- stapler, small
- straws, straight plastic (2)
- tape, masking
- thumbtack
- watch (or clock) that indicates seconds

SAFETY

Ask a Question

1 How can I construct a device to measure wind speed?

Form a Hypothesis

2 Write a possible answer for the question above. Explain your reasoning.

Test the Hypothesis

3 Cut off the rolled edges of all five paper cups. They will then be lighter so that they can spin more easily.

4 Measure and place four equally spaced markings 1 cm below the rim of one of the paper cups.

5 Use the hole punch to punch a hole at each mark so that the cup has four equally spaced holes. Use the sharp pencil to carefully punch a hole in the center of the bottom of the cup.

6 Push a straw through two opposite holes in the side of the cup.

7 Repeat step 5 for the other two holes. The straws should form an X.

8 Measure 3 cm from the bottom of the remaining paper cups, and mark each spot with a dot.

9 At each dot, punch a hole in the paper cups with the hole punch.

10 Color the outside of one of the four cups.

Terry J. Rakes
Elmwood Jr. High
Rogers, Arkansas

11 Slide a cup on one of the straws by pushing the straw through the punched hole. Rotate the cup so that the bottom faces to the right.

12 Fold the end of the straw, and staple it to the inside of the cup directly across from the hole.

13 Repeat steps 11–12 for each of the remaining cups.

14 Push the tack through the intersection of the two straws.

15 Push the eraser end of a pencil through the bottom hole in the center cup. Push the tack as far as it will go into the end of the eraser.

16 Push the sharpened end of the pencil into some modeling clay to form a base. The device will then be able to stand up without being knocked over, as shown at right.

17 Blow into the cups so that they spin. Adjust the tack so that the cups can freely spin without wobbling or falling apart. Congratulations! You have just constructed an anemometer.

18 Find a suitable area outside to place the anemometer vertically on a surface away from objects that would obstruct the wind, such as buildings and trees.

19 Mark the surface at the base of the anemometer with masking tape. Label the tape "starting point."

20 Hold the colored cup over the starting point while your partner holds the watch.

21 Release the colored cup. At the same time, your partner should look at the watch or clock. As the cups spin, count the number of times the colored cup crosses the starting point in 10 s.

Analyze the Results

1 How many times did the colored cup cross the starting point in 10 s?

2 Divide your answer in step 21 by 10 to get the number of revolutions in 1 s.

3 Measure the diameter of your anemometer (the distance between the outside edges of two opposite cups) in centimeters. Multiply this number by 3.14 to get the circumference of the circle made by the cups of your anemometer.

4 Multiply your answer from step 3 by the number of revolutions per second (step 2). Divide that answer by 100 to get wind speed in meters per second.

5 Compare your results with those of your classmates. Did you get the same results? What could account for any slight differences in your results?

Draw Conclusions

6 Could Daniel fly his bicycle today? Why or why not?

CHAPTER RESOURCES

Chapter Resource File

- Datasheet for LabBook
- Lab Notes and Answers

Skills Practice Lab

Watching the Weather

Teacher's Notes

Time Required

One 45-minute class period

Lab Ratings

EASY ——————————→ HARD

Teacher Prep △
Student Set-Up △
Concept Level △△
Clean Up △

MATERIALS

The only material required in this lab is a pencil. Have students complete the lab individually.

Skills Practice Lab

MATERIALS
- pencil

Watching the Weather

Imagine that you own a private consulting firm that helps people plan for big occasions, such as weddings, parties, and celebrity events. One of your duties is making sure the weather doesn't put a damper on your clients' plans. In order to provide the best service possible, you have taken a crash course in reading weather maps. Will the celebrity golf match have to be delayed on account of rain? Will the wedding ceremony have to be moved inside so the blushing bride doesn't get soaked? It is your job to say yea or nay.

Procedure

1. Study the station model and legend shown on the next page. You will use the legend to interpret the weather map on the final page of this activity.

2. Weather data is represented on a weather map by a station model. A station model is a small circle that shows the location of the weather station along with a set of symbols and numbers around the circle that represent the data collected at the weather station. Study the table below.

Weather-Map Symbols					
Weather conditions		**Cloud cover**		**Wind speed (mph)**	
••	Light rain	○	No clouds	◎	Calm
∴	Moderate rain	◑	One-tenth or less	3–8
⁞•	Heavy rain	◕	Two- to three-tenths	9–14
,	Drizzle	◑	Broken	15–20
✳ ✳	Light snow	◑	Nine-tenths	21–25
✳✳	Moderate snow	●	Overcast	32–37
ᚱ	Thunderstorm	⊗	Sky obscured	44–48
∿	Freezing rain		**Special Symbols**	55–60
∞	Haze	▲▲▲▲ Cold front		66–71
≡	Fog	●●●● Warm front		
		H	High pressure	
		L	Low pressure	
		૬	Hurricane	

Station Model

Wind speed is represented by whole and half tails.

A line indicates the direction the wind is coming from.

Air temperature

A symbol represents the current weather conditions. If there is no symbol, there is no precipitation.

Dew point temperature

Shading indicates the cloud coverage.

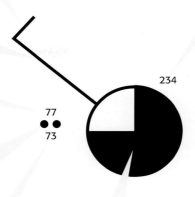

77

73

234

Atmospheric pressure in millibars (mbar). This number has been shortened on the station model. To read the number properly you must follow a few simple rules.

- If the first number is greater than 5, place a 9 in front of the number and a decimal point between the last two digits.

- If the first number is less than or equal to 5, place a 10 in front of the number and a decimal point between the last two digits.

Interpreting Station Models

The station model below is for Boston, Massachusetts. The current temperature in Boston is 42°F, and the dew point is 39°F. The barometric pressure is 1011.0 mbar. The sky is overcast, and there is moderate rainfall. The wind is coming from the southwest at 15–20 mph.

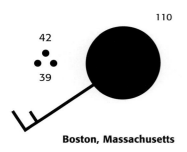

42

39

110

Boston, Massachusetts

Lab Notes

You may want to go over the different weather symbols with students and discuss how to convert the abbreviated form of atmospheric pressure to its actual measure. Before the lab, have students review the different kinds of fronts. Students may enjoy creating a weather report based on the weather report provided in this lab. Students can present this report to the class as a "live" studio show or through a videotape they create in their own time.

CHAPTER RESOURCES

Chapter Resource File

- Datasheet for LabBook
- Lab Notes and Answers

Analyze the Results

1. It's the winter. A cold front is coming through. Temperatures are low where the cold front has passed.

2. The temperature is 42°F. The dewpoint is 36°F. There is broken cloud cover, the wind is from the northwest at 3–8 mph, and the barometric pressure is 1,024.6 mb.

3. As the cold front approaches, the wind is generally from the south, temperatures are warmer and the barometric pressure is low. As the cold front passes, the wind is from the northwest, temperatures are much cooler, and the pressure rises.

Draw Conclusions

4. The temperature is 45°F. The barometric pressure is 965.4 mb, the dewpoint is 38°F, the sky is obscured, there is a thunderstorm, and the wind is from the south at 21–25 mph.

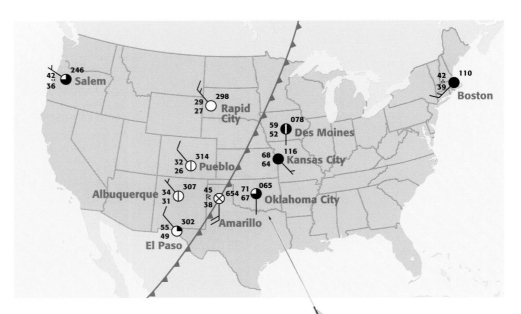

Analyze the Results

1. Based on the weather for the entire United States, what time of year is it? Explain your answer.

2. Interpret the station model for Salem, Oregon. What is the temperature, dew point, cloud coverage, wind direction, wind speed, and atmospheric pressure? Is there any precipitation? If so, what kind?

3. What is happening to wind direction, temperature, and pressure as the cold front approaches? as it passes?

Draw Conclusions

4. Interpret the station model for Amarillo, Texas.

Skills Practice Lab

Let It Snow!

Although an inch of rain might be good for your garden, 7 cm or 8 cm could cause an unwelcome flood. But what about snow? How much snow is too much? A blizzard might drop 40 cm of snow overnight. Sure it's up to your knees, but how does this much snow compare with rain? This activity will help you find out.

Procedure

1 Pour 50 mL of shaved ice into your beaker. Do not pack the ice into the beaker. This ice will represent your snowfall.

2 Use the ruler to measure the height of the snow in the beaker.

3 Turn on the hot plate to a low setting. **Caution:** Wear heat-resistant gloves and goggles when working with the hot plate.

4 Place the beaker on the hot plate, and leave it there until all of the snow melts.

5 Pour the water into the graduated cylinder, and record the height and volume of the water.

6 Repeat steps 1–5 two more times.

Analysis

1 What was the difference in height before and after the snow melted in each of your three trials? What was the average difference?

2 Why did the volume change after the ice melted?

3 What was the ratio of snow height to water height?

4 Use the ratio you found in step 3 of the Analysis to calculate how much water 50 cm of this snow would produce. Use the following equation to help.

$$\frac{\text{measured height of snow}}{\text{measured height of water}} = \frac{50 \text{ cm of snow}}{? \text{ cm of water}}$$

5 Why is it important to know the water content of a snowfall?

MATERIALS

- beaker, 100 mL
- gloves, heat-resistant
- graduated cylinder
- hot plate
- ice, shaved, 150 mL
- ruler, metric

SAFETY

Applying Your Data

Shaved ice isn't really snow. Research to find out how much water real snow would produce. Does every snowfall produce the same ratio of snow height to water depth?

CHAPTER RESOURCES

Chapter Resource File

- Datasheet for LabBook
- Lab Notes and Answers

Walter Woolbaugh
Manhattan School System
Manhattan, Montana

Applying Your Data

Every snowfall does not produce the same ratio of snow height to water depth. The ratio of snow height to water depth is dependent on several variables, including whether the snow is wet or dry.

Skills Practice Lab

Let It Snow!

Teacher's Notes

Time Required

One 45-minute class period

Lab Ratings

EASY ————————→ HARD

Teacher Prep 🧪
Student Set-Up 🧪🧪
Concept Level 🧪
Clean Up 🧪

MATERIALS

The materials listed on the student page are enough for a group of 3 to 4 students.

Safety Caution

Remind students to review all safety cautions and icons before beginning this lab activity.

Analyze the Results

1. Answers may vary according to the water content of the ice or snow sample.

2. The volume changed because the water changed from a solid to a liquid.

3. Answers may vary.

4. Answers may vary

5. Sample answer: The water content of a snowfall—whether it is relatively wet or relatively dry—affects how much flooding may occur as the snow melts. A "wetter" snow has more water per volume and may cause more flooding than a "drier" snow.

Model-Making Lab

Gone with the Wind

Teacher's Notes

Time Required
One 45-minute class period

Lab Ratings
EASY ———————————→ HARD

Teacher Prep 🧪🧪
Student Set-Up 🧪🧪
Concept Level 🧪🧪
Clean Up 🧪

MATERIALS
The materials listed on the student page are enough for a group of 2 to 3 students.

Safety Caution
Remind students to review all safety cautions and icons before beginning this lab activity.

Preparation Notes
You might want to watch your local weather station in order to schedule this experiment on a windy day. Use a magnetic compass to find magnetic north. Then, use masking tape or chalk to mark the sidewalk or parking lot with an arrow pointing toward magnetic north. Before the activity, ask students if they have ever seen a weather vane. Also, have them list several reasons why knowing the wind direction might be helpful.

Model-Making Lab

Gone with the Wind

Pilots at the Fly Away Airport need your help—fast! Last night, lightning destroyed the orange windsock. This windsock helped pilots measure which direction the wind was blowing. But now the windsock is gone with the wind, and an incoming airplane needs to land. The pilot must know which direction the wind is blowing and is counting on you to make a device that can measure wind direction.

MATERIALS

- card, index
- compass, drawing
- compass, magnetic
- pencil, sharpened
- plate, paper
- protractor
- rock, small
- ruler, metric
- scissors
- stapler
- straw, straight plastic
- thumbtack (or pushpin)

SAFETY

Ask a Question

1 How can I measure wind direction?

Form a Hypothesis

2 Write a possible answer to the question above.

Test the Hypothesis

3 Find the center of the plate by tracing around its edge with a drawing compass. The pointed end of the compass should poke a small hole in the center of the plate.

4 Use a ruler to draw a line across the center of the plate.

5 Use a protractor to help you draw a second line through the center of the plate. This new line should be at a 90° angle to the line you drew in step 4.

6 Moving clockwise, label each line "N," "E," "S," and "W."

7 Use a protractor to help you draw two more lines through the center of the plate. These lines should be at a 45° angle to the lines you drew in steps 4 and 5.

Walter Woolbaugh
Manhattan School System
Manhattan, Montana

8 Moving clockwise from *N,* label these new lines "NE," "SE," "SW," and "NW." The plate now resembles the face of a magnetic compass. The plate will be the base of your wind-direction indicator. It will help you read the direction of the wind at a glance.

9 Measure and mark a 5 cm × 5 cm square on an index card, and cut out the square. Fold the square in half to form a triangle.

10 Staple an open edge of the triangle to the straw so that one point of the triangle touches the end of the straw.

11 Hold the pencil at a 90° angle to the straw. The eraser should touch the balance point of the straw. Push a thumbtack or pushpin through the straw and into the eraser. The straw should spin without falling off.

12 Find a suitable area outside to measure the wind direction. The area should be clear of trees and buildings.

13 Press the sharpened end of the pencil through the center hole of the plate and into the ground. The labels on your paper plate should be facing the sky, as shown on this page.

14 Use a compass to find magnetic north. Rotate the plate so that the *N* on the plate points north. Place a small rock on top of the plate so that the plate does not turn.

15 Watch the straw as it rotates. The triangle will point in the direction the wind is blowing.

Analyze the Results

1 From which direction is the wind coming?

2 In which direction is the wind blowing?

Draw Conclusions

3 Would this be an effective way for pilots to measure wind direction? Why or why not?

4 What improvements would you suggest to Fly Away Airport to measure wind direction more accurately?

Applying Your Data

Use this tool to measure and record wind direction for several days. What changes in wind direction occur as a front approaches? as a front passes?

Review magnetic declination in the chapter entitled "Maps as Models of the Earth." How might magnetic declination affect your design for a tool to measure wind direction?

Analyze the Results

1. Answers may vary.

2. Answers may vary.

Draw Conclusions

3. Answers may vary. Accept all reasonable responses.

4. Answers may vary. Accept all reasonable responses.

Applying Your Data

Answers may vary. (Wind direction varies according to the type of front that is moving through.)

Sample answer: You have to adjust the weather vane to account for the difference between magnetic north and true north. The adjustment will vary depending on where you live.

CHAPTER RESOURCES

Chapter Resource File

• Datasheet for LabBook

• Lab Notes and Answers

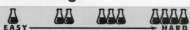

Skills Practice Lab

Global Impact

Teacher's Notes

Time Required

One 45-minute class period

Lab Ratings

EASY ——————→ HARD

Teacher Prep 🧪
Student Set-Up 🧪🧪🧪
Concept Level 🧪🧪
Clean Up 🧪

MATERIALS

The materials listed on the student page are enough for 1 student.

Preparation Notes

This activity requires graphing skills. Students may need a review of graphing, analyzing data from a graph, and calculating the slope of a graph.

Analyze the Results

1. Students will notice that temperatures fluctuated over the last 100 years but have increased in the last 30 years.

2. Sample answer: The larger the sample size, the more precise your analysis will be. The average temperature for a certain year might not be representative for the entire decade. There were very few similarities among the graphs.

Skills Practice Lab

Global Impact

For years, scientists have debated the topic of global warming. Is the temperature of the Earth actually getting warmer? In this activity, you will examine a table to determine if the data indicate any trends. Be sure to notice how much the trends seem to change as you analyze different sets of data.

MATERIALS

- pencils, colored (4)
- ruler, metric

Procedure

1. The table below shows average global temperatures recorded over the last 100 years.

2. Draw a graph. Label the horizontal axis "Time." Mark the grid in 5-year intervals. Label the vertical axis "Temperature (°C)," with values ranging from 13°C to 15°C.

3. Starting with 1900, use the numbers in red to plot the temperature in 20-year intervals. Connect the dots with straight lines.

4. Using a ruler, estimate the average slope for the temperatures. Draw a red line to represent the slope.

5. Using different colors, plot the temperatures at 10-year intervals and 5-year intervals on the same graph. Connect each set of dots, and draw the average slope for each set.

Analyze the Results

1. Examine your completed graph, and explain any trends you see in the graphed data. Was there an increase or a decrease in average temperature over the last 100 years?

2. What similarities and differences did you see between each set of graphed data?

Draw Conclusions

3. What conclusions can you draw from the data you graphed in this activity?

4. What would happen if your graph were plotted in 1-year intervals? Try it!

Average Global Temperatures											
Year	°C	Year	°C	Year	°C	Year	°C	Year	°C	Year	°C
1900	14.0	1917	13.6	1934	14.0	1951	14.0	1968	13.9	1985	14.1
1901	13.9	1918	13.6	1935	13.9	1952	14.0	1969	14.0	1986	14.2
1902	13.8	1919	13.8	1936	14.0	1953	14.1	1970	14.0	1987	14.3
1903	13.6	1920	13.8	1937	14.1	1954	13.9	1971	13.9	1988	14.4
1904	13.5	1921	13.9	1938	14.1	1955	13.9	1972	13.9	1989	14.2
1905	13.7	1922	13.9	1939	14.0	1956	13.8	1973	14.2	1990	14.5
1906	13.8	1923	13.8	1940	14.1	1957	14.1	1974	13.9	1991	14.4
1907	13.6	1924	13.8	1941	14.1	1958	14.1	1975	14.0	1992	14.1
1908	13.7	1925	13.8	1942	14.1	1959	14.0	1976	13.8	1993	14.2
1909	13.7	1926	14.1	1943	14.0	1960	14.0	1977	14.2	1994	14.3
1910	13.7	1927	14.0	1944	14.1	1961	14.1	1978	14.1	1995	14.5
1911	13.7	1928	14.0	1945	14.0	1962	14.0	1979	14.1	1996	14.4
1912	13.7	1929	13.8	1946	14.0	1963	14.0	1980	14.3	1997	14.4
1913	13.8	1930	13.9	1947	14.1	1964	13.7	1981	14.4	1998	14.5
1914	14.0	1931	14.0	1948	14.0	1965	13.8	1982	14.1	1999	14.5
1915	14.0	1932	14.0	1949	13.9	1966	13.9	1983	14.3	2000	14.5
1916	13.8	1933	13.9	1950	13.8	1967	14.0	1984	14.1	2001	14.5

CHAPTER RESOURCES

Chapter Resource File

- **Datasheet for LabBook**
- **Lab Notes and Answers**

Janel Guse
West Central Middle School
Hartford, South Dakota

Draw Conclusions

3. Sample answer: You can conclude that a larger data set gives you a more complete picture of what is happening. Global temperatures have gradually increased in the last 100 years.

4. Sample answer: Global temperatures would appear to fluctuate more.

Skills Practice Lab

For the Birds

You and a partner have a new business building birdhouses. But your first clients have told you that birds do not want to live in the birdhouses you have made. The clients want their money back unless you can solve the problem. You need to come up with a solution right away!

You remember reading an article about microclimates in a science magazine. Cities often heat up because the pavement and buildings absorb so much solar radiation. Maybe the houses are too warm! How can the houses be kept cooler?

You decide to investigate the roofs; after all, changing the roofs would be a lot easier than building new houses. In order to help your clients and the birds, you decide to test different roof colors and materials to see how these variables affect a roof's ability to absorb the sun's rays.

One partner will test the color, and the other partner will test the materials. You will then share your results and make a recommendation together.

MATERIALS

- cardboard (4 pieces)
- paint, black, white, and light blue tempera
- rubber, beige or tan
- thermometers, Celsius (4)
- watch (or clock)
- wood, beige or tan

SAFETY

Part A: Color Test

Ask a Question

1 What color would be the best choice for the roof of a birdhouse?

Form a Hypothesis

2 Write down the color you think will keep a birdhouse coolest.

Test the Hypothesis

3 Paint one piece of cardboard black, another piece white, and a third light blue.

4 After the paint has dried, take the three pieces of cardboard outside, and place a thermometer on each piece.

5 In an area where there is no shade, place each piece at the same height so that all three receive the same amount of sunlight. Leave the pieces in the sunlight for 15 min.

6 Leave a fourth thermometer outside in the shade to measure the temperature of the air.

7 Record the reading of the thermometer on each piece of cardboard. Also, record the outside temperature.

CHAPTER RESOURCES

Chapter Resource File

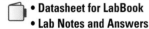

- Datasheet for LabBook
- Lab Notes and Answers

Larry Tackett
Andrew Jackson Middle School
Cross Lanes, West Virginia

LabBook

Skills Practice Lab

For the Birds

Teacher's Notes

Time Required
One 45-minute class period

Lab Ratings

EASY			HARD

Teacher Prep 🔬
Student Set-Up 🔬🔬
Concept Level 🔬🔬
Clean Up 🔬🔬

MATERIALS

The materials listed on the student page are enough for a group of 4 to 5 students.

Safety Caution

Remind students to review all safety cautions and icons before beginning this lab activity.

Part A
Analyze the Results

1. Sample answer: no, The thermometers recorded different temperatures. The black and blue pieces of cardboard, particularly the black one, caused the temperature to increase.

2. Sample answer: The temperature of the black cardboard was much higher than the outside temperature. Students should find that the temperature of the other colors was also different from the outside temperature.

Part A
Draw Conclusions

3. Answers may vary. Accept all reasonable responses.

Analyze the Results

1 Did each of the three thermometers record the same temperature after 15 min? Explain.

2 Were the temperature readings on each of the three pieces of cardboard the same as the reading for the outside temperature? Explain.

Draw Conclusions

3 How do your observations compare with your hypothesis?

Part B: Material Test

Ask a Question

1 Which material would be the best choice for the roof of a birdhouse?

Form a Hypothesis

2 Write down the material you think will keep a birdhouse coolest.

Test the Hypothesis

3 Take the rubber, wood, and the fourth piece of cardboard outside, and place a thermometer on each.

4 In an area where there is no shade, place each material at the same height so that they all receive the same amount of sunlight. Leave the materials in the sunlight for 15 min.

5 Leave a fourth thermometer outside in the shade to measure the temperature of the air.

6 Record the temperature of each material. Also, record the outside temperature. After you and your partner have finished your investigations, take a few minutes to share your results.

Analyze the Results

1 Did each of the thermometers on the three materials record the same temperature after 15 min? Explain.

2 Were the temperature readings on the rubber, wood, and cardboard the same as the reading for the outside temperature? Explain.

Draw Conclusions

3 How do your observations compare with your hypothesis?

4 Which material would you use to build the roofs for your birdhouses? Why?

5 Which color would you use to paint the new roofs? Why?

Part B
Analyze the Results

1. Sample answer: no, The temperatures were different. The temperature of the rubber was higher than that of the other two materials.

2. Sample answer: no, The temperature of the rubber was higher than the outside temperature. Accept all other reasonable answers for the other materials.

Part B
Draw Conclusions

3. Answers may vary. Accept all reasonable answers.

4. Sample answer: The wood would be the coolest. The cardboard would be a possible alternative.

5. Sample answer: The white roof would be the coolest. A light blue roof would be a possible alternative.

Applying Your Data

Answers may vary. Accept all reasonable interpretations of the data collected.

✓ *Reading Check* Answers

Chapter 1 The Atmosphere

Section 1

Page 4: Water can be liquid (rain), solid (snow or ice), or gas (water vapor).

Page 6: The troposphere is the layer of turning or change. The stratosphere is the layer in which gases are layered and do not mix vertically. The mesosphere is the middle layer. The thermosphere is the layer in which temperatures are highest.

Page 8: The thermosphere does not feel hot because air molecules are spaced far apart and cannot collide to transfer much thermal energy.

Section 2

Page 11: Cold air is more dense than warm air, so cold air sinks and warm air rises. This produces convection currents.

Page 13: A greenhouse gas is a gas that absorbs thermal energy in the atmosphere.

Section 3

Page 15: Sinking air causes areas of high pressure because sinking air presses down on the air beneath it.

Page 16: the westerlies

Page 19: At night, the mountains cool faster than the valleys. The cold mountain air is denser than the warm valley air, so the mountain air blows down the valleys at night.

Section 4

Page 20: Sample answer: smoke, dust and sea salt

Page 23: Answers may vary. Acid precipitation may decrease the soil nutrients that are available to plants.

Page 24: Powdered lime is used to counteract the effects of acidic snowmelt from snow that accumulated during the winter.

Page 26: Allowance trading establishes allowances for a certain type of pollutant. Companies are permitted to release their allowance of the pollutant, but if they exceed the allowance, they must buy additional allowances or pay a fine.

Chapter 2 Understanding Weather

Section 1

Page 38: The water cycle is the continuous movement of water from Earth's oceans and rivers into the atmosphere, into the ground, and back into the oceans and rivers.

Page 40: A psychrometer is used to measure relative humidity.

Page 41: The bulb of a wet-bulb thermometer is covered with moistened material. The bulb cools as water evaporates from the material. If the air is dry, more water will evaporate from the material, and the temperature recorded by the thermometer will be low. If the air is humid, less water will evaporate from the material, and the temperature recorded by the thermometer will be higher.

Page 43: Altostratus clouds form at middle altitudes.

Section 2

Page 47: A maritime tropical air mass causes hot and humid summer weather in the midwestern United States.

Page 49: An occluded front produces cool temperatures and large amounts of rain.

Page 51: An anticyclone can produce dry, clear weather.

Section 3

Page 53: A severe thunderstorm is a thunderstorm that produces high winds, hail, flash floods, or tornadoes.

Page 55: Hurricanes are also called *typhoons* or *cyclones.*

Page 56: Hurricanes get their energy from the condensation of water vapor.

Section 4

Page 60: Meteorologists use weather balloons to collect atmospheric data above Earth's surface.

Chapter 3   Climate

Section 1

Page 74: Climate is the average weather condition in an area over a long period of time. Weather is the condition of the atmosphere at a particular time.

Page 76: Locations near the equator have less seasonal variation because the tilt of the Earth does not change the amount of energy these locations receive from the sun.

Page 78: The atmosphere becomes less dense and loses its ability to absorb and hold thermal energy, at higher elevations.

Page 79: The Gulf Stream current carries warm water past Iceland, which heats the air and causes milder temperatures.

Page 80: Each biome has a different climate and different plant and animals communities.

Section 2

Page 82: You would find the tropical zone from 23.5° north latitude to 23.5° south latitude.

Page 85: Answers may vary. Sample answer: rats, lizards, snakes, and scorpions.

Section 3

Page 86: The temperate zone is located between the Tropics and the polar zone.

Page 88: Temperate deserts are cold at night because low humidity and cloudless skies allow energy to escape.

Page 91: Cities have higher temperatures than the surrounding rural areas because buildings and pavement absorb solar radiation instead of reflecting it.

Section 4

Page 93: Changes in the Earth's orbit and the tilt of the Earth's axis are the two things that Milankovitch says cause ice ages.

Page 94: Dust, ash, and smoke from volcanic eruptions block the sun's rays, which causes the Earth to cool.

Page 97: The deserts would receive less rainfall, making it harder for plants and animals in the desert to survive.

Study Skills

FoldNote Instructions

Have you ever tried to study for a test or quiz but didn't know where to start? Or have you read a chapter and found that you can remember only a few ideas? Well, FoldNotes are a fun and exciting way to help you learn and remember the ideas you encounter as you learn science!

FoldNotes are tools that you can use to organize concepts. By focusing on a few main concepts, FoldNotes help you learn and remember how the concepts fit together. They can help you see the "big picture." Below you will find instructions for building 10 different FoldNotes.

Pyramid

1. Place a sheet of paper in front of you. Fold the lower left-hand corner of the paper diagonally to the opposite edge of the paper.

2. Cut off the tab of paper created by the fold (at the top).

3. Open the paper so that it is a square. Fold the lower right-hand corner of the paper diagonally to the opposite corner to form a triangle.

4. Open the paper. The creases of the two folds will have created an X.

5. Using scissors, cut along one of the creases. Start from any corner, and stop at the center point to create two flaps. Use tape or glue to attach one of the flaps on top of the other flap.

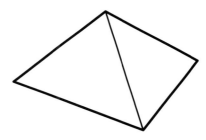

Double Door

1. Fold a sheet of paper in half from the top to the bottom. Then, unfold the paper.

2. Fold the top and bottom edges of the paper to the crease.

Booklet

1. Fold a sheet of paper in half from left to right. Then, unfold the paper.

2. Fold the sheet of paper in half again from the top to the bottom. Then, unfold the paper.

3. Refold the sheet of paper in half from left to right.

4. Fold the top and bottom edges to the center crease.

5. Completely unfold the paper.

6. Refold the paper from top to bottom.

7. Using scissors, cut a slit along the center crease of the sheet from the folded edge to the creases made in step 4. Do not cut the entire sheet in half.

8. Fold the sheet of paper in half from left to right. While holding the bottom and top edges of the paper, push the bottom and top edges together so that the center collapses at the center slit. Fold the four flaps to form a four-page book.

Layered Book

1. Lay one sheet of paper on top of another sheet. Slide the top sheet up so that 2 cm of the bottom sheet is showing.

2. Hold the two sheets together, fold down the top of the two sheets so that you see four 2 cm tabs along the bottom.

3. Using a stapler, staple the top of the FoldNote.

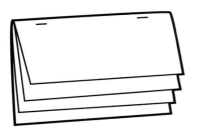

Key-Term Fold

1. Fold a sheet of lined notebook paper in half from left to right.

2. Using scissors, cut along every third line from the right edge of the paper to the center fold to make tabs.

Four-Corner Fold

1. Fold a sheet of paper in half from left to right. Then, unfold the paper.

2. Fold each side of the paper to the crease in the center of the paper.

3. Fold the paper in half from the top to the bottom. Then, unfold the paper.

4. Using scissors, cut the top flap creases made in step 3 to form four flaps.

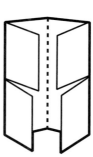

Three-Panel Flip Chart

1. Fold a piece of paper in half from the top to the bottom.

2. Fold the paper in thirds from side to side. Then, unfold the paper so that you can see the three sections.

3. From the top of the paper, cut along each of the vertical fold lines to the fold in the middle of the paper. You will now have three flaps.

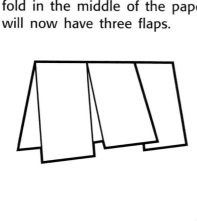

Table Fold

1. Fold a piece of paper in half from the top to the bottom. Then, fold the paper in half again.

2. Fold the paper in thirds from side to side.

3. Unfold the paper completely. Carefully trace the fold lines by using a pen or pencil.

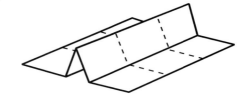

Two-Panel Flip Chart

1. Fold a piece of paper in half from the top to the bottom.

2. Fold the paper in half from side to side. Then, unfold the paper so that you can see the two sections.

3. From the top of the paper, cut along the vertical fold line to the fold in the middle of the paper. You will now have two flaps.

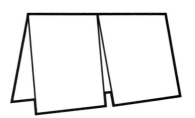

Tri-Fold

1. Fold a piece a paper in thirds from the top to the bottom.

2. Unfold the paper so that you can see the three sections. Then, turn the paper sideways so that the three sections form vertical columns.

3. Trace the fold lines by using a pen or pencil. Label the columns "Know," "Want," and "Learn."

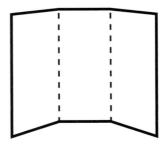

Appendix

Graphic Organizer Instructions

Have you ever wished that you could "draw out" the many concepts you learn in your science class? Sometimes, being able to *see* how concepts are related really helps you remember what you've learned. Graphic Organizers do just that! They give you a way to draw or map out concepts.

All you need to make a Graphic Organizer is a piece of paper and a pencil. Below you will find instructions for four different Graphic Organizers designed to help you organize the concepts you'll learn in this book.

Spider Map

1. Draw a diagram like the one shown. In the circle, write the main topic.

2. From the circle, draw legs to represent different categories of the main topic. You can have as many categories as you want.

3. From the category legs, draw horizontal lines. As you read the chapter, write details about each category on the horizontal lines.

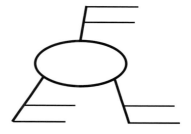

Comparison Table

1. Draw a chart like the one shown. Your chart can have as many columns and rows as you want.

2. In the top row, write the topics that you want to compare.

3. In the left column, write characteristics of the topics that you want to compare. As you read the chapter, fill in the characteristics for each topic in the appropriate boxes.

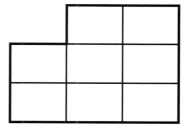

Chain-of-Events-Chart

1. Draw a box. In the box, write the first step of a process or the first event of a timeline.

2. Under the box, draw another box, and use an arrow to connect the two boxes. In the second box, write the next step of the process or the next event in the timeline.

3. Continue adding boxes until the process or timeline is finished.

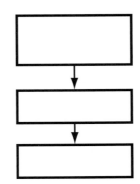

Concept Map

1. Draw a circle in the center of a piece of paper. Write the main idea of the chapter in the center of the circle.

2. From the circle, draw other circles. In those circles, write characteristics of the main idea. Draw arrows from the center circle to the circles that contain the characteristics.

3. From each circle that contains a characteristic, draw other circles. In those circles, write specific details about the characteristic. Draw arrows from each circle that contains a characteristic to the circles that contain specific details. You may draw as many circles as you want.

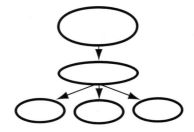

SI Measurement

The International System of Units, or SI, is the standard system of measurement used by many scientists. Using the same standards of measurement makes it easier for scientists to communicate with one another.

SI works by combining prefixes and base units. Each base unit can be used with different prefixes to define smaller and larger quantities. The table below lists common SI prefixes.

SI Prefixes

Prefix	Symbol	Factor	Example
kilo-	k	1,000	kilogram, 1 kg = 1,000 g
hecto-	h	100	hectoliter, 1 hL = 100 L
deka-	da	10	dekameter, 1 dam = 10 m
		1	meter, liter, gram
deci-	d	0.1	decigram, 1 dg = 0.1 g
centi-	c	0.01	centimeter, 1 cm = 0.01 m
milli-	m	0.001	milliliter, 1 mL = 0.001 L
micro-	μ	0.000 001	micrometer, 1 μm = 0.000 001 m

SI Conversion Table

SI units	From SI to English	From English to SI
Length		
kilometer (km) = 1,000 m	1 km = 0.621 mi	1 mi = 1.609 km
meter (m) = 100 cm	1 m = 3.281 ft	1 ft = 0.305 m
centimeter (cm) = 0.01 m	1 cm = 0.394 in.	1 in. = 2.540 cm
millimeter (mm) = 0.001 m	1 mm = 0.039 in.	
micrometer (μm) = 0.000 001 m		
nanometer (nm) = 0.000 000 001 m		
Area		
square kilometer (km^2) = 100 hectares	1 km^2 = 0.386 mi^2	1 mi^2 = 2.590 km^2
hectare (ha) = 10,000 m^2	1 ha = 2.471 acres	1 acre = 0.405 ha
square meter (m^2) = 10,000 cm^2	1 m^2 = 10.764 ft^2	1 ft^2 = 0.093 m^2
square centimeter (cm^2) = 100 mm^2	1 cm^2 = 0.155 in.^{2}	1 in.^{2} = 6.452 cm^2
Volume		
liter (L) = 1,000 mL = 1 dm^3	1 L = 1.057 fl qt	1 fl qt = 0.946 L
milliliter (mL) = 0.001 L = 1 cm^3	1 mL = 0.034 fl oz	1 fl oz = 29.574 mL
microliter (μL) = 0.000 001 L		
Mass		
kilogram (kg) = 1,000 g	1 kg = 2.205 lb	1 lb = 0.454 kg
gram (g) = 1,000 mg	1 g = 0.035 oz	1 oz = 28.350 g
milligram (mg) = 0.001 g		
microgram (μg) = 0.000 001 g		

Temperature Scales

Temperature can be expressed by using three different scales: Fahrenheit, Celsius, and Kelvin. The SI unit for temperature is the kelvin (K).

Although 0 K is much colder than 0°C, a change of 1 K is equal to a change of 1°C.

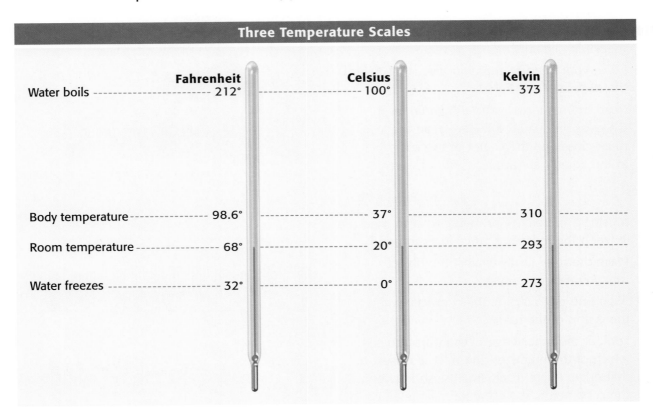

Three Temperature Scales

	Fahrenheit	Celsius	Kelvin
Water boils	212°	100°	373
Body temperature	98.6°	37°	310
Room temperature	68°	20°	293
Water freezes	32°	0°	273

Temperature Conversions Table

To convert	Use this equation:	Example
Celsius to Fahrenheit °C → °F	$°F = \left(\dfrac{9}{5} \times °C \right) + 32$	Convert 45°C to °F. $°F = \left(\dfrac{9}{5} \times 45°C \right) + 32 = 113°F$
Fahrenheit to Celsius °F → °C	$°C = \dfrac{5}{9} \times (°F - 32)$	Convert 68°F to °C. $°C = \dfrac{5}{9} \times (68°F - 32) = 20°C$
Celsius to Kelvin °C → K	$K = °C + 273$	Convert 45°C to K. $K = 45°C + 273 = 318\ K$
Kelvin to Celsius K → °C	$°C = K - 273$	Convert 32 K to °C. $°C = 32K - 273 = -241°C$

Measuring Skills

Using a Graduated Cylinder

When using a graduated cylinder to measure volume, keep the following procedures in mind:

1. Place the cylinder on a flat, level surface before measuring liquid.

2. Move your head so that your eye is level with the surface of the liquid.

3. Read the mark closest to the liquid level. On glass graduated cylinders, read the mark closest to the center of the curve in the liquid's surface.

Using a Meterstick or Metric Ruler

When using a meterstick or metric ruler to measure length, keep the following procedures in mind:

1. Place the ruler firmly against the object that you are measuring.

2. Align one edge of the object exactly with the 0 end of the ruler.

3. Look at the other edge of the object to see which of the marks on the ruler is closest to that edge. (Note: Each small slash between the centimeters represents a millimeter, which is one-tenth of a centimeter.)

Using a Triple-Beam Balance

When using a triple-beam balance to measure mass, keep the following procedures in mind:

1. Make sure the balance is on a level surface.

2. Place all of the countermasses at 0. Adjust the balancing knob until the pointer rests at 0.

3. Place the object you wish to measure on the pan. **Caution:** Do not place hot objects or chemicals directly on the balance pan.

4. Move the largest countermass along the beam to the right until it is at the last notch that does not tip the balance. Follow the same procedure with the next-largest countermass. Then, move the smallest countermass until the pointer rests at 0.

5. Add the readings from the three beams together to determine the mass of the object.

6. When determining the mass of crystals or powders, first find the mass of a piece of filter paper. Then, add the crystals or powder to the paper, and remeasure. The actual mass of the crystals or powder is the total mass minus the mass of the paper. When finding the mass of liquids, first find the mass of the empty container. Then, find the combined mass of the liquid and container. The mass of the liquid is the total mass minus the mass of the container.

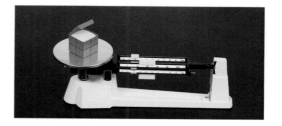

Scientific Methods

The ways in which scientists answer questions and solve problems are called **scientific methods.** The same steps are often used by scientists as they look for answers. However, there is more than one way to use these steps. Scientists may use all of the steps or just some of the steps during an investigation. They may even repeat some of the steps. The goal of using scientific methods is to come up with reliable answers and solutions.

Six Steps of Scientific Methods

1 Ask a Question

Good questions come from careful **observations.** You make observations by using your senses to gather information. Sometimes, you may use instruments, such as microscopes and telescopes, to extend the range of your senses. As you observe the natural world, you will discover that you have many more questions than answers. These questions drive investigations.

Questions beginning with *what, why, how,* and *when* are important in focusing an investigation. Here is an example of a question that could lead to an investigation.

Question: How does acid rain affect plant growth?

2 Form a Hypothesis

After you ask a question, you need to form a **hypothesis.** A hypothesis is a clear statement of what you expect the answer to your question to be. Your hypothesis will represent your best "educated guess" based on what you have observed and what you already know. A good hypothesis is testable. Otherwise, the investigation can go no further. Here is a hypothesis based on the question, "How does acid rain affect plant growth?"

Hypothesis: Acid rain slows plant growth.

The hypothesis can lead to predictions. A prediction is what you think the outcome of your experiment or data collection will be. Predictions are usually stated in an if-then format. Here is a sample prediction for the hypothesis that acid rain slows plant growth.

Prediction: If a plant is watered with only acid rain (which has a pH of 4), then the plant will grow at half its normal rate.

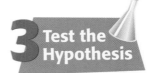

3 Test the Hypothesis

After you have formed a hypothesis and made a prediction, your hypothesis should be tested. One way to test a hypothesis is with a controlled experiment. A **controlled experiment** tests only one factor at a time. In an experiment to test the effect of acid rain on plant growth, the **control group** would be watered with normal rain water. The **experimental group** would be watered with acid rain. All of the plants should receive the same amount of sunlight and water each day. The air temperature should be the same for all groups. However, the acidity of the water will be a variable. In fact, any factor that is different from one group to another is a **variable.** If your hypothesis is correct, then the acidity of the water and plant growth are *dependant variables.* The amount a plant grows is dependent on the acidity of the water. However, the amount of water each plant receives and the amount of sunlight each plant receives are *independent variables.* Either of these factors could change without affecting the other factor.

Sometimes, the nature of an investigation makes a controlled experiment impossible. For example, the Earth's core is surrounded by thousands of meters of rock. Under such circumstances, a hypothesis may be tested by making detailed observations.

4 Analyze the Results

After you have completed your experiments, made your observations, and collected your data, you must analyze all the information you have gathered. Tables and graphs are often used in this step to organize the data.

5 Draw Conclusions

After analyzing your data, you can determine if your results support your hypothesis. If your hypothesis is supported, you (or others) might want to repeat the observations or experiments to verify your results. If your hypothesis is not supported by the data, you may have to check your procedure for errors. You may even have to reject your hypothesis and make a new one. If you cannot draw a conclusion from your results, you may have to try the investigation again or carry out further observations or experiments.

6 Communicate Results

After any scientific investigation, you should report your results. By preparing a written or oral report, you let others know what you have learned. They may repeat your investigation to see if they get the same results. Your report may even lead to another question and then to another investigation.

Scientific Methods in Action

Scientific methods contain loops in which several steps may be repeated over and over again. In some cases, certain steps are unnecessary. Thus, there is not a "straight line" of steps. For example, sometimes scientists find that testing one hypothesis raises new questions and new hypotheses to be tested. And sometimes, testing the hypothesis leads directly to a conclusion. Furthermore, the steps in scientific methods are not always used in the same order. Follow the steps in the diagram, and see how many different directions scientific methods can take you.

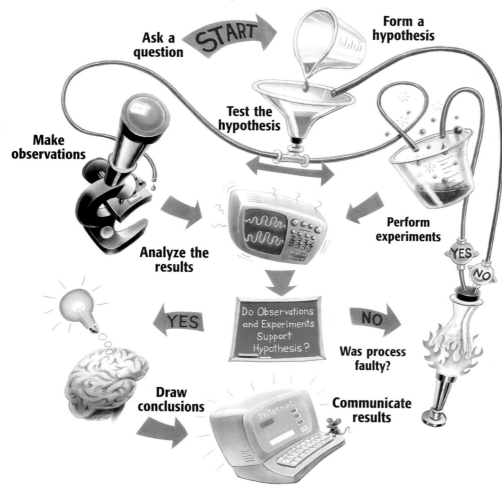

Making Charts and Graphs

Pie Charts

A pie chart shows how each group of data relates to all of the data. Each part of the circle forming the chart represents a category of the data. The entire circle represents all of the data. For example, a biologist studying a hardwood forest in Wisconsin found that there were five different types of trees. The data table at right summarizes the biologist's findings.

Wisconsin Hardwood Trees	
Type of tree	Number found
Oak	600
Maple	750
Beech	300
Birch	1,200
Hickory	150
Total	3,000

How to Make a Pie Chart

1 To make a pie chart of these data, first find the percentage of each type of tree. Divide the number of trees of each type by the total number of trees, and multiply by 100.

$$\frac{600 \text{ oak}}{3,000 \text{ trees}} \times 100 = 20\%$$

$$\frac{750 \text{ maple}}{3,000 \text{ trees}} \times 100 = 25\%$$

$$\frac{300 \text{ beech}}{3,000 \text{ trees}} \times 100 = 10\%$$

$$\frac{1,200 \text{ birch}}{3,000 \text{ trees}} \times 100 = 40\%$$

$$\frac{150 \text{ hickory}}{3,000 \text{ trees}} \times 100 = 5\%$$

2 Now, determine the size of the wedges that make up the pie chart. Multiply each percentage by 360°. Remember that a circle contains 360°.

$20\% \times 360° = 72°$ $25\% \times 360° = 90°$

$10\% \times 360° = 36°$ $40\% \times 360° = 144°$

$5\% \times 360° = 18°$

3 Check that the sum of the percentages is 100 and the sum of the degrees is 360.

$20\% + 25\% + 10\% + 40\% + 5\% = 100\%$

$72° + 90° + 36° + 144° + 18° = 360°$

4 Use a compass to draw a circle and mark the center of the circle.

5 Then, use a protractor to draw angles of 72°, 90°, 36°, 144°, and 18° in the circle.

6 Finally, label each part of the chart, and choose an appropriate title.

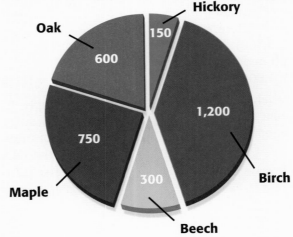

A Community of Wisconsin Hardwood Trees

Line Graphs

Line graphs are most often used to demonstrate continuous change. For example, Mr. Smith's students analyzed the population records for their hometown, Appleton, between 1900 and 2000. Examine the data at right.

Because the year and the population change, they are the *variables*. The population is determined by, or dependent on, the year. Therefore, the population is called the **dependent variable,** and the year is called the **independent variable.** Each set of data is called a **data pair.** To prepare a line graph, you must first organize data pairs into a table like the one at right.

Population of Appleton, 1900–2000	
Year	Population
1900	1,800
1920	2,500
1940	3,200
1960	3,900
1980	4,600
2000	5,300

How to Make a Line Graph

1 Place the independent variable along the horizontal (*x*) axis. Place the dependent variable along the vertical (*y*) axis.

2 Label the *x*-axis "Year" and the *y*-axis "Population." Look at your largest and smallest values for the population. For the *y*-axis, determine a scale that will provide enough space to show these values. You must use the same scale for the entire length of the axis. Next, find an appropriate scale for the *x*-axis.

3 Choose reasonable starting points for each axis.

4 Plot the data pairs as accurately as possible.

5 Choose a title that accurately represents the data.

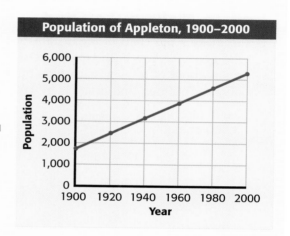

How to Determine Slope

Slope is the ratio of the change in the *y*-value to the change in the *x*-value, or "rise over run."

1 Choose two points on the line graph. For example, the population of Appleton in 2000 was 5,300 people. Therefore, you can define point *a* as (2000, 5,300). In 1900, the population was 1,800 people. You can define point *b* as (1900, 1,800).

2 Find the change in the *y*-value.
(*y* at point *a*) − (*y* at point *b*) = 5,300 people − 1,800 people = 3,500 people

3 Find the change in the *x*-value.
(*x* at point *a*) − (*x* at point *b*) = 2000 − 1900 = 100 years

4 Calculate the slope of the graph by dividing the change in *y* by the change in *x*.

$$slope = \frac{change\ in\ y}{change\ in\ x}$$

$$slope = \frac{3,500\ people}{100\ years}$$

$$slope = 35\ people\ per\ year$$

In this example, the population in Appleton increased by a fixed amount each year. The graph of these data is a straight line. Therefore, the relationship is **linear.** When the graph of a set of data is not a straight line, the relationship is **nonlinear.**

Using Algebra to Determine Slope

The equation in step 4 may also be arranged to be

$$y = kx$$

where y represents the change in the y-value, k represents the slope, and x represents the change in the x-value.

$$slope = \frac{change\ in\ y}{change\ in\ x}$$

$$k = \frac{y}{x}$$

$$k \times x = \frac{y \times x}{x}$$

$$kx = y$$

Bar Graphs

Bar graphs are used to demonstrate change that is not continuous. These graphs can be used to indicate trends when the data cover a long period of time. A meteorologist gathered the precipitation data shown here for Hartford, Connecticut, for April 1–15, 1996, and used a bar graph to represent the data.

Precipitation in Hartford, Connecticut April 1–15, 1996			
Date	Precipitation (cm)	Date	Precipitation (cm)
April 1	0.5	April 9	0.25
April 2	1.25	April 10	0.0
April 3	0.0	April 11	1.0
April 4	0.0	April 12	0.0
April 5	0.0	April 13	0.25
April 6	0.0	April 14	0.0
April 7	0.0	April 15	6.50
April 8	1.75		

How to Make a Bar Graph

1 Use an appropriate scale and a reasonable starting point for each axis.

2 Label the axes, and plot the data.

3 Choose a title that accurately represents the data.

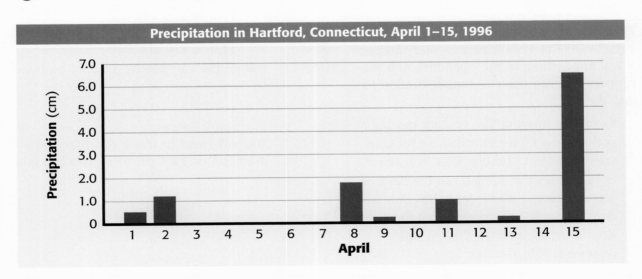

Precipitation in Hartford, Connecticut, April 1–15, 1996

Math Refresher

Science requires an understanding of many math concepts. The following pages will help you review some important math skills.

Averages

An **average**, or **mean**, simplifies a set of numbers into a single number that *approximates* the value of the set.

> **Example:** Find the average of the following set of numbers: 5, 4, 7, and 8.

Step 1: Find the sum.

$$5 + 4 + 7 + 8 = 24$$

Step 2: Divide the sum by the number of numbers in your set. Because there are four numbers in this example, divide the sum by 4.

$$\frac{24}{4} = 6$$

The average, or mean, is **6.**

Ratios

A **ratio** is a comparison between numbers, and it is usually written as a fraction.

> **Example:** Find the ratio of thermometers to students if you have 36 thermometers and 48 students in your class.

Step 1: Make the ratio.

$$\frac{36 \text{ thermometers}}{48 \text{ students}}$$

Step 2: Reduce the fraction to its simplest form.

$$\frac{36}{48} = \frac{36 \div 12}{48 \div 12} = \frac{3}{4}$$

The ratio of thermometers to students is **3 to 4,** or $\frac{3}{4}$. The ratio may also be written in the form 3:4.

Proportions

A **proportion** is an equation that states that two ratios are equal.

$$\frac{3}{1} = \frac{12}{4}$$

To solve a proportion, first multiply across the equal sign. This is called *cross-multiplication*. If you know three of the quantities in a proportion, you can use cross-multiplication to find the fourth.

> **Example:** Imagine that you are making a scale model of the solar system for your science project. The diameter of Jupiter is 11.2 times the diameter of the Earth. If you are using a plastic-foam ball that has a diameter of 2 cm to represent the Earth, what must the diameter of the ball representing Jupiter be?

$$\frac{11.2}{1} = \frac{x}{2 \text{ cm}}$$

Step 1: Cross-multiply.

$$\frac{11.2}{1} \diagdown\!\!\!\!\!\diagup \frac{x}{2}$$

$$11.2 \times 2 = x \times 1$$

Step 2: Multiply.

$$22.4 = x \times 1$$

Step 3: Isolate the variable by dividing both sides by 1.

$$x = \frac{22.4}{1}$$

$$x = 22.4 \text{ cm}$$

You will need to use a ball that has a diameter of **22.4** cm to represent Jupiter.

Percentages

A **percentage** is a ratio of a given number to 100.

Example: What is 85% of 40?

Step 1: Rewrite the percentage by moving the decimal point two places to the left.

0.85

Step 2: Multiply the decimal by the number that you are calculating the percentage of.

0.85 × 40 = 34

85% of 40 is **34.**

Decimals

To **add** or **subtract decimals,** line up the digits vertically so that the decimal points line up. Then, add or subtract the columns from right to left. Carry or borrow numbers as necessary.

Example: Add the following numbers: 3.1415 and 2.96.

Step 1: Line up the digits vertically so that the decimal points line up.

3.1415
+ 2.96

Step 2: Add the columns from right to left, and carry when necessary.

1 1
3.1415
+ 2.96
6.1015

The sum is **6.1015.**

Fractions

Numbers tell you how many; **fractions** tell you *how much of a whole.*

Example: Your class has 24 plants. Your teacher instructs you to put 5 plants in a shady spot. What fraction of the plants in your class will you put in a shady spot?

Step 1: In the denominator, write the total number of parts in the whole.

$\dfrac{?}{24}$

Step 2: In the numerator, write the number of parts of the whole that are being considered.

$\dfrac{5}{24}$

So, $\dfrac{5}{24}$ of the plants will be in the shade.

Reducing Fractions

It is usually best to express a fraction in its simplest form. Expressing a fraction in its simplest form is called *reducing* a fraction.

Example: Reduce the fraction $\dfrac{30}{45}$ to its simplest form.

Step 1: Find the largest whole number that will divide evenly into both the numerator and denominator. This number is called the *greatest common factor* (GCF).

Factors of the numerator 30:
1, 2, 3, 5, 6, 10, **15,** 30

Factors of the denominator 45:
1, 3, 5, 9, **15,** 45

Step 2: Divide both the numerator and the denominator by the GCF, which in this case is 15.

$$\frac{30}{45} = \frac{30 \div 15}{45 \div 15} = \frac{2}{3}$$

Thus, $\dfrac{30}{45}$ reduced to its simplest form is $\dfrac{2}{3}$.

Adding and Subtracting Fractions

To **add** or **subtract fractions** that have the **same denominator,** simply add or subtract the numerators.

Examples:

$$\frac{3}{5} + \frac{1}{5} = ? \text{ and } \frac{3}{4} - \frac{1}{4} = ?$$

Step 1: Add or subtract the numerators.

$$\frac{3}{5} + \frac{1}{5} = \frac{4}{\ } \text{ and } \frac{3}{4} - \frac{1}{4} = \frac{2}{\ }$$

Step 2: Write the sum or difference over the denominator.

$$\frac{3}{5} + \frac{1}{5} = \frac{4}{5} \text{ and } \frac{3}{4} - \frac{1}{4} = \frac{2}{4}$$

Step 3: If necessary, reduce the fraction to its simplest form.

$\frac{4}{5}$ cannot be reduced, and $\frac{2}{4} = \frac{1}{2}$.

To **add** or **subtract fractions** that have **different denominators,** first find the least common denominator (LCD).

Examples:

$$\frac{1}{2} + \frac{1}{6} = ? \text{ and } \frac{3}{4} - \frac{2}{3} = ?$$

Step 1: Write the equivalent fractions that have a common denominator.

$$\frac{3}{6} + \frac{1}{6} = ? \text{ and } \frac{9}{12} - \frac{8}{12} = ?$$

Step 2: Add or subtract the fractions.

$$\frac{3}{6} + \frac{1}{6} = \frac{4}{6} \text{ and } \frac{9}{12} - \frac{8}{12} = \frac{1}{12}$$

Step 3: If necessary, reduce the fraction to its simplest form.

The fraction $\frac{4}{6} = \frac{2}{3}$, and $\frac{1}{12}$ cannot be reduced.

Multiplying Fractions

To **multiply fractions,** multiply the numerators and the denominators together, and then reduce the fraction to its simplest form.

Example:

$$\frac{5}{9} \times \frac{7}{10} = ?$$

Step 1: Multiply the numerators and denominators.

$$\frac{5}{9} \times \frac{7}{10} = \frac{5 \times 7}{9 \times 10} = \frac{35}{90}$$

Step 2: Reduce the fraction.

$$\frac{35}{90} = \frac{35 \div 5}{90 \div 5} = \frac{7}{18}$$

Dividing Fractions

To **divide fractions,** first rewrite the divisor (the number you divide by) upside down. This number is called the *reciprocal* of the divisor. Then multiply and reduce if necessary.

Example:

$$\frac{5}{8} \div \frac{3}{2} = ?$$

Step 1: Rewrite the divisor as its reciprocal.

$$\frac{3}{2} \rightarrow \frac{2}{3}$$

Step 2: Multiply the fractions.

$$\frac{5}{8} \times \frac{2}{3} = \frac{5 \times 2}{8 \times 3} = \frac{10}{24}$$

Step 3: Reduce the fraction.

$$\frac{10}{24} = \frac{10 \div 2}{24 \div 2} = \frac{5}{12}$$

Scientific Notation

Scientific notation is a short way of representing very large and very small numbers without writing all of the place-holding zeros.

> **Example:** Write 653,000,000 in scientific notation.

Step 1: Write the number without the place-holding zeros.

653

Step 2: Place the decimal point after the first digit.

6.53

Step 3: Find the exponent by counting the number of places that you moved the decimal point.

6.53000000

The decimal point was moved eight places to the left. Therefore, the exponent of 10 is positive 8. If you had moved the decimal point to the right, the exponent would be negative.

Step 4: Write the number in scientific notation.

$$6.53 \times 10^8$$

Area

Area is the number of square units needed to cover the surface of an object.

> **Formulas:**
>
> *area of a square = side × side*
> *area of a rectangle = length × width*
> *area of a triangle = $\frac{1}{2}$ × base × height*
>
> **Examples:** Find the areas.

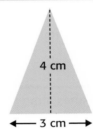

Triangle

area = $\frac{1}{2}$ × base × height

area = $\frac{1}{2}$ × 3 cm × 4 cm

*area = **6 cm²***

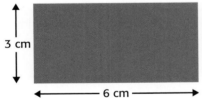

Rectangle

area = length × width
area = 6 cm × 3 cm
*area = **18 cm²***

Square

area = side × side
area = 3 cm × 3 cm
*area = **9 cm²***

Volume

Volume is the amount of space that something occupies.

> **Formulas:**
>
> *volume of a cube =*
> *side × side × side*
>
> *volume of a prism =*
> *area of base × height*
>
> **Examples:**
>
> Find the volume of the solids.

Cube

volume = side × side × side
volume = 4 cm × 4 cm × 4 cm
*volume = **64 cm³***

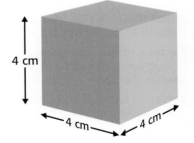

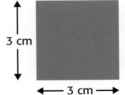

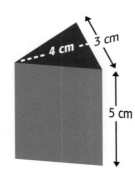

Prism

volume = area of base × height
volume = (area of triangle) × height
volume = ($\frac{1}{2}$ × 3 cm × 4 cm) × 5 cm
volume = 6 cm² × 5 cm
*volume = **30 cm³***

Appendix

Glossary

A

acid precipitation rain, sleet, or snow that contains a high concentration of acids (23)

air mass a large body of air where temperature and moisture content are similar throughout (46)

air pollution the contamination of the atmosphere by the introduction of pollutants from human and natural sources (20)

air pressure the measure of the force with which air molecules push on a surface (5)

anemometer an instrument used to measure wind speed (61)

anticyclone the rotation of air around a high-pressure center in the direction opposite to Earth's rotation (50)

atmosphere a mixture of gases that surrounds a planet or moon (4)

B

barometer an instrument that measures atmospheric pressure (61)

biome a large region characterized by a specific type of climate and certain types of plant and animal communities (79)

C

climate the average weather conditions in an area over a long period of time (74)

cloud a collection of small water droplets or ice crystals suspended in the air, which forms when the air is cooled and condensation occurs (42)

condensation the change of state from a gas to a liquid (41)

convection the transfer of thermal energy by the circulation or movement of a liquid or gas (11)

Coriolis effect the apparent curving of the path of a moving object from an otherwise straight path due to the Earth's rotation (16)

cyclone an area in the atmosphere that has lower pressure than the surrounding areas and has winds that spiral toward the center (50)

E

elevation the height of an object above sea level (78)

F

front the boundary between air masses of different densities and usually different temperatures (48)

G

global warming a gradual increase in average global temperature (12, 96)

greenhouse effect the warming of the surface and lower atmosphere of Earth that occurs when water vapor, carbon dioxide, and other gases absorb and reradiate thermal energy (12, 96)

H

humidity the amount of water vapor in the air (39)

hurricane a severe storm that develops over tropical oceans and whose strong winds of more than 120 km/h spiral in toward the intensely low-pressure storm center (55)

I

ice age a long period of climate cooling during which ice sheets cover large areas of Earth's surface; also known as a *glacial period* (92)

J

jet stream a narrow belt of strong winds that blow in the upper troposphere (18)

L

latitude the distance north or south from the equator; expressed in degrees (75)

lightning an electric discharge that takes place between two oppositely charged surfaces, such as between a cloud and the ground, between two clouds, or between two parts of the same cloud (53)

M

mesosphere the layer of the atmosphere between the stratosphere and the thermosphere and in which temperature decreases as altitude increases (7)

microclimate the climate of a small area (90)

P

polar easterlies prevailing winds that blow from east to west between 60° and 90° latitude in both hemispheres (16)

polar zone the North or South Pole and the surrounding region (89)

precipitation any form of water that falls to the Earth's surface from the clouds (44)

prevailing winds winds that blow mainly from one direction during a given period (76)

R

radiation the transfer of energy as electromagnetic waves (10)

relative humidity the ratio of the amount of water vapor in the air to the maximum amount of water vapor the air can hold at a set temperature (39)

S

stratosphere the layer of the atmosphere that is above the troposphere and in which temperature increases as altitude increases (7)

surface current a horizontal movement of ocean water that is caused by wind and that occurs at or near the ocean's surface (79)

T

temperate zone the climate zone between the Tropics and the polar zone (86)

thermal conduction the transfer of energy as heat through a material (11)

thermometer an instrument that measures and indicates temperature (61)

thermosphere the uppermost layer of the atmosphere, in which temperature increases as altitude increases (8)

thunder the sound caused by the rapid expansion of air along an electrical strike (53)

thunderstorm a usually brief, heavy storm that consists of rain, strong winds, lightning, and thunder (52)

tornado a destructive, rotating column of air that has very high wind speeds, is visible as a funnel-shaped cloud, and touches the ground (54)

trade winds prevailing winds that blow northeast from 30° north latitude to the equator and that blow southeast from 30° south latitude to the equator (16)

tropical zone the region that surrounds the equator and that extends from about 23° north latitude to 23° south latitude (82)

troposphere the lowest layer of the atmosphere, in which temperature decreases at a constant rate as altitude increases (7)

W

weather the short-term state of the atmosphere, including temperature, humidity, precipitation, wind, and visibility (38, 74)

westerlies prevailing winds that blow from west to east between 30° and 60° latitude in both hemispheres (16)

wind the movement of air caused by differences in air pressure (14)

Spanish Glossary

A

acid precipitation/precipitación ácida lluvia, agua-nieve o nieve que contiene una alta concentración de ácidos (23)

air mass/masa de aire un gran volumen de aire que tiene una temperatura y contenido de humedad similar en toda su extensión (46)

air pollution/contaminación del aire la contaminación de la atmósfera debido a la introducción de contaminantes provenientes de fuentes humanas y naturales (20)

air pressure/presión del aire la medida de la fuerza con la que las moléculas del aire empujan contra una superficie (5)

anemometer/anemómetro un instrumento que se usa para medir la rapidez del viento (61)

anticyclone/anticiclón la rotación del aire alrededor de un centro de alta presión en dirección opuesta a la rotación de la Tierra (50)

atmosphere/atmósfera una mezcla de gases que rodea un planeta o una luna (4)

B

barometer/barómetro un instrumento que mide la presión atmosférica (61)

biome/bioma una región extensa caracterizada por un tipo de clima específico y ciertos tipos de comunidades de plantas y animales (79)

C

climate/clima las condiciones promedio del tiempo en un área durante un largo período de tiempo (74)

cloud/nube un conjunto de pequeñas gotitas de agua o cristales de hielo suspendidos en el aire, que se forma cuando el aire se enfría y ocurre condensación (42)

condensation/condensación el cambio de estado de gas a líquido (41)

convection/convección la transferencia de energía térmica mediante la circulación o el movimiento de un líquido o gas (11)

Coriolis effect/efecto de Coriolis la desviación aparente de la trayectoria recta que experimentan los objetos en movimiento debido a la rotación de la Tierra (16)

cyclone/ciclón un área de la atmósfera que tiene una presión menor que la de las áreas circundantes y que tiene vientos que giran en espiral hacia el centro (50)

E

elevation/elevación la altura de un objeto sobre el nivel del mar (78)

F

front/frente el límite entre masas de aire de diferentes desidades y, normalmente, diferentes temperaturas (48)

G

global warming/calentamiento global un aumento gradual de la temperatura global promedio (12, 96)

greenhouse effect/efecto de invernadero el calentamiento de la superficie y de la parte más baja de la atmósfera, el cual se produce cuando el vapor de agua, el dióxido de carbono y otros gases absorben y vuelven a irradiar la energía térmica (12, 96)

H

humidity/humedad la cantidad de vapor de agua que hay en el aire (39)

hurricane/huracán tormenta severa que se desarrolla sobre océanos tropicales, con vientos fuertes que soplan a más de 120 km/h y que se mueven en espiral hacia el centro de presión extremadamente baja de la tormenta (55)

I

ice age/edad de hielo un largo período de tiempo frío durante el cual grandes áreas de la superficie terrestre están cubiertas por capas de hielo; también conocido como período glacial (92)

J

jet stream/corriente en chorro un cinturón delgado de vientos fuertes que soplan en la parte superior de la troposfera (18)

L

latitude/latitud la distancia hacia el norte o hacia el sur del ecuador; se expresa en grados (75)

lightning/relámpago una descarga eléctrica que ocurre entre dos superficies que tienen carga opuesta, como por ejemplo, entre una nube y el suelo, entre dos nubes o entres dos partes de la misma nube (53)

M

mesosphere/mesosfera la capa de la atmósfera que se encuentra entre la estratosfera y la termosfera, en la cual la temperatura disminuye al aumentar la altitud (7)

microclimate/microclima el clima de un área pequeña (90)

P

polar easterlies/vientos polares del este vientos preponderantes que soplan de este a oeste entre los 60° y los 90° de latitud en ambos hemisferios (16)

polar zone/zona polar el Polo Norte y el Polo Sur y la región circundante (89)

precipitation/precipitación cualquier forma de agua que cae de las nubes a la superficie de la Tierra (44)

prevailing winds/vientos prevalecientes vientos que soplan principalmente de una dirección durante un período de tiempo determinado (76)

R

radiation/radiación la transferencia de energía en forma de ondas electromagnéticas (10)

relative humidity/humedad relativa la proporción de la cantidad de vapor de agua que hay en el aire respecto a la cantidad máxima de vapor de agua que el aire puede contener a una temperatura dada (39)

S

stratosphere/estratosfera la capa de la atmósfera que se encuentra encima de la troposfera y en la que la temperatura aumenta al aumentar la altitud (7)

surface current/corriente superficial un movimiento horizontal del agua del océano que es producido por el viento y que ocurre en la superficie del océano o cerca de ella (79)

T

temperate zone/zona templada la zona climática ubicada entre los trópicos y la zona polar (86)

thermal conduction/conducción térmica la transferencia de energía en forma de calor a través de un material (11)

thermometer/termómetro un instrumento que mide e indica la temperatura (61)

thermosphere/termosfera la capa más alta de la atmósfera, en la cual la temperatura aumenta a medida que la altitud aumenta (8)

thunder/trueno el sonido producido por la expansión rápida del aire a lo largo de una descarga eléctrica (53)

thunderstorm/tormenta eléctrica una tormenta fuerte y normalmente breve que consiste en lluvia, vientos fuertes, relámpagos y truenos (52)

tornado/tornado una columna destructiva de aire en rotación cuyos vientos se mueven a velocidades muy altas; se ve como una nube con forma de embudo y toca el suelo (54)

trade winds/vientos alisios vientos preponderantes que soplan hacia el noreste a partir de los 30° de latitud norte hacia el ecuador y que soplan hacia el sureste a partir de los 30° de latitud sur hacia el ecuador (16)

tropical zone/zona tropical la región que rodea el ecuador y se extiende desde aproximadamente 23° de latitud norte hasta 23° de latitud sur (82)

troposphere/troposfera la capa inferior de la atmósfera, en la que la temperatura disminuye a una tasa constante a medida que la altitud aumenta (7)

W

weather/tiempo el estado de la atmósfera a corto plazo que incluye la temperatura, la humedad, la precipitación, el viento y la visibilidad (38, 74)

westerlies/vientos del oeste vientos preponderantes que soplan de oeste a este entre 30° y 60° de latitud en ambos hemisferios (16)

wind/viento el movimiento de aire producido por diferencias en la presión barométrica (14)

Spanish Glossary

Index

Index

Index

Credits

PHOTOGRAPHY

Front Cover Douglas E. Walker/Masterfile

Skills Practice Lab Teens Sam Dudgeon/HRW

Connection to Astrology Corbis Images; **Connection to Biology** David M. Phillips/Visuals Unlimited; **Connection to Chemistry** Digital Image copyright © 2005 PhotoDisc; **Connection to Environment** Digital Image copyright © 2005 PhotoDisc; **Connection to Geology** Letraset Phototone; **Connection to Language Arts** Digital Image copyright © 2005 PhotoDisc; **Connection to Meteorology** Digital Image copyright © 2005 PhotoDisc; **Connection to Oceanography** © ICONOTEC; **Connection to Physics** Digital Image copyright © 2005 PhotoDisc

Table of Contents iv (cl), Goddard Space Flight Center Scientific Visualization Studio/NASA; iv (b), NASA; v (tl), Index Stock; v (tr), Doug Mills/AP/Wide World Photos; x (bl), Sam Dudgeon/HRW; xi (tl), John Langford/HRW; xi (b), Sam Dudgeon/HRW; xii (tl), Victoria Smith/HRW; xii (bl), Stephanie Morris/HRW; xii (br), Sam Dudgeon/HRW; xiii (tl), Patti Murray/Animals, Animals; xiii (tr), Jana Birchum/HRW; xiii (b), Peter Van Steen/HRW

Chapter One 2–3, Robert Holmes/CORBIS; 5, Peter Van Steen/HRW; 7 (t), SuperStock; 7 (b), NASA; 8, Image Copyright ©2005 PhotoDisc, Inc.; 9, Patrick J. Endres/Alaskaphotographics.com; 14, Terry Renna/AP/Wide World Photos; 15 (b), Moredun Animal Health Ltd./Science Photo Library/Photo Researchers, Inc.; 18 (t), NASA/Science Photo Library/Photo Researchers, Inc.; 20 (c), Argus Fotoarchiv/Peter Arnold, Inc.; 464 (r), David Weintraub/Photo Researchers, Inc; 464 (l), Digital Image copyright © 2005 PhotoDisc/Getty Images; 21 (bl), Steve Starr/CORBIS; 21 (r), Corbis Images; 23, Simon Fraser/SPL/Photo Researchers, Inc.; 24 (t), Goddard Space Flight Center Scientific Visualization Studio/NASA; 24 (b), Goddard Space Flight Center Scientific Visualization Studio/NASA; 25, Tampa Electric; 26, Francis Dean/The Image Works; 27, Tampa Electric; 28, 29, Sam Dudgeon/HRW; 31 (t), Goddard Space Flight Center Scientific Visualization Studio/NASA; 34 (b), James McInnis/Los Alamos National Laboratories; 34 (t), Jonathan Blair/CORBIS; 35 (r), Fred Hirschmann; 35 (bl), Fred Hirschmann

Chapter Two 36–37, Tim Chapman/Miami Herald/NewsCom; 40, Sam Dudgeon/HRW; 41, Victoria Smith/HRW; 42 (tc), NOAA; 42 (tr), Joyce Photographics/Photo Researchers, Inc.; 42 (tl), Corbis Images; 44, Gene E. Moore; 44 (tl), Gerben Oppermans/Getty Images/Stone; 45 (c), Corbis Images; 45 (t), Victoria Smith/HRW; 47, Image Copyright ©2005 PhotoDisc, Inc.; 47 (t), Reuters/Gary Wiepert/NewsCom; 50, NASA; 52, William H. Edwards/Getty Images/The Image Bank; 53 (br), Jean–Loup Charmet/Science Photo Library/Photo Researchers, Inc.; 54 (all), Howard B. Bluestein/Photo Researchers, Inc.; 55 (t), Red Huber/Orlando Sentinel/SYGMA/CORBIS; 55 (b), NASA; 500 (tl), NASA/Science Photo Library/Photo Researchers, Inc.; 57, Dave Martin/AP/Wide World Photos; 58 (b), Joe Raedle/NewsCom; 58 (t), Will Chandler/Anderson Independent–Mail/AP/Wide World Photos; 59 (t), Jean–Loup Charmet/Science Photo Library/Photo Researchers, Inc.; 59 (c), NASA/Science Photo Library/Photo Researchers, Inc.; 60, Graham Neden/Ecoscene/CORBIS; 61, Sam Dudgeon/HRW; 61 (br), G.R. Roberts Photo Library; 61 (t), Guido Alberto Rossi/Getty Images/The Image Bank; 62, National Weather Service/NOAA; 66, Sam Dudgeon/HRW; 67 (tr), Corbis Images; 70 (tr), Lightscapes Photography, Inc./CORBIS; 67 (b), Joyce Photographics/Photo Researchers, Inc.; 71 (t), Michael Lyon; 71 (bl), Corbis Images

Chapter Three 72–73, Steve Bloom Images; 74 (bkgd), Tom Van Sant, Geosphere Project/Planetary Visions/Science Photo Library/Photo Researchers, Inc.; 74 (tl), G.R. Roberts Photo Library; 74 (tr), Index Stock; 74 (c), Yva Momatiuk & John Eastcott; 74 (bl), Gary Retherford/Photo Researchers, Inc.; 74 (br), SuperStock; 75 (tr), CALLER–TIMES/AP/Wide World Photos; 75 (tc), Doug Mills/AP/Wide World Photos; 77 (b), Tom Van Sant, Geosphere Project/Planetary Visions/Science Photo Library/Photo Researchers, Inc.; 78 (bl), Larry Ulrich Photography; 78 (br), Paul Wakefield/Getty Images/Stone; 81, Index Stock; 82 (br), Tom Van Sant/Geosphere Project, Santa Monica/Science Photo Library/Photo Researchers, Inc.; 83 (tl), Carlos Navajas/Getty Images/The Image Bank; 83 (tr), Michael Fogden/Bruce Coleman, Inc.; 84, Nadine Zuber/Photo Researchers, Inc.; 85, Larry Ulrich Photography; 86 (br), Tom Van Sant/Geosphere Project, Santa Monica/Science Photo Library/Photo Researchers, Inc.; 87 (b), Tom Bean/Getty Images/Stone; 87 (t), CORBIS Images/HRW; 88 (b), Steven Simpson/Getty Images/FPG International; 88 (t), Fred Hirschmann; 89 (b), Harry Walker/Alaska Stock; 89 (tr), Tom Van Sant/Geosphere Project, Santa Monica/Science Photo Library/Photo Researchers, Inc.; 90, SuperStock; 94 (br), Roger Werth/Woodfin Camp & Associates; 95, D. Van Ravenswaay/Photo Researchers, Inc.; 100, Gunter Ziesler/Peter Arnold, Inc.; 101, SuperStock; 104, Roger Ressmeyer/CORBIS; 104 (b), Terry Brandt/Grant Heilman Photography, Inc.; 105 (t), Courtesy of The University of Michigan

Lab Book/Appendix 106, Sam Dudgeon/HRW; 109, Kuni Stringer/AP/Wide World Photos; 110, Victoria Smith/HRW; 111, Jay Malonson/AP/Wide World Photos; 113, 116, Sam Dudgeon/HRW; 117, Andy Christiansen/HRW

TEACHER EDITION CREDITS

1E (b), NASA; 1F (bl), NASA/Science Photo Library/Photo Researchers, Inc.; 1F (r), Digital Image copyright © 2005 PhotoDisc/Getty Images; 35E (l), Gene E. Moore; 35E (br), Howard B. Bluestein/Photo Researchers, Inc.; 35F (t), NASA; 35F (br), Graham Neden/Ecoscene/CORBIS; 71E (tl), CALLER-TIMES/AP/Wide World Photos; 71E(tr), Doug Mills/AP/Wide World Photos; 71E (b), Tom Van Sant, Geosphere Project/Planetary Visions/Science Photo Library/Photo Researchers, Inc.

Answers to Concept Mapping Questions

The following pages contain sample answers to all of the concept mapping questions that appear in the Chapter Reviews. Because there is more than one way to do a concept map, your students' answers may vary.

CHAPTER 1   The Atmosphere

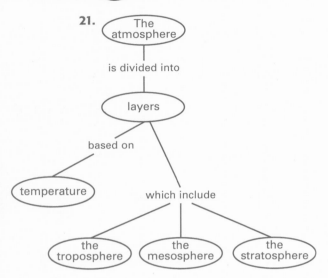

21.

The atmosphere → *is divided into* → layers → *based on* → temperature / *which include* → the troposphere, the mesosphere, the stratosphere

CHAPTER 2   Understanding Weather

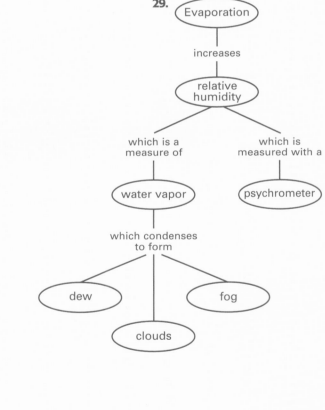

29.

Evaporation → *increases* → relative humidity → *which is a measure of* → water vapor / *which is measured with a* → psychrometer

water vapor → *which condenses to form* → dew, clouds, fog

CHAPTER 3   Climate

17.

Changes in climate → *such as* → global warming, ice ages

global warming → *might be caused by* → greenhouse effect → *which might be related to* → deforestation

ice ages → *might be explained by* → Milankovitch theory